Measuring the Distance
between Locke and Toland

Measuring the Distance *between* Locke and Toland

Reason, Revelation, and Rejection during the Locke-Stillingfleet Debate

JONATHAN S. MARKO

☙PICKWICK *Publications* • Eugene, Oregon

MEASURING THE DISTANCE BETWEEN LOCKE AND TOLAND
Reason, Revelation, and Rejection during the Locke-Stillingfleet Debate

Copyright © 2017 Jonathan S. Marko. All rights reserved. Except for brief quotations in critical publications or reviews, no part of this book may be reproduced in any manner without prior written permission from the publisher. Write: Permissions, Wipf and Stock Publishers, 199 W. 8th Ave., Suite 3, Eugene, OR 97401.

Pickwick Publications
An Imprint of Wipf and Stock Publishers
199 W. 8th Ave., Suite 3
Eugene, OR 97401

www.wipfandstock.com

PAPERBACK ISBN: 978-1-4982-1895-5
HARDCOVER ISBN: 978-1-4982-1897-9
EBOOK ISBN: 978-1-4982-1896-2

Cataloguing-in-Publication data:

Names: Marko, Jonathan S.

Title: Measuring the distance between Locke and Toland : reason, revelation, and rejection during the Locke-Stillingfleet debate / Jonathan S. Marko.

Description: Eugene, OR: Pickwick Publications, 2017 | Includes bibliographical references.

Identifiers: ISBN 978-1-4982-1895-5 (paperback) | ISBN 978-1-4982-1897-9 (hardcover) | ISBN 978-1-4982-1896-2 (ebook)

Subjects: LCSH: Locke, John, 1632–1704 | Stillingfleet, Edward, 1635–1699 | Toland, John, 1670–1722 | Philosophy, English—17th century | England—Religion—17th century | Faith and reason

Classification: B1297 M18 2017 (paperback) | B1297 (ebook)

Manufactured in the U.S.A.   01/31/17

To Meagan
Proverbs 31:10–31

"What partly pleases, totally will shock:
I question much, if *Toland* would be *Locke*."

—discarded couplet from Alexander Pope's *An Essay on Man*

Contents

Acknowledgments | ix

1 Introduction | 1
2 The Locke-Stillingfleet Controversy: From False Start to Footing for Exploring Locke's and Toland's Epistemologies | 13
3 Locke's Incorporation of Faith and Revelation within Reason | 61
4 Toland's Incorporation of Faith and Revelation within Reason | 123
5 Conclusions and Implications | 174

Bibliography | 189
Index | 199

Acknowledgments

I AM VERY THANKFUL for all of the people who were instrumental to my writing and completion of this book. Firstly, much thanks goes to my dissertation committee: Ronald J. Feenstra, Richard A. Muller, Lee Hardy, and Alan P. F. Sell. They helped me to fine-tune my dissertation and encouraged me to develop it into this book. I am especially indebted to the former two, from Calvin Theological Seminary, in whose offices and seminars I had the privilege of developing into a better scholar over the course of a few years. And it was they who introduced me to the writings of John Locke and the so-called deists. I would also like to express my gratitude to Cornerstone University. The administrators and my colleagues there have helped this project come to fruition in a timely manner through a variety of ways. Furthermore, I am thankful for all of the support provided to me through the years by my family, local church, and friends. Finally, I cannot thank Meagan, my wife, enough for all that she has done to enable me to pursue my scholarly projects amidst the busyness of raising three daughters together and through all the joys and difficulties that life brings. I dedicate this book to her.

1

Introduction

A REASONABLE NARRATIVE FROM MYSTERIOUS PREMISES

ANY HISTORY OF PHILOSOPHY that covers the rise of deism or the rise of natural religion in England will inevitably juxtapose John Locke (1632–1704) and John Toland (1670–1722). John Locke was perhaps *the* great mind of his time and his magnum opus, *An Essay Concerning Human Understanding* (*Essay*), still piques the interest and draws the scrutiny of historians, philosophers, and theologians alike. Because Locke looms so large and draws the focus of so many, those who became attached to him in one way or another were effectively saved from the indefinite limbo of historical obscurity. This is the case with John Toland. His work *Christianity Not Mysterious* (*CNM*) is best known for its use of Lockean principles with a few modifications in a scathing critique of the then-current religious establishments. While Locke cultivated religious mysteries with his epistemological ploughshare, Toland beats it into a sword and lops away the mysterious fruits of revelation growing above the soil of reason. Thus Toland is the first of a generation of so-called deists who use and modify Locke's epistemology to promulgate natural religion and critique Christianity, or so the story goes.

It is not just the philosophical differences between Locke and Toland that make an exploration of Toland enticing, but also the personal characteristics attributed to him in the histories of philosophy. In these accounts we are often introduced to Locke the Reputable and Toland the

Disreputable. Whatever other adjectives one might apply to Locke, such as heretical or orthodox, he is consistently portrayed as brilliant and honest. He is the venerable gentleman at Oates earnestly trying to make sense of religion and reason come what may. Portrayals of Toland, while various, are rarely complimentary. For instance, Leslie Stephen introduces Toland with the following description:

> From his earliest days Toland was a mere waif and stray, hanging loose upon society, retiring at intervals into the profoundest recesses of Grub Street, emerging again by fits to candalize the whole respectable world, and then once more sinking back into tenfold obscurity. His career is made more pathetic by his incessant efforts to clutch at various supports, which always gave way as he grasped at them.

And subsequently, where Stephen discusses *CNM* as being the root cause of the embittered debate between Locke and Edward Stillingfleet (1635–99), he calculates, "we may fancy Toland chuckling with all the vanity of gratified mischief."[1]

With such descriptions of Toland circulating in important historical works such as Stephen's, it is easy to imagine in *CNM* the significant and cleverly subtle epistemological deviations from the *Essay* that are alluded to in Toland scholarship. The converse is true as well. But before adopting the contours of this narrative a few basic questions are in order. How, exactly, do Locke's and Toland's epistemologies differ? Tiresome quick descriptions, such as that Locke accepts religious mysteries and Toland does not, simply lack definitive boundaries and create more questions. Locke can be a large, quick, and elusive quarry. And if Toland is tethered to him, Locke must be caught before trying to measure the distance between the two.

OVERALL ARGUMENT

This book will compare the epistemologies of John Locke and John Toland based upon Locke's *Essay* and Toland's *CNM* and their related works. In so doing, it will also evaluate Bishop Edward Stillingfleet's comparison of the two works. This book contends that the differences between Locke and Toland with respect to their epistemologies are not based upon or evidenced by their respective categorizations of propositions, but rather on Toland's attempt at working out the implications of Locke's epistemological principles in conjunction with Toland's interpretations of certain

---

1. Stephen, *History of English Thought*, 1:101–2; 1:111.

biblical passages and certain theological preferences and presuppositions. Had Locke ordered propositions according to his preferred consideration of reason, his categorization of propositions would be the same ascribed to Toland. The resultant, substantial differences between Locke and Toland in their understandings of epistemology are connected with Toland's definite or likely rejections of theological and philosophical positions that Locke does not dismiss: post-New Testament original revelation and miracles, non-materialism of the soul, and prior-to-the-close-of-the-New-Testament divine revelation requiring a supernaturally bestowed faculty and private miracles for believers.[2]

THE STATE OF THE PROBLEM

John Toland penned numerous books on a variety of topics in his nearly three decades of writing, but the book that brought him the most notoriety was his very first, *CNM*.[3] In it he borrows heavily from John Locke's *Essay*, a book that by then had made a considerable and largely favorable impression on the educated.[4] Bishop Edward Stillingfleet, who was in a heated debate with the Unitarians at the time, spied in Toland's *CNM* what he thought was a defense of the Unitarians against him on certain points and an attack on the doctrine of the Trinity. Stillingfleet also noticed the numerous Lockean appropriations in *CNM*. In *A Discourse in Vindication of the Doctrine of the Trinity* (*Discourse*), Stillingfleet fixes his guns on *CNM* and parts of Locke's

---

2. Toland would reject any claim of a private miracle that occurred in the presence of an unbeliever that was not to have been done by the God of the Bible and for the purpose of helping the unbeliever with her unbelief. John Locke does not specifically discuss the claims of believers in non-biblical religions regarding miracles done in favor of their religion.

3. Toland, *Christianity Not Mysterious*, 2nd ed. This is a slightly enlarged version of the original and anonymously published first edition. From here onward, the page numbers of *CNM*, 2nd ed., will be referenced parenthetically. The first edition of the work will be referenced in the footnotes when needed. Works directly related to *CNM*: *Apology*, *Defence*, and *Vindicius*. The second edition of *CNM* is also printed with the *Apology* in 1702.

4. Locke, *Essay*, 3rd ed; Rogers, introduction to *The Philosophy of Edward Stillingfleet*, 1:vii–x. According to G. A. J. Rogers, Stillingfleet only owned the second edition (1694) of the *Essay*. But the 1695 edition is essentially a page for page reprint of the 1694 edition. Both have been consulted and there are no important differences that are of concern here. Also, the third edition (1695) is the latest edition that John Toland would have been able to consult prior to the publication of *CNM*. Also consulted is the critical edition of the *Essay*, edited by Nidditch. From here onward the book number, chapter, and section of the third edition (1695) will be referenced parenthetically. Other editions of the work will be referenced in the footnotes when appropriate.

Essay from which he sees Toland building his case for the notion that we can only have certainty of clear and distinct ideas and only reason about them. While Locke himself was not charged with heresy, Stillingfleet accuses Locke of paving the way—albeit unwittingly—for it. That is, Stillingfleet believed that Toland had shown the unorthodox conclusions of the foundational, epistemological principles of the *Essay*, to which Locke, its very author, only loosely adhered. Locke felt he and his *Essay* were under fire, and despite advice to the contrary, two of the great theological and philosophical minds of their generation became embroiled in a rigorous debate. John Toland essentially became a bystander in this particular controversy, allowing Locke to clarify grossly misinterpreted parts of *CNM* for Stillingfleet.[5]

Despite the glaring mistakes Locke points out in Stillingfleet's understanding of the notions of ideas, certainty, and knowledge found in the *Essay* and Toland's *CNM*, Toland is still to this day portrayed somewhat as Stillingfleet paints him. While originally portrayed by Stillingfleet as having brought the *Essay's* foundational principles to their true unorthodox end, namely that certainty can only be had by and reasoning could only be done with clear and distinct ideas, Toland is now portrayed as having largely borrowed from the *Essay* and having adapted it to his own heretical ends. This altered picture stands because most are skeptical of or deny the accuracy of Stillingfleet's reading of Locke and the *Essay* in light of Locke's defense, but for some reason assume that the bishop's reading of Toland's *CNM* is correct.[6]

---

5. Stillingfleet, *Discourse*, 2nd ed. There are no pertinent differences between the first and second editions that concern this book. The subsequent works in or referencing the debate are, in order of dissemination: Locke, *Letter to Edward*; Stillingfleet, *Bishop of Worcester's Answer*; Locke, *Mr. Locke's Reply . . . Answer to His Letter*; Stillingfleet, *Bishop of Worcester's Answer to Mr. Locke's Second Letter*; Locke, *Mr. Locke's Reply . . . Answer to His Second Letter*.

6. If these scholars are not simply assuming Stillingfleet is correct in his reading of Toland—that he claimed certainty can only be had with clear and distinct ideas—there is no compelling evidence that they have investigated the matter. In fact, most do not demonstrate that they even grasp what clear and distinct ideas means. Sullivan, *John Toland*, 76–77. The following quote of Sullivan suggests a lack of understanding of Locke's notions of ideas and certainty central to the Locke-Stillingfleet debate's launch: "Toland was faithful to Locke in insisting that, in order to acknowledge anything, one must have first a clear and distinct idea of it" (76). As will be shown this is inaccurate. On the next page, Sullivan makes it clear he thinks Stillingfleet's reading of Toland on clear and distinct ideas is correct (77). Beiser, *Sovereignty of Reason*, 250–51. Beiser oddly finds Locke's explanation of ideas "more peculiar and obscure" than Toland's. The only thing that I can think of that can account for that is that he thinks Stillingfleet has read Toland correctly and not read Locke correctly. His explanation of Toland's use of clear, distinct, and adequate ideas is clearly flawed as will be shown (250n77). He later states that certainty can only be had with clear and distinct ideas. There he describes

Scholarly assessments of Toland tend to abound with a few major, intertwined problems related to this prevailing view that Stillingfleet correctly read *CNM* and that Toland did greatly diverge from Locke despite the fact that both built on similar foundations. Supporting or resulting from this view are three common assertions often made regarding the juxtaposition of Locke and Toland: 1) Toland appropriates the foundational principles of Locke's *Essay* to a significant degree, 2) Locke accepts above reason propositions, while Toland does not, and 3) Locke accepts divine revelation and Toland rejects, or essentially rejects, divine revelation by subordinating it to reason.[7]

These three assertions, which are related to the prevailing view of *CNM*, are teeming with problems. Assertion one—that Toland appropriates the foundational principles of Locke's *Essay* to a significant degree or that Toland is dependent on Locke—is vague but widely held.

Assertion two—that Locke accepts above reason propositions, while Toland does not—is the most widely known. There is seemingly clear textual evidence that Locke accepts "above reason" things and Toland rejects them. On the one hand, Locke discusses above reason propositions in multiple places (IV.xvii.23; IV.xviii.7–8) and affirms them. On the other hand, the full title of Toland's *CNM* is *Christianity Not Mysterious: or, A Treatise Shewing, That There is Nothing in the Gospel Contrary to Reason, Nor Above It: and That No Christian Doctrine Can Be Properly Call'd a Mystery*. In fact, it seems as though this textual evidence clearly supports the prevailing view that Toland, the disciple, attacked his master. But, due to the lack of specificity of assertion one, an imposing assumption actually undergirds assertion two. The assumption is that Locke and Toland are operating with

---

clear and distinct ideas as being ideas that can be described in "clear and simple terms," an imprecise and unhelpful definition (251). Helm, "Locke on Faith and Knowledge," 58–59. Helm operates with the understanding that Stillingfleet has read Toland correctly (58–59). Helm is one of the few scholars who think Stillingfleet could be correct about Locke (59). Biddle, "Locke's Critique of Innate Principles," 419–20. It appears as though Biddle agrees with Stillingfleet's assessment in his portrayal of Toland's *CNM*. While citing Toland's *CNM* for support, that which he brings out is not explained in context but rather pieced together to comport with Stillingfleet's reading of *CNM*.

7. Toland scholarship supporting the three assertions: Sullivan, *John Toland*; Beiser, *Sovereignty of Reason*, 220–65; Leask, "Personation and Immanent Undermining"; Livingston, *Modern Christian Thought*, 1:18–21; Fouke, *Philosophy and Theology*, 23, 81–86, 221–40, 237–38; Cragg, *Church and the Age of Reason*, 78, 160; Cragg, *Reason and Authority*, 67, 78, 83; Welch, *Protestant Thought*, 1:36–38; McGuinness, "Christianity Not Mysterious and the Enlightenment"; Stephen, *History of English Thought*, 1:94–118; Turner, *Without God, Without Creed*, 51–63; Biddle, "Locke's Critique of Innate Principles"; Higgins-Biddle, introduction to *The Reasonableness of Christianity*; Randall, Jr., *Making of the Modern Mind*, 285–89; Lucci, *Scripture and Deism*, 72–73, 81–82.

the same notion of reason in Locke's acceptance of things that are above reason and Toland's rejection of things that are above reason. Yet, as will be demonstrated, Locke operates with two rather distinct understandings of reason in the chapters of the *Essay* that are most often juxtaposed with *CNM*. What is more, no one has attempted an in depth explanation of Toland's understanding of reason, which is needed to be able to compare it to Locke's. To operate as if it is the same as Locke's is not only presumptuous but problematic since Locke's understanding of reason is one of the most contested topics in Locke scholarship. In addition, in Locke scholarship there is general confusion precisely as to what above reason propositions are.[8] To even begin to get a handle on Toland's understanding of reason, the center of his epistemology, one would have to seriously explore the more fundamental aspects of his epistemology such as ideas and certainty, which few have attempted.[9]

Furthermore, due to the lack of comparison of Locke's and Toland's foundational, epistemological principles and their respective views of reason, assertion three is made—Locke accepts divine revelation and Toland rejects, or essentially rejects, divine revelation by subordinating it to reason. In fact, some incorrectly identify above reason propositions and revelation making assertions two and three identical.[10] But of those who understand

---

8. The complex categorization of scholars into various groups based on the similarities of their treatments of Locke that is undertaken in chapter 3 will not be rehearsed here. Most of the explorations of Locke's reason are more specifically about the relationship between reason and faith or reason and revelation. Livingston, *Modern Christian Thought*, 1:18–21; Welch, *Protestant Thought*, 1:35–36; Sullivan, *John Toland*, 79; Cragg, *The Church and the Age of Reason*, 13; Copleston, *History of Philosophy*, 5:69–70; Randall, Jr., *Making of the Modern Mind*, 285–89; O'Higgins, *Anthony Collins*, 52; Uzgalis, "Anthony Collins"; Kuehn, "Reason and Understanding"; Biddle, "Locke's Critique of Innate Principles"; Leask, "Personation and Immanent Undermining"; Ashcraft, "Faith and Knowledge"; Sell, *John Locke*, 97; Polinska, "Faith and Reason"; Losonsky, "Locke and Leibniz"; Helm, "Locke on Faith and Knowledge"; Snyder, "Faith and Reason"; Woolhouse, *Locke*, 140–43; Jolley, "Locke on Faith and Reason"; LoLordo, *Locke's Moral Man*; Ayers, *Locke*, 1:121; Wolterstorff, *John Locke and the Ethics of Belief*; Wolterstorff, "John Locke's Epistemological Piety."

9. As said above, most assume Stillingfleet has a correct read on Toland, but not on Locke. Leask is one scholar who has attempted a more in depth comparison of Locke and Toland on ideas, among other topics. Leask, "Personation and Immanent Undermining."

10. A possible example of this is ibid., 243–44. This book attempts to give Leask the most charitable reading possible and will thus give the alternative to this reading of his article. Technically speaking, revelation reports things that humans could have, at least, arguably, discovered on their own whereas above reason things, curtly stated, are beyond our discovery. The two terms may have a synecdochic relationship depending on the writer.

above reason propositions to be a subset of revelation or think the two to be overlapping somehow, they appear to think assertions two and three are mutually supportive for one reason or another.

Together the three assertions are coherent and they give a slightly more detailed explanation of the prevailing view's claim that Toland did greatly diverge from Locke. But while Locke scholarship is fraught with detailed analyses that work toward answering important questions that bear on the relationship between Locke and Toland, this is clearly not the case in Toland scholarship. It is riddled with reliance on second-hand information on and readings of Toland, which is likely due to the prolixity of the Locke-Stillingfleet debate and *CNM*'s hard-to-follow style. The potentially fatal assumptions that *CNM* claims that certainty can only be had with clear and distinct ideas and that Toland and Locke have the same notion in mind when using the term reason are only two of several. Another significant assumption that is made that reinforces one of the assumptions named above is that when Toland says that faith is knowledge, by knowledge he means the Lockean knowledge that only comes about by intuition and demonstration.[11] This is incorrect and just reinforces the popular, but incorrect Stillingfleet reading of Toland that he teaches that only certainty can be had by clear and distinct ideas. It also reduces Christianity to a natural religion of morality since morality is demonstrable according to Locke's *Essay*.[12] Two other very important terms used by Toland that are not investigated thoroughly enough are experience and evidence. When Toland says that experience is the means of information, which serves as the common stock of all of our knowledge, some incorrectly understand him to mean experiences in the contemporary, modern-day vernacular. In other words, they think that Toland is advocating a verifiability criterion such that if one cannot verify something it cannot be believed.[13] On a related issue, evidence,

---

11. Ibid., 245; Sullivan, *John Toland*, 126; Lucci, *Scripture and Deism*, 81–82; Beiser, *Sovereignty of Reason*, 251–52. Beiser is possibly tripped up by Toland's calling faith knowledge. Champion, *Republican Learning*, 79–80. Champion portrays Toland as not being so concerned with theology: "Toland, as we will see, was concerned with epistemological certainty too, but the context for the performance of that certainty was not theological but a broader social community" (79). Champion's work is appreciated as it is a very interesting historical account of Toland, but it does not say much about the philosophical and theological points made by *CNM*. Cf. Champion, "Enlightened Erudition and the Politics of Reading."

12. Locke, *Essay* IV.iii.18. There he explicitly notes that he thinks "*Morality amongst the Sciences capable of Demonstration.*"

13. Beiser, *Sovereignty of Reason*, 250–52; Leask, "Personation and Immanent Undermining," 245. The verifiability criterion is connected to Toland's calling faith knowledge in Leask and possibly in Beiser.

an extremely important term in *CNM*, is taken wrongly to mean empirical proof, which greatly distorts what Toland is attempting to convey.[14] In short, there are numerous problems in Locke and especially Toland scholarship, some named above, which have caused Locke and Toland to be viewed as very similar in some respects but greatly different in others.

This book also will interact with two historical narratives found in Locke and Toland scholarship, one involving Toland and the other involving Locke and Toland, which quickly and undeservedly became matters of "fact." The first is that Toland was actually a pantheistic materialist his entire life and thus *CNM* and its related works are a cover of sorts to his true religious, or irreligious, views. Variations of this view have been commonplace since its first mature promulgation in Robert E. Sullivan's *John Toland and the Deist Controversy*.[15] Despite the fact that Rhoda Rappaport clearly shows how Sullivan's greatest piece of evidence for his view is based on circular reasoning, few seem to care.[16] It fits too well with Toland's mischievous persona.

The other historical narrative, which is accepted as a matter of fact though based upon a mere suggestion without any further investigation, originated from the pen of John C. Higgins-Biddle. He thinks it possible that Locke had a copy of *CNM* prior to its publication. If so, Higgins-Biddle reasons, Locke's observation of its epistemological connections to his *Essay* and its deistic conclusions might have caused him to write *ROC*, in part, to show his *Essay* does not end up in deism, but, on the contrary, is against it.[17] The conjectured motivations for Locke's writing of *ROC* pertaining to Toland lose their force when it is seen that the gulf between the *Essay* and *CNM* is not as wide as once thought.

---

14. Beiser, *Sovereignty of Reason*, 254.

15. Sullivan, *John Toland*, 43–47, 114–19; Beiser, *Sovereignty of Reason*, 243–44; Champion, *Republican Learning*, 35, 250–56; Berman, "Deism, Immortality, and the Art"; Berman, "Disclaimers as Offence Mechanisms"; Berman, "Toland, John"; Fouke, *Philosophy and Theology*, 12, 187; Israel, *Radical Enlightenment*, 609–14; cf. Berman, *History of Atheism*.

16. Rappaport, "Questions of Evidence." Rappaport cites Giancarlo Carabelli as making the possible connection between Toland and the *Two Essays*. Giancarlo Carabelli, *Tolandiana*, 20–21; L.P., *Two Essays*.

17. Higgins-Biddle, introduction to *The Reasonableness of Christianity*, xxvii–xxxvii; Biddle, "Locke's Critique of Innate Principles."

METHODOLOGY AND OUTLINE

The aim of this book is to understand the religious epistemologies promulgated in the *Essay* and *CNM* and grasp in what respects they differ.[18] Thus, this book will focus primarily on the *Essay*, *CNM*, their respective defenses, and *The Reasonableness of Christianity* (*ROC*), which Toland was likely able to read prior to the publication of his two 1696 editions of *CNM*, and *ROC*'s two vindications. While all editions have been consulted, the third edition of the *Essay* (1695), the second edition of *ROC* (1696), and the second edition (enlarged) of *CNM* (1696) are the editions of choice.[19] Caution will be exercised by checking earlier editions against the choice versions in case a particular thinker actually had only an earlier edition of another's work. While both thinkers have numerous other works apart from those with a historical link to the uproar caused by *CNM* for both Toland and Locke, these are the ones of interest. While each thinker was likely changing his opinion on points throughout his writing career, the defenses and vindications of their 1695–96 religious works will be approached as conveying honest commentary on their thoughts, at least, as they stood during this two-year window, when *ROC*, *CNM*, and the third edition of the *Essay* were published. Moreover, due to the abundant citations from and references to the *Essay* and *CNM*, these works will be parenthetically referenced.

Another important figure's works that come into play in this book are those of Bishop Edward Stillingfleet pertaining to his debate with Locke,

---

18. While the evidence points to these works being indicative of Locke's and Toland's personal epistemological and religious opinions, the merits of this book do not hinge on it. It will be primarily shown that Locke's *Essay* and Toland's *CNM* are much more individually coherent and comparatively consistent than anyone has previously thought or demonstrated.

19. *ROC* came out prior to Toland's *CNM*. Locke became embroiled in a verbose debate with John Edwards that resulted in two vindications of *ROC* penned also by him. Cf. Locke, *Reasonableness of Christianity*, crit. ed. This Higgins-Biddle's critical edition of *ROC* is based upon, but not slavishly, the "Harvard copy" of *ROC*. The Harvard copy is a first edition *ROC* that contains Locke's notes, emendations, and corrections. Higgins-Biddle, introduction to *The Reasonableness of Christianity*, cxxxiv. I have researched both and there are no pertinent differences that are of importance for this book. The page numbers of the second edition (1696) are recorded in the footnotes. The following work was published along with the second edition (1696) of *ROC*: Locke, *Vindication*. Not long after Locke published: Locke, *Second Vindication*. For a work aimed at reconciling what are thought to be discordant aspects of *ROC* and the *Essay*: Marko, "Promulgation of Right Morals." Moreover, there are other important works pertinent to the *Essay* found in Locke's *Posthumous Works* such as *Of the Conduct of the Understanding*, *A Discourse of Miracles*, and *A Paraphrase and Notes on the Epistles of St. Paul to the Galatians, Romans, 1 & II Corinthians, Ephesians*.

especially his *Discourse* (the second edition is the edition of choice). The fact that Stillingfleet only had the second edition (1694) of Locke's *Essay* is not important as there is little difference between the second and third editions. Regardless, as stated before, all editions will be consulted. There will also be works and letters discussed from those beyond the focus figures of Locke and Toland, such as John Tillotson (1630–94), Anthony Collins (1676–1729), William Molyneux (1656–98), and Matthew Tindal (1657–1733); but Stillingfleet is the most important figure outside of Locke and Toland. It was his *Discourse* that forever associated the two in the histories of philosophy.

There will be substantial interaction with secondary scholarship that investigates the epistemologies of Locke and Toland. There are several sources that investigate both figures on key elements and there are other resources that concentrate primarily on one or the other. Some of the more significant figures who will be interacted with are Nicholas Wolterstorff, Nicholas Jolley, Alan P. F. Sell, Violetta Polinska, John C. Higgins-Biddle, Richard Ashcraft, Paul Helm, Robert E. Sullivan, Ian Leask, and Frederick Beiser. There are numerous others, but those named prove to be especially helpful dialogue partners.

Most of the investigated Stillingfleet, Locke, and Toland scholars and this book's understanding of their views will be discussed in depth in each chapter's state of the question section and during the course of the argument. While the actual interpretation of Locke and Toland is the primary focus of the book, understanding how long-held and popular erroneous views appeared and perpetuated is an important historiographical accent to the book. It was definitely one of the most intriguing aspects of the research and writing process. In short, patient exposition of related Stillingfleet, Locke, and Toland works *and* demonstration of the careful dismantling of scholarly arguments are both necessary to disabuse scholarship of such long-held erroneous readings of Locke and Toland and the resultant, general narrative that has found its way into every account mentioning the two.

This book consists of five chapters. The next chapter investigates the Locke-Stillingfleet debate. The lack of investigation into this important debate seems odd and is probably the most significant source of confusion regarding the interpretation of *CNM* and the *Essay*. Until one understands what both Locke and Toland are saying about ideas and certainty, one cannot expect to make the right connections when investigating their notions of reason, faith, and revelation. The key questions that will be asked in the chapter are the following: 1) Is Stillingfleet correct in connecting Locke and Toland and does he get them right?; 2) How and why do Locke and Toland respond the way that they do?; and 3) What are the salient points of this debate's historical reception? Chapter 2 argues that Stillingfleet is correct in asserting agreement between Locke's and Toland's notions of ideas and certainty but misinterprets what both thinkers are conveying about these notions when he treats them in the *Discourse*. While Locke's clarifications on ideas and certainty made in the course of the debate are helpful, the controversy as a whole and its reception leaves little resolved regarding a comparison of Locke's and Toland's respective epistemologies.

Chapter 3 focuses solely on the religious epistemology of John Locke. It builds upon the epistemological investigation of Locke started in chapter 2 and is necessary for allowing a point-for-point comparison with Toland's epistemology in chapter 4. The primary questions being asked in chapter 3 are: 1) According to Locke, what is reason?; 2) What is its relationship to faith?; and 3) What is its relationship to revelation? The chapter argues that to understand Locke's description of reason, and thus the relationships between reason and faith and reason and revelation, one must acknowledge that in the *Essay* Locke primarily conceives of the mind employing the faculty of reason working in reason's proper office or scope, which entails the considerations of natural as well as supernatural sources of information (the propositions of the latter trumping the probable propositions of the former) and a corresponding proper faith that pertains to probable (uncertain) propositions from the same sources. In *Essay* IV.xviii, however, he conceives of the mind employing reason in a diminished office, or concerning only natural sources, and a corresponding vulgar faith, concerned with only supernatural sources; but he does this partly, at least, to show that such an antithetical framing of the two fails to maintain definitive boundaries. As a result, faith in or assent to a proposition from *any* source and the determination of divine revelation as such morally *ought* to be the result of the mind employing its power of reason in its full scope or office.

Chapter 4 aims at exploring the same questions asked in chapter 3, but regarding Toland, and an additional point-for-point comparison with Locke started in chapter 2 and made possible by the epistemological investigation of Locke done in chapter 3. Chapter 4 argues that the differences between Locke and Toland with respect to their understandings of reason, its related faculties, faith, and revelation are not based upon or evidenced by their respective categorizations of propositions, but are based upon Toland's attempt at working out the implications of Locke's epistemological principles in conjunction with Toland's interpretations of certain biblical passages and certain theological preferences and presuppositions. Had Locke ordered propositions according to his preferred consideration of reason, his categorization of propositions would be the same ascribed to Toland. The resultant, substantial differences between Locke and Toland in their understandings of epistemology are connected with Toland's definite or likely rejections of theological and philosophical positions that Locke does not dismiss: post-New Testament original revelation and miracles, non-materialism of the soul, and prior-to-the-close-of-the-New-Testament divine revelation requiring a supernaturally bestowed faculty and private miracles for believers.[20]

Chapter 5 concentrates on conclusions and implications. Part I of the chapter revisits the argument laid out in the book and the new narrative that arises from it. Part II focuses on a number of historical implications. In that respect a series of sifting questions for categorizing thinkers in the narrative of the rise of natural religion in England will be suggested, corresponding suggestions for the study of certain figures will follow, and implications for the well-accepted Biddle hypothesis regarding the writing of *ROC* will be articulated. Part III discusses this books findings on doctrines and propositions said to be above reason, while IV focuses on the implications of Locke's and Toland's hermeneutics regarding the influences of biblical criticism and the natural sciences. Comments related to Toland's alleged mischievous persona and corresponding claims that he employed a covert style of writing will be made in Part V. Finally, part VI will make suggestions for a study that could build upon this book to give a fuller sense of Locke's and Toland's prolegomena.

---

20. Again, Toland would reject any claim of a private miracle that occurred in the presence of an unbeliever that was not to have been done by the God of the Bible and for the purpose of helping the unbeliever with her unbelief (*CNM* 151). John Locke does not specifically discuss the claims of believers in non-biblical religions regarding miracles done in favor of their religion.

2

The Locke-Stillingfleet Controversy
From False Start to Footing for Exploring Locke's and Toland's Epistemologies

INTRODUCTION

As stated in the last chapter, the juxtaposition of John Locke and John Toland is a common feature of many histories of philosophy. John Locke is fashioned as the more orthodox of the two, defending revelation's authority and doctrines above reason, while Toland, himself a Lockean, dismisses anything above reason and subordinates revelation to reason. This juxtaposition finds its roots in Bishop Stillingfleet's assertion, in the *Discourse*, of a connection between Locke's and Toland's respective treatments of ideas and certainty. Not only did Stillingfleet's observation spark a lengthy, multivolume debate with Locke, but he forever tethered him with Toland in the annals.

This chapter will explore the Locke-Stillingfleet debate in its historical context and perform the comparative, epistemological spadework necessary for analyzing and comparing Locke's and Toland's understandings of reason and its relationship to faith and revelation that will be done in chapters 3 and 4. Thus, a few overarching questions will be asked. First, is Stillingfleet correct in connecting Locke and Toland and does he get them right? Second, how and why do Locke and Toland respond the way that they do? And, finally, what are the salient points of this debate's historical reception?

This chapter will suggest that Stillingfleet is correct in asserting agreement between Locke's and Toland's notions of ideas and certainty but misinterprets what both thinkers are conveying about these notions when he treats them in the *Discourse*. While the clarifications on ideas and certainty Locke makes in the course of the debate are helpful, the controversy as a whole and its reception leaves little resolved regarding a comparison of Locke's and Toland's respective epistemologies.

This chapter will be comprised of four parts in addition to a conclusion. Part I will rehearse a brief narrative of the Locke-Stillingfleet debate to give us historical grounding and to position the primary literature. Part II will serve as the state of the question regarding the secondary literature. Part III will focus on ideas, knowledge, and certainty. There the chapter will give an analysis and exposition of Locke's *Essay* on ideas, knowledge, and certainty followed by a demonstration that Toland's *CNM* comports with the *Essay* on the same issues. The part will conclude with Stillingfleet's interpretations of Locke's *Essay* and Toland's *CNM* and this chapter's comments on them. The goal of part III is to demonstrate the first part of the chapter's argument: Stillingfleet is correct in asserting agreement between Locke's and Toland's notions of ideas and certainty but misinterprets what both thinkers are conveying about them when he comments on them in the *Discourse*. Part IV will focus on responses and receptions: Locke's responses to Stillingfleet on said issues and *CNM*, Toland's response, and contemporary receptions of the controversy. The goal of part IV is to demonstrate the need for further exploration and a comparison of Locke's and Toland's epistemologies, and thus the second part of this chapter's argument: While the clarifications on ideas and certainty Locke makes in the course of the debate are helpful, the controversy as a whole and its reception leaves little resolved regarding a comparison of Locke's and Toland's respective epistemologies.

PART I: A BRIEF HISTORY OF THE CONTROVERSY'S INCEPTION AND THE ENSUING DEBATE

John Locke's *Essay* received notoriety and fair sales in its first three editions, the first of which was published in 1690. It found its way, with the help of friends and admirers, into Dublin University and Oxford University in abridged form as a textbook[1]; and in a 1694 letter, written to Philip van Limborch, Locke notes: "The second edition of my book on the Human Understanding is selling faster than I could have believed, nor, however

---

1. Christophersen, *Bibliographical Introduction*, 28–29.

heterodox it may be, has that dissertation as yet found an assailant."[2] Locke's denial of innate ideas drew significant attention with its first publication, being censured in print by John Norris in 1690 and James Lowde in 1694.[3] Unless memory failed Locke in his letter to Limborch, these censures were not of sufficient gravity in guile or content to mark their penmen as "assailants." Locke's tenor is markedly different, however, just over two years later as seen in a letter dated February 22nd, 1697, to William Molyneux:

> My book crept into the world about six or seven years ago, without any opposition, and has since passed amongst some for useful, and, the least favourable, for innocent. But, as it seems to me, it is agreed by some men that it should no longer do so. Something, I know not what, is at last spyed out in it, that is like to be troublesome, and therefore it must be an ill book, and be treated accordingly. 'Tis not that I know any thing in particular, but some things that have hapned [sic] at the same time together, seem to suggest this: what it will produce, time will shew.[4]

By this time, Edward Stillingfleet, Lord Bishop of Worcester, had published his *Discourse*. Although in this book he never charges Locke with heresy, he does claim Locke's *Essay* paved the way for the allegedly heterodox *CNM*, a book that is now mentioned alongside the *Essay* in nearly every history of philosophy text up to the present-day.

The designs of John Toland's *CNM* as perceived by Stillingfleet were to undermine the doctrine of the holy Trinity among others.[5] Stillingfleet understands Toland to claim that certainty and reason only concern clear and distinct ideas. Furthermore, clear and distinct ideas find their origin only in sensation and reflection. The bishop reasons that these claims amount to the denial of the "certainty of Faith" in matters where clear and distinct ideas cannot be had.[6] What is more, Stillingfleet remarks that one cannot form a clear and distinct idea of the notion of substance from the ideas that we have from sensation or reflection; rather the notion of substance is an implication

---

2. Locke, "L1804: Locke to Phillipus van Limborch," 174; cf. Woolhouse, *Locke*, 498n35. Christophersen, biographer of Locke and chronicler of his works and debates, remarks, "To the great distribution of the Essay corresponded an equally extensive opposition." Christophersen, *Bibliographical Introduction*, 29.

3. Christophersen, *Bibliographical Introduction*, 29–34.

4. Locke, "L2202: Locke to William Molyneux," 6; cf. Woolhouse, *Locke: A Bibliography*, 371.

5. Stillingfleet, *Discourse*, 272. Here, Stillingfleet explicitly states that the author of *CNM* is striking at the doctrine of the Trinity. Stillingfleet never once uses Toland's name, even though it appears on the second edition (1696) of *CNM*.

6. Ibid., 232–33.

of the "Repugnancy to our first Conceptions of things, that *Modes* or *Accidents* should subsist by themselves."[7] This means that one cannot be certain of or reason about substance according to *CNM*. Therefore, and here is the rub, according to Stillingfleet, if we are to follow the reasoning promulgated in *CNM*, we can have no certainty of the doctrine of the Trinity as that doctrine "depends upon our Knowledge of the Nature of *Substance*, and *Person* and the *Distinction* between them."[8]

It is within this delineation of the problems above that the *Essay* is brought into juxtaposition with *CNM*. Stillingfleet explicitly lumps together Locke and Toland and unites them under one noxious designation: "And therefore I do not wonder, that the *Gentlemen of this new way of reasoning*, have almost discarded Substance out of the reasonable part of the World" (emphasis mine).[9] His subsequent citations from the *Essay* concerning the origin of ideas and the way they bear on notions of substances are intended to show from where Toland received the notions that troubled Stillingfleet and that now find themselves under the bishop's scrutiny.[10] Although the premises from which the author of *CNM* works are from the *Essay*, he is more consistent with them in his conclusions, according to Stillingfleet, than Locke is. The bishop believes the upshot of Locke's discourse on spiritual and corporeal substances is that we can be certain that there are spiritual and bodily substances, albeit without clear and distinct ideas.[11] Therein lies Locke's inconsistency (and evidence of no heretical intent):

> But, if our Reason depend upon our *clear and distinct Idea's*; how is this possible? We cannot reason without *clear Idea's*, and yet we may be certain without them: Can we be certain without Reason? Or doth our Reason give us true Notions of things without these *Idea's*? If it be so, this new *Hypothesis* about Reason must appear to be very unreasonable.[12]

Although Stillingfleet teases out further problematic implications from the *Essay* and assails *CNM* in the remainder of the chapter, all of it stems from what has already been stated: according to Stillingfleet, the *Essay* maintains that we can only have certainty of and reason about clear and distinct ideas, and while Locke does not see the irreligious implications of his claims, the

---

7. Ibid., 236.
8. Ibid., 233.
9. Ibid., 234.
10. Ibid., 234–39.
11. Ibid., 239.
12. Ibid., 239–40.

author of *CNM* does and employs them as weapons against the doctrine of the Trinity.

That was the beginning of a fascinating philosophical debate. Even though Stillingfleet's *Discourse* could not have been in print for more than a few months, Locke quickly responded with *A Letter to Edward Ld Bishop of Worcester, etc.* (*L1*), dated January 7th, 1696/7.[13] Stillingfleet responds rapidly in kind with *The Bishop of Worcester's Answer to Mr. Locke's Letter, etc.*, dated April 26th, 1697. Locke volleys back *Mr. Locke's Reply to the Right Reverend the Lord Bishop of Worcester's Answer to His Letter, etc.* (*L2*), dated June 29th, 1697. Attached to its end is a brief work entitled, *An Answer to Remarks upon An Essay Concerning Humane Understanding* (*L3*) that does reference the debate but is directed at another Lockean opponent. Stillingfleet's next and final riposte, dated September 22nd, 1697, is entitled, *The Bishop of Worcester's Answer to Mr. Locke's Second Letter, etc.* The final work in the debate, which comes from Locke, is dated May of 1698: *Mr. Locke's Reply to the Right Reverend Lord Bishop of Worcester's Answer to His Second Letter, etc.* (*L4*). If it were not for Edward Stillingfleet's death in March of 1699, the debate might have continued.

One voice that is virtually absent in the proceedings is that of John Toland. Toland makes little mention of Stillingfleet's charges in the three works that serve as vindications of his *CNM*: *An Apology for Mr. Toland, etc.* (*Apology*), *A Defence of Mr. Toland in a Letter to Himself* (*Defence*), and *Vindicius Liberius: or, M. Toland's Defence of Himself, etc.* (*Vindicius*). He does incorporate an excerpt from *The Agreement of the Unitarians with the Catholick Church*, written by Stephen Nye (one of Stillingfleet's opponents), in the *Apology* and *Defence*. The excerpt indicates, among other things, Stillingfleet's distortion of what *CNM* teaches. Even when he briefly mentions the debate over twenty years later, he presents some quotes from Locke, with approval, that simply demonstrate Locke thinks Toland was sorely handled by Stillingfleet.[14]

---

13. It is of interest to note that the date of the completion of this response is before William Molyneux advises Locke to let the matter between him and Stillingfleet rest for the time-being. Cf. "L2189: William Molyneux to Locke," 766–67. The editor of Locke's correspondences notes that Stillingfleet's *Discourse* was being advertised in November 1696 and both editions are dated as 1697 (766–67n2). Cf. Woolhouse, *Locke: A Bibliography*, 370.

14. John Toland has three vindications or defenses of *CNM*. Stillingfleet is mentioned in all three but his only response comes through a quote from noted Unitarian Stephen Nye. Toland, *Apology*; Toland, *Defence*; Toland, *Vindicius*; Toland, *Collection of Several Pieces*, 1:lxxiii–lxxvi. These pages show Toland's positive appraisal of his handling by Locke in response to Fr. Hare. These pages reference pp. 438, 440, & 443 of vol. 1 of the 1714 *Works of John Locke*; Fr. Hare, *Church Authority Vindicated*; Champion,

PART II: STATE OF THE QUESTION

There are precious few who have done work on the Locke-Stillingfleet debate (or the thought of Bishop Stillingfleet for that matter). On the one hand, this is somewhat surprising considering how often it is mentioned in the histories of philosophy. On the other hand, it is not so shocking considering the characteristics of the debate: this debate is truncated, it consists of over 1,200 pages not including *CNM* and the *Essay*, and its alternation from one of the many issues to another likely appears desultory to the unwary reader. Thankfully some luminaries such as Alan P. F. Sell, Roger Woolhouse, Paul Schuurman, and Gerard Reedy have made strides in setting the debate into its intellectual milieu and the trajectories leading in and out of it.[15] A smaller contingent that is worthy of distinction, consisting of M. A. Stewart, Richard Popkin, and G. A. J. Rogers, has done important work in gaining traction in the mind of the oft-mentioned but often under-studied Edward Stillingfleet.[16]

There are a few worrisome characteristics found in other scholarly literature, which concentrates on Locke's and Toland's epistemologies, pertinent to the debate. In light of the little attention Stillingfleet's works actually receive, it is peculiar to see the frequency of the secondary literature's agreement with one of Stillingfleet's assessments of *CNM*: that we can only be certain about clear and distinct ideas. This is actually suspect because in the course of the lengthy debate not only does Locke express perplexity at Stillingfleet's reading that the *Essay* claims certainty can only be had about that which one has clear and distinct ideas, but he expresses perplexity how Stillingfleet attributes the same description to *CNM*. In short, if Locke and Toland scholars are thoroughly investigating the debate to assess Locke as misinterpreting Toland and Stillingfleet as interpreting him correctly, one would think that a defense of Stillingfleet's reading on the matter would be existent and referenced. Also, few Toland scholars have even done what can be considered a fair examination of what Toland says on certainty and ideas. An examination done by Ian Leask argues that Toland teaches that some ideas are innate—a point that will be argued against in this chapter—but that does not necessarily go against Stillingfleet's reading of Toland.[17] The

---

Republican Learning. Champion interacts with 1:lxxiii–lxxvi of *Collection of Several Pieces* (79); Stephen Nye, *Agreement of the Unitarians*.

15. Sell, *John Locke*; Woolhouse, *Locke: A Biography*; Schuurman, "Vision in God"; Reedy, "Socinians, John Toland."

16. Stewart, "Stillingfleet and the Way of Ideas"; Popkin, "The Philosophy of Bishop Stillingfleet"; Rogers, introduction to *The Philosophy of Edward Stillingfleet*.

17. Leask, "Personation and Imminent Undermining," 231–56.

most likely conclusion is that scholars have been assuming Stillingfleet read Toland correctly. Likely suspects are Robert E. Sullivan, author of Toland's noted biography, Paul Helm, Frederick C. Beiser, and John C. Biddle.[18]

Another point of concern regarding current scholarship is the universal claim that Toland subordinates revelation to reason in one way or another. It is likely that most take it as a matter of fact because no one has investigated precisely what Toland means by reason; and those that comment on Toland in relation to Locke assume both thinkers operate with the same conception of reason. Some who strive to offer their reasoning for the notion that Toland subordinates revelation to reason build on the assumption that Stillingfleet read Toland correctly. For instance, the notion that revelation is subordinate to reason, for those like Sullivan, has a direct link, at least, to Stillingfleet's reading of Toland: we can only have certainty of and reason about clear and distinct ideas. He writes:

> . . . his epistemological assumptions were irreconcilable with allowing divine inspiration a role in the creation of humanity's religious opinions. His conviction—that, should God use this means of information, the intelligence He conveyed would have to conform to the canons of human reason by presenting

---

18. As stated earlier, if these scholars are not simply assuming Stillingfleet is correct in his reading of Toland—that he claimed certainty can only be had with clear and distinct ideas—there is no compelling evidence that they have investigated the matter. In fact, most do not even appear to grasp precisely what clear and distinct ideas means in Locke or Toland. Sullivan, *John Toland*, 76–77. The following quote of Sullivan points to possible confusion over Locke's notions of ideas and certainty central to the Locke-Stillingfleet debates launch: "Toland was faithful to Locke in insisting that, in order to *acknowledge* anything, one must have first a clear and distinct idea of it" (76) (emphasis mine). On the next page, Sullivan makes it clear he thinks Stillingfleet's reading of Toland on clear and distinct ideas is correct (77). Frederick C. Beiser, *Sovereignty of Reason*, 250–51. Beiser oddly finds Locke's explanation of ideas "more peculiar and obscure" than Toland's (Locke gives chapters to his explanation and Toland never gives a formal treatment of the notion). The only thing that I can think that can account for Beiser's claim is that he thinks Stillingfleet has read Toland correctly and not read Locke correctly. His explanation of Toland's use of clear, distinct, and adequate ideas is flawed, but that will be shown later (250n77). He later states that certainty can only be had with clear and distinct ideas. There he describes clear and distinct ideas as being ideas that can be described in "clear and simple terms," an imprecise and unhelpful definition (251). Helm, "Locke on Faith and Knowledge," 58–59. Helm operates with the understanding that Stillingfleet has read Toland correctly (58–59). Interestingly, Helm is one of the few scholars that think Stillingfleet could be correct about Locke (59). John C. Biddle, "Locke's Critique of Innate Principles," 419–20. It appears as though Biddle agrees with Stillingfleet's assessment and portrayal of Toland's *CNM*. While citing Toland's *CNM* for support, that which he brings out is not explained in context but rather evidently pieced together to comport with Stillingfleet's reading of *CNM*.

clear and distinct ideas, rather than mysteries—precluded any discoveries.[19]

In other words, because of reason's need for clear and distinct ideas revelation cannot provide us with novelty or mystery if it is to be considered as such. Again, this reading of Toland is likely, for Sullivan at least, based on the assumption that Stillingfleet read Toland correctly. Others, like Roger Woolhouse, find other or additional support for the notion that Toland subordinates revelation to reason from another place. In his important biography on Locke, Woolhouse assumes that Locke's charge (leveled at Stillingfleet in the course of the debate) that Stillingfleet's arguments involving the immortality of the soul actually undercut revelation, "a position diametrically opposed to his starting point," is Toland's position. Differently stated, Woolhouse understands that Locke charges Stillingfleet with subordinating revelation to natural reason at one point in the debate, a notion that Stillingfleet condemns in others, and Woolhouse believes these "others" include Toland.[20] The problem is, even if the others did include Toland, Locke is not stating that Stillingfleet is accusing Toland *rightly*. For the vast majority of scholars who comment on Toland's subordination of revelation to reason without any evident consideration, but who did not take it as a matter of fact in their research, likely follow Woolhouse's or Sullivan's reasoning on the points above, or both.

There is another very important reading of Toland that has an association with the assumption that Stillingfleet reads Toland correctly that is worth mentioning. A significant assumption that is made that reinforces one of the assumptions named above is that when Toland says that faith is knowledge, by knowledge, in that context, he means the Lockean knowledge that only comes about by intuition and demonstration.[21] This is incor-

19. Sullivan, *John Toland*, 216. Sullivan notes that this is not the only way in which Toland tries to undermine the authority of Scripture. This makes more sense of his otherwise cryptic earlier statement regarding Toland but not Locke: "Toland was faithful to Locke in insisting that, in order to *acknowledge* anything, one must first have a clear and distinct idea of it" (emphasis mine) (76).

20. Woolhouse, *Locke: A Biography*, 408–9.

21. This reduces Christianity to mere natural religion or morality. Leask, "Personation and Immanent Undermining," 245; Sullivan, *John Toland*, 126; 81–82; Beiser, *Sovereignty of Reason*, 251–52. Beiser is possibly tripped up initially by Toland's calling faith knowledge. Beiser notes that Toland makes clear and distinct ideas a requirement for faith and knowledge; but he thinks Toland is sometimes inconsistent and makes clear and distinct ideas necessary for knowledge alone (252). Champion, *Republican Learning*, 79–86. I am admittedly perplexed by his assessment of Toland's writing that faith is knowledge. He seems to get Toland correctly on this point: "Faith was shorthand for indicating that an individual understood what they believed" (84). That statement

rect and just reinforces the popular, but incorrect Stillingfleet reading of Toland that he teaches that only certainty can be had with clear and distinct ideas; that is, both assumptions greatly limit certainty in matters of the faith. It is also for some an explanation of the way by which Toland subordinates revelation to reason or evidence of it.[22] In fact, it will be shown that Toland is appropriating one of Locke's uses of the term knowledge when he says faith is knowledge, but not the use that Beiser, Sullivan, and Leask think.

The approaches of the scholars who actually are investigating Toland, discussed above, are often the same. It is assumed that Stillingfleet read Toland correctly. Evidence is then looked for supporting these views and found. The evidence as construed, however, cannot be supported by the context from which it was pulled. Possibly sensing this, Leask's recent article

---

is correct. Prior to this, however, he says that Toland "was to collapse Locke's distinction by the assertion that 'Faith is knowledge'" (79). Lucci, *Scripture and Deism*, 72–73, 81–82. Lucci acknowledges that he has read Champion's work, even using Champion's social assessment of Toland's identification of faith and knowledge (ibid., 81–82; Champion, *Republican Learning*, 79–80). Champion portrays Toland as not being concerned so much with theology: "Toland, as we will see, was concerned with epistemological certainty too, but the context for the performance of that certainty was not theological but a broader social community" (79, quoted by Lucci, *Scripture and Deism*, 81–82). Lucci's manner of using Toland's own words and other scholars' quotes on Toland on this issue—Toland's admitting faith can be called knowledge—without comment makes it difficult to understand what *he* thinks. There will be no interaction with Champion and Lucci on this point.

22. Sullivan, *John Toland*, 126; Leask, "Personation and Imminent Undermining," 242–46; Beiser, *Sovereignty of Reason*, 250–54. Sullivan thinks that Toland's identification of faith and knowledge is a/the way that he rules out revelation with novelty as being divine. Both Leask and Beiser believe that they have spotted a verifiability criterion in Toland, and that is a/the way that he subordinates revelation to reason. They both think that one must reason from her personal experience—experience being another understudied term in *CNM*—before assenting to a proposition. That is, they both think of experience in a common, modern-day sense of the term and believe it points to a verifiability criterion. It is in this sense that Leask reads Toland's identification of faith and knowledge: "Toland, as we have just seen, has no such qualms about maintaining the priority of reason—to that extent that he will even declare an *identity* of faith and knowledge" (245). Leask also appears to think that *CNM* flatly rejects revelation with novelty (243–44, 246). It is not clear whether or not he thinks that this novelty restriction and the verifiability criterion are the same restriction. Either way, they both result in a subordination of revelation to reason, albeit with slight differences as will be touched on briefly in chapter 4. Beiser's understanding of what Toland means by faith is knowledge is wrapped up in the verifiability criterion as well. He also might think that his verifiability criterion has the same results as Sullivan's novelty restriction. On a related issue, evidence, an extremely important term in *CNM*, is taken wrongly to mean empirical proof, by at least Beiser, which greatly distorts what Toland is attempting to convey (254).

comparing the epistemologies of John Locke and John Toland makes a commendable effort in exegeting the works of the respective thinkers.

Investigating and comparing Locke's and Toland's ideas and their notions of reason, not to mention the other heavily intertwined issues, and their connections, is too cumbersome for one chapter. Therefore ideas and certainty and the related issue of knowledge will be investigated here. It is important to mention that this chapter will not critique Locke or Toland, nor will it focus on the contemporary discussions over Locke's so-called representative theory of perception.[23] The exploration of Locke and Toland on the issue of reason and its relationship to faith and revelation, as said earlier, will be treated in later chapters. The implication of this is that this chapter can only index the beginning of the aforementioned problematic, scholarly assessments of Toland's epistemology and the difficulties that plague Locke scholarship on the issues of reason, faith, and revelation.

PART III: IDEAS, KNOWLEDGE, AND CERTAINTY

Locke's *Essay* on Ideas, Knowledge, and Certainty

Ideas are foundational to the *Essay*. They are what the mind utilizes in thinking; they are mental representations (II.i.1). They are all ultimately derived from our experience or observation, no ideas being innate: "Our Observation employ'd either about *external, sensible Objects; or about the internal Operations of our Minds, perceived and reflected on by our selves, is that, which supplies our Understandings with all the materials of thinking*" (II.i.2). On the one hand, from our senses we obtain simple ideas from external objects such as colors, taste, etc. In fact, most of our simple ideas come from sensation (II.i.3). On the other hand, some fundamental or simple ideas come about by reflection, "that notice which the Mind takes of its own Operations, and the manner of them, by reason whereof, there come to be *Ideas* of these Operations in the Understanding." Examples of these ideas that come from observing ourselves from within are: perception, thinking, doubting, believing, reasoning, knowing, and willing. Locke also includes passions, such as satisfaction and uneasiness that might arise from any thought, in these operations (II.i.4).

Ideas can be divided into two primary categories: simple ideas and complex ideas. Simple ideas are the ones outlined above that come only from sensation and reflection. Humans can no more invent a new simple idea than they can picture a color that has not been before seen. Complex

---

23. Cf. Yolton, "Way of Ideas"; Yolton, *John Locke*.

ideas are combinations of simple ideas. They find their construction in the mind as it observes an object or situation or when it thinks about something that is not simple while not under the present influence of an external object (II.ii). In addition, while the mind is wholly passive in the reception of simple ideas, this is not the case in forming complex ideas, where it "uses some kind of Liberty." If not, what else would explain the differences among people regarding their ideas of gold or justice (II.xxx.3)?

There are a number of non-mutually-exclusive, helpful ways that ideas, namely complex ideas, can be further categorized: clear versus obscure, distinct versus confused, real versus fantastical, adequate versus inadequate, and true versus false. The first two categorization pairs are closely interconnected: clear versus obscure and distinct versus confused. Of clear and obscure ideas, Locke says that they are the same in the mind as they are in the sight (II.xxix.2). Simple ideas, the foundation of our complex ideas, are clear. "*Complex Ideas*, as they are made up of Simple ones: so they are *clear*, when the *Ideas*, that go to their Composition, are clear; and the Number and Order of those Simple *Ideas*, that are Ingredients of any Complex one, is determinate and certain" (II.xxix.2). Also, "As a *clear Idea* is that whereof the Mind has a full and evident perception, so a *distinct idea* is that wherein the Mind perceives a difference from all other; and a *confused Idea* is such an one, as is not sufficiently distinguishable from another, from which it ought to be different" (II.xxix.4). So, curtly stated, a clear complex idea is clear by virtue of the certainty of order and permanency of its simple idea ingredients (simple ideas are always clear). Otherwise the complex idea is obscure. It is distinct depending on whether or not it can be distinguished from similar ideas from which it ought to be different (typically alerted by virtue of their different names) (II.xxix.5–6). Otherwise it is confused (with another idea from which it ought to be distinct). Thus, one might have a clear idea of something but the complex idea does not have enough elements to distinguish it from another particular idea. The clear idea will be confused with that other idea from which it ought to be distinct and at the same time be distinct from all other ideas. In short, when it is said that two ideas are confused, the situation is really such that two words that are supposed to indicate two distinct ideas are anchored to the same idea.

Obscure ideas deserve additional comment. Locke does not explain these thoroughly. Some guess can be made at what he would say. Again, a clear complex idea is clear by virtue of the order and permanency of its simple idea ingredients. When a complex idea is said to be obscure, in truth the situation involves a number of ideas that are intended by the mind to be the same but are not due to one or a combination of the following: spatial distance, environment (such as lighting color, consistency, and brightness), memory capacity, and sensory capacity. Also, an obscure idea's obscurity most assuredly, in many situations, has something to do with our mind's typical procedure of filling-in-the-gaps, so to speak, with what we would expect to preside in the object focused on by the mind from similar ideas we retain in our memories. While in the case of "confused ideas" there is really one idea with two names, in the case of an "obscure idea" the scenario truly involves different ideas that the mind intends to be identical.

The issue is more interesting, however, when concentrating on the fact that some complex ideas can be clear and distinct in part and obscure and confused in another. Locke uses different examples to illustrate this. For instance a 1,000-sided polygon is distinct from a 999-sided polygon in number of sides but not in its figure. Or, in other words, we could know we are looking at a polygon but could not distinguish the two aforementioned polygons from one another simply by looking at them. We would have to count their sides. Their figures in comparison by sight become confused. Likewise, we have clear ideas about certain lengths, comparison of lengths, duration, etc. But the idea of boundlessness or parts so small we cannot see with the naked eye, although clear in part—such as the consideration of certain lengths, addition, and subtraction—are obscure and confused in another—such as how they appear to the mind or the eye (II.xxix.13–16).

Moreover, clear and distinct often are coupled together while obscure and confused often go hand-in-hand. A clear idea has better potential to be distinct from another idea that is like it. As said above, obscurity is simply the lack of certainty of order and permanency of its simple ingredients. This can be due to the environment, one's memory, or both. Regarding the environment, the lighting might be such that the details keep changing as one looks at something far off. With respect to the memory, obscure ideas are the product of the memory's inability to reframe an intended idea consistently with the same permanency and order, making the intended idea mutable; and thus in actuality the intended idea is represented by multiple ideas. This often results in producing confused ideas because two somewhat obscure intended ideas that ought to be distinct, and sometimes are in the mind, will at times be perceived to be the same.

Next, Locke looks at three other categorizations of ideas that evolve from considerations of the ideas "in reference to things from whence they are taken, or which they may be supposed to represent," namely real versus fantastical ideas, adequate versus inadequate ideas, and true versus false ideas (II.xxx.1). Locke explains real and fantastical ideas first. Real ideas have conformity to the archetype, which is or can be found in nature; whereas fantastical ideas have no foundation in nature (II.xxx.1). Simple ideas are always real as they agree to the power of the things which produce them in our minds—our minds being in a passive state of reception. Complex ideas, called mixed modes, like courage, or an idea of a square, and complex ideas of relations between two ideas, have a *possibility* of existing in reality so they are real. Substance is not so easy to categorize. The ideas of substances are real when "they are such Combinations of simple *Ideas*, as are really united, and co-exist in Things without us" (II.xxx.5).

Locke then makes a distinction within real ideas: adequate and inadequate ideas. "Those I call *Adequate*, which perfectly represent those Archetypes, which the Mind supposes them taken from; which it intends them to stand for; and to which it refers them. *Inadequate Ideas* are such, which are but a partial, or incomplete representation of those Archetypes to which they are referred" (II.xxxi.1). Simple ideas are adequate as they cannot be produced at will and answer exactly (as intended by God) to the power of things (II.xxxi.2). Our complex ideas of modes that are created from the human mind itself cannot be but adequate because they can only reference what they are intended to reference, itself. They can be inadequate only in the sense that they are intended to correspond to the adequate ideas held by another but do not (II.xxxi.3–5).

Substances are included in the adequate-inadequate discussion as well. They can refer to a supposed real essence of a species of things or they are intended only to be representations of things that exist via the "*Ideas* of those qualities that are discoverable in them." Both instances only ever result in imperfect and inadequate ideas. The complex ideas of the substance cannot be the real essence of any substance, for the properties we discover in that body would be deducible from those ideas and the necessary connections between the properties would be known if they were. This can be contrasted with the complex idea of a triangle: "as all Properties of a Triangle depend on, and, as far as they are discoverable, are deducible from the complex *Idea* of three Lines, including a Space." In natural objects we do not have the ability to discover the essence from which all properties flow. Therefore, when we think about their real essences we have no distinct idea (II.xxxi.6). It follows that the "Ideas of *Substances* must be *all inadequate* in that respect, as not containing in them that real Essence, which the Mind intends they should" (II.xxxi.7). Secondly, even the ideas of substance as an acknowledged mere representation of things that exist, which come closer to what the mind in that case can actually yield versus substances considered as essences of species, are inadequate because we cannot know all of the thing's powers and qualities; thus they do not fully conform to their archetype. For instance the qualities of gold continue to be discovered today and we do not have an indubitable connection between the properties (II.xxxi.8–9). In short, whatever is intended by our complex ideas of substances will always be inadequate (II.xxxi.11) and simply be a so-called nominal essence (II.xxxi.12–14). This would be the same for mathematical figures if we simply collected their properties. But, we do know the essence of these figures. One can know the geometric formula of an ellipse and how all of a given ellipse's measurements cohere: "Whereas having in our plain *Idea*, the whole Essence of that Figure, we from thence discover those Properties, and demonstratively see how they flow, and are inseparable from it" (II.xxxi.11).

The final distinction Locke makes within real ideas is: true versus false ideas. Since ideas are but bare appearances they cannot be properly true and false (II.xxxii.1). They can, however, be considered true or false when the mind passes judgment on them, affirming or denying something about them. In other words, when they become the subject of propositions they can be true or false (II.xxxii.3). In short, "When-ever the mind refers any of its *Ideas* to any thing extraneous to them, they are then *capable to be called true or false*" (II.xxxii.4). For instance, an idea one holds in one's mind may be true or false if it is supposed to be conformable to that found in the mind of another person. Also, if the mind supposes the idea to be conformable to something in real existence it can be true or false. An example is: the idea of a centaur thought actually to be roaming the woods or, at least having once existed, is false. A third source of falsity deals with the ideas of substances generally: "When the Mind *referrs* any of its *Ideas to* that *real* Constitution, and *Essence* of any thing, whereon all its properties depend: and thus the greatest part, if not all our *Ideas* of Substances, are false" (II.xxxii.5). The complex idea of a substance is false when it is supposed to be the mental representation of the unknown essence. When "substance" is considered as a collection of simple ideas that refer to patterns in things, this "substance" can be false if it includes a property that does not actually coexist with the others. If it negates a property that is constantly found in the thing, it is not false but ought to simply be called imperfect and inadequate (II.xxxii.18).

In short, Locke uses various categories for ideas. Simple ideas are always clear, distinct, real, adequate, and true. The situation with complex ideas is more complicated. Firstly, complex ideas can be described as clear or obscure in part. If there is as little as one clear simple idea that is certain and permanent within a complex idea such that that complex idea is distinct from a similar complex idea, the ideas are then distinct, at least in relation to each other. Otherwise the two ideas are in the mind identical and therefore confused. Ideas can be put in the remaining categories in considering them in reference to something. So thirdly, complex ideas can be real or fantastical, and fourthly, real ideas can be categorized as adequate or inadequate. Finally, complex ideas can be true or false when the mind is affirming or denying something about them.

Knowledge is another important term that Locke uses. The first sense of the word that he uses is explained by the following definition: "*Knowledge* then seems to me to be nothing but the *perception of the connection and agreement, or disagreement and repugnancy of any of our Ideas* (IV.i.2)." Regarding this agreement and disagreement he lists four sorts: identity and diversity, relation in general, co-existence or necessary connection, and real existence (IV.i.3). Locke notes that the first act of the mind is to perceive its ideas, know each one, and perceive their difference. While Locke could divide these related actions up further, he does not. This—the identity and diversity sort of knowledge—is the fundamental sense of knowledge and that without which we could have no knowledge in the below senses. We have no need of maxims but the mind immediately perceives identity and diversity as soon as two ideas are perceived clearly (IV.i.4).

Locke explains the other sorts of knowledge briefly. Relation is nothing more than the perception of the relationship between two ideas (IV.i.5). It is the agreement the mind sees between two different ideas in various respects (IV.i.5). Co-existence (or non-co-existence) is simply the mind's seeing the presence (or absence) of ideas within larger ideas. This sort of knowledge "belongs particularly to Substances." For instance, the idea of yellow co-exists with the idea of gold (IV.i.6). Identity and co-existence knowledge are nothing more than relation knowledge but Locke believes that they deserve their own distinct head. Knowledge of real existence simply regards whether something exists or not. He gives the following examples of the four sorts: "Thus *Blue is not Yellow*, is of Identity. *Two Triangles upon equal Basis, between two Parallels are equal*, is of Relation. *Iron is susceptible of magnetical Impressions*, is of Co-existence, *God is*, is of real Existence" (IV.i.7).

The other topic that is of importance to consider here is certainty. But certainty is only given by knowledge, of which there are three degrees or methods—intuition, demonstration, and sensation—by which we arrive at one of the four sorts of knowledge. If knowledge is immediate it is called intuitive (IV.ii.1). One simply "sees" the truth without mental discourse, and does so by the faculty of distinct perception (IV.ii.5). Intuition is the clearest degree of knowledge and gives the most certainty of which the human faculties are capable (IV.ii.1). The next degree of knowledge is demonstration and it builds on intuition. It is not immediate but requires reasoning and indubitable proofs (IV.ii.2).[24] "Those intervening *Ideas*, which serve to shew the agreement of any two others, are called *Proofs*; and where the agreement, or disagreement, is by this means plainly and clearly perceived, it is called *Demonstration*, it being *shewn* to the Understanding, and the Mind

---

24. This is the first time an allusion to reason is mentioned in book IV of the *Essay*.

made see that it is so." The quickness of the mind to find these intermediate ideas and apply them rightly is called sagacity (IV.ii.3). Demonstrative knowledge is not as bright and clear and is without the full assurance that always accompanies intuition. This is because demonstrative knowledge requires hard work, involves initial doubt, and requires more memory the longer the indubitable proof is—this last characteristic being culpable for causing many to embrace falsehoods (IV.ii.6–7). It is important here to note Michael Ayers's description of Locke's degrees of knowledge:

> The notion of degrees of knowledge does not imply that the "perception" involved in demonstration and sensitive knowledge is fallible. What Locke supposed to vary in degree, since it is not probability, seems to be security from a certain sort of error: not the error of perceiving what is false, for that is impossible, but the error of taking ourselves to perceive (or have perceived) what is not (or was not) really perceived. We may mistake "falsehood for demonstration."

Ayers continues and explains that it is not the faculty of knowledge that assents wrongly but the faculty of judgment that believes falsehoods.[25]

Then there is sensitive Knowledge, "which going beyond her probability, and yet not reaching perfectly to either of the foregoing degrees of Certainty" (IV.ii.14), gives us "an assurance that *deserves the name of Knowledge*" (IV.xi.3). The existence of the observed external objects are doubted by some, but that doubt should be dissipated because of the qualitative difference between the ideas generated, for instance, by a hot stove that one perceives her hand to be on presently versus thinking back to that painful experience. The certainty of things without "is not only *as great* as our frame can attain to, but *as our Condition needs*," as ordained by God (IV.xi.8). Locke notes that it is by intuition that we have knowledge of ourselves, by demonstration that we can have knowledge of God, and it is through sensation that we have knowledge of other things (IV.ix–xi).

In sum, this section has so far explored a number of interrelated topics. First, it investigated Locke's treatment of ideas, including his various categorizations of them. The categories are as follows: simple versus complex, clear versus obscure, distinct versus confused, real versus fantastical, adequate versus inadequate, and true versus false. Next, it explored some of the various senses of the term knowledge employed in the *Essay*, the notion of certainty, and how knowledge and certainty relate. While Locke has four sorts of knowledge, there are three methods by which it comes about. Certainty is only produced by and supervenes upon knowledge.

25. Ayers, *Locke*, 1:95.

Toland's *CNM* on Ideas, Knowledge, and Certainty

Having reviewed Locke's position on ideas, knowledge, and certainty, this chapter will now turn to John Toland's *CNM* and explore his treatment of the same topics. The question that will be asked is: How does Toland's treatment of ideas, knowledge, and certainty compare to Locke's in the *Essay*? The answer will be shown to be: *CNM*'s treatment of those topics is not as detailed as the *Essay's* nor does it always use the same terminology, but *CNM* definitely comports with the *Essay* on these topics. This is in opposition to important Toland scholarship, most of which claims that Toland collapses faith into Lockean knowledge and a lone voice that believes Toland incorporates innate ideas into *CNM*. These scholars will be responded to in the course of the explanation of Toland's notions of ideas, knowledge, and certainty.

As Stillingfleet noticed, John Toland's discourse on ideas seems in many respects Lockean. By ideas Toland means "*the immediate Object of the Mind when it thinks, or any Thought that the Mind imploys about any thing*" (11). Toland's ideas, like Locke's, are mental representations or "Representative Beings" (19; cf. 11). What is more, these ideas, like Locke's, can be deemed simple or complex. Toland notes that simple and distinct ideas—what Locke would merely call simple, distinct being understood—"are the sole Matter and Foundation of all our *Reasoning*" (11–12). These simple ideas are derived from the same two sources Locke notes, sensation and reflection, although the former thinker does not use the term reflection; Toland writes:

> But the bare Act of receiving Ideas into the Mind, whether *by the Intromission of the Senses*, as Colours, Figures, Sounds, Smells, *etc.* or whether those Ideas be *the simple Operations of the Soul* about what it thus gets from without, as meer *Consciousness* for Example, *Knowing, Affirming*, or *Denying*, without any farther Considerations: This bare Act, I say, of receiving such Ideas into the Mind, is not strictly *Reason*, because the soul herein is purely passive (9–10).

And, as Toland says above, these simple ideas are received passively, just as Locke had said before him. There is no liberty there. Toland goes on to expand his explanation slightly by clarifying that we receive these ideas from external objects that bear on the human senses and from the consciousness or awareness of the operations of our minds that we notice from being confronted with external objects: "*Knowing, Perceiving, Affirming, Denying, Considering, Willing, Desiring,* and the Ideas of all the other Operations of the Mind, which are thus occasion'd by the Antecedent Impressions of sensible Objects" (9–10).

At one point, Toland discusses *"Means of Information"* or *"those Ways whereby any thing comes barely to our Knowledg, without necessarily commanding our Assent."* He notes two main types, experience and authority. He goes on to make a distinction between external and internal experience, which is important here: *"Experience is either external, which furnished us with the Ideas of sensible Objects; or internal, which helps us to the Ideas of the Operations of our own minds. This is the common Stock of all our Knowledg; nor can we possibly have Ideas any other way without new Organs or Faculties"* (16–17).[26] Thus, it is clear that we are limited to the simple ideas that are produced by our present organs and faculties.

Toland's explanation of complex ideas is very brief but also comports with Locke's explanation of them. When Toland notes that simple and distinct ideas are stored up in the "great Repository of the Understanding" and are the sole matter and foundation of reasoning also, he follows with: "For the Mind does upon occasion compare them together, compound them into complex Ideas, and enlarge, contract, or separate them, as it discovers their Circumstances capable or not" (12–13). Moreover, Toland explains that these complex ideas are not just of complex objects we see or with which we come into direct contact with, but others such as God, created spirits, arguing, suspension, and so on. That is, they also include *"meerly intellectual or abstracted Thought"* (11).

The further explanations of ideas are peppered throughout *CNM* and Toland never comes close to the depth and detail of coverage that Locke affords them. Whereas Locke discusses a number of not-mutually-exclusive ways that ideas can be categorized—clear versus obscure, distinct versus confused, real versus fantastical, adequate versus inadequate, and true versus false—Toland simply employs the categories he needs and any explanations given are either brief or inferred from how he is using them. Apparently, Toland *intended* his explanations of ideas and other terms to be just detailed enough to allow his philosophically untrained readers to understand what he is saying without burdening them with details impertinent to the discussions at hand. Hence, in the preface of *CNM*, Toland remarks, *"I have in many Places made explanatory Repetitions of difficult Words, by synonymous Terms of a more general and known Use. This Labour, I grant, is of no Benefit to Philosophers, but it is of considerable Advantage to the Vulgar, which I'm far from neglecting"* (xvii). This quote speaks to his desire to be readable to

---

26. It is doubtful that simple and distinct ideas are intended by Toland to exhaust the category of experience. They are the foundation of and are included in the category, however.

the common public; and this chapter's treatments (and those of the other chapters as well) of his categories of ideas, knowledge, and other notions will hopefully convey something of the brevity of his attention to and explanation of the various concepts.

Toland employs the categories of clear versus obscure and distinct versus confused. The way in which he couples them even comports with Locke's coupling. Regarding clear versus obscure ideas, Toland does juxtapose clear and obscure ideas or conceptions explicitly (60). Toland's understanding of *clear* agrees with Locke's. It means they are conceivable or imaginable. Toland writes:

> For Perspicuity and Obscurity are relative Terms, and what is either to me may be the quite contrary to another. If Things be deliver'd in Words not understood by the Hearer, nor demonstrated to agree with other Truths already very clear, or now so made to him, he cannot conceive 'em" (23–24).

Put another way, the words attached to various ideas must be understood and the various ideas reconcilable with other truths for the larger idea proposed to be conceivable. Furthermore, if it is conceivable it cannot be inherently contradictory (25–29). Moreover, Toland understands some ideas to be clear in part and obscure in others. In fact, he uses the idea of eternity, just as Locke does, as an example. There are certain aspects that are clear, like subtraction of bounds, but the thing is not perfectly imaginable (80–81). Whatever is the case, the little he conveys about clear versus obscure ideas does not disagree with what Locke teaches.

While Toland does not use the word "confused" with ideas, he does use the term "distinct" on occasion. He writes of our God-given design including our inability to be deceived by *"clear and distinct Ideas."* And he also uses "clear and distinct" with no comment on what he means (25, 85–86). The one place where he uses it and gives an example is evidence that his use of "clear and distinct" comports with Locke's use. There he writes, "The Idea of the *Soul* then is every whit as clear and distinct as that of the *Body*" (85). If Toland differs in the ways he uses or conceives of what he calls clear, obscure, and distinct ideas compared to Locke, it is not apparent in *CNM*.

The categories of inadequate versus adequate ideas are the only other category pair Toland explicitly employs in *CNM* and it comports with Locke's notions and treatments of the same pair. Toland includes the associated categories into a chapter entitled, "That Nothing Ought to Be Call'd a Mystery, because We Have Not an Adequate Idea of All Its Properties, Nor Any at All of Its Essence" (74). His argument in this chapter is explicit: *"nothing can be said to be a Mystery, because we have not an adequate Idea* of it, or a distinct View of all its Properties at once; for then every thing would be a Mystery" (74). There are no mysteries in nature or religion for lack of an adequate idea (cf. 87). Although Toland does not give a definition of adequate and inadequate ideas, his description of it is akin to Locke's as Toland calls an adequate idea a complete one: "*because we have not an adequate or compleat Idea of whatever belongs to it*" (79). Toland notes that God's attributes, namely his eternity, are not mysterious for lack of an adequate or complete notion (80–81). Furthermore, and again, like Locke, Toland focuses a significant portion of his incorporation of adequate and inadequate ideas on substance. Toland argues that the fact that we cannot know all of the properties of any substance or know any real essences of a substance (that which from all properties naturally flow or result), two assertions pointed out by Locke, ought not to mean things are to be called mysteries. Toland forces the reader to ponder the following question: If not having an adequate idea of things were grounds for calling them mysteries, what would not be a mystery (cf. 79)? Toland explains further why we ought not call bodies mysteries: "The Reason is, because *knowing nothing of Bodies but their Properties, God has wisely provided we should understand no more of these than are useful and necessary for us*; which is all our present Condition needs" (75–76). (Even this reasoning is strikingly similar to Locke's, who, although not arguing against calling things mysteries, does point out that what we are capable of sensing is all for our well-being [IV.xi.8].) God should not be called a mystery for lack of knowing his real essence either. Again, the same explanation is given: "I remark'd in the Beginning of this Chapter, that we know nothing of things, but such of the Properties as were *necessary* and *useful*. We may say the same of *God*; for every Act of our Religion is directed by the Consideration of some of his Attributes, without ever thinking of his *Essence*" (86).[27] There is a final point that is worth noting that connects Toland and Locke in the discussion of adequate and inadequate ideas. When discussing nominal and real essences, he notes that he distinguishes nominal essences from real essences "after an excellent modern Philosopher" (82). All commentators acknowledge this to be a reference to Locke.

There are a few conclusions we can draw so far regarding Toland's and Locke's respective treatments of ideas. First, Toland employs clear versus obscure, distinct versus confused, and adequate versus inadequate distinctions that agree with Locke's categorical distinctions that go by the same names. Second, he, it is widely thought, points to Locke as being important

---

27. Cf. Toland, *Vindicius*, 84–89. There Toland comments on *CNM*'s chapter explored here.

to his distinction of real and nominal essences. Third, that Toland does not explicitly use the true versus false or the real versus fantastical ideas is no reason to think he rejects those distinctions. It is more likely that there was no reason to bring them up or to complicate matters with relatively pedantic distinctions.

The pages that follow will continue an exploration of Toland's fundamental epistemological notions, concentrating on knowledge and certainty, and interact with scholars on what this section suggests are serious misreadings on Toland's various uses of the term knowledge. Scholarly readings of Toland's teachings on knowledge are highly problematic. As indicated in part II, many noted scholars understand Toland to be using the term knowledge in the Lockean sense that refers to the knowledge that comes by the method of intuition and demonstration when Toland claims that faith can be called knowledge. For some, their misreading of Toland on this point fuels the notion that Toland rejects any revelation as such that asserts novelty, an effective subordination of revelation to reason. Another aforementioned misreading pertaining to Toland's notion of immediate knowledge has been recently promulgated. This scholar believes there is evidence that *CNM*'s treatment of immediate knowledge conflates innate and intuitive ideas in opposition to Locke. In short, the pages that follow will contain exposition of Toland as well as interactions with the relevant scholarship.

Toland's discussion of knowledge falls within the bounds of what Locke discusses, but Toland's treatment, like his treatment of ideas, although conformable, is much less detailed. Toland's definition of knowledge is: "nothing else but *the Perception of the Agreement or Disagreement of our Ideas in a greater or lesser Number, whereinsoever this Agreement or Disagreement may consist*" (12). This is conceptually the same as Locke's given in the *Essay* IV.i.2: "*Knowledge* then seems to me to be nothing but *the perception of the connection and agreement, or disagreement and repugnancy of any of our ideas.*" Whereas Locke goes on to define four sorts of knowledge—identity and diversity, relation, co-existence or necessary connection, and real existence—Toland does not.

The connotation of knowledge Toland employs often and which causes much mischief for interpreters is, however, akin to Locke's description of knowledge in the identity and diversity sense. In the *Essay*, Locke writes: "As to the first sort of Agreement or Disagreement, *viz. Identity, or Diversity*. 'Tis the first Act of the Mind, when it has any Sentiments or *Ideas* at all, to perceive its *Ideas*, and so far as it perceives them, to know each what it is, and thereby also to perceive their difference, and that one is not another" (IV.i.4). Thus, simply to perceive or understand or frame an idea is to *know* that idea in a qualified sense. Likewise one could *know* a false proposition in that sense as well. It is in this manner of speaking that Toland often employs knowledge, even for things such as particular religious doctrines of which we can have no certainty but only probability. It is this manner of speaking about probable things that misdirects Toland scholars.

Two scholars who misinterpret what Toland intends by using the term knowledge with regard to that which is only subject to belief are Leask and Sullivan. Referencing a particular passage of *CNM,* Leask writes: "Toland, as we have just seen, has no such qualms about maintaining the priority of reason—to the extent that he will even declare an *identity* of faith and knowledge." Leask says this to drive home his argument that Toland's epistemology runs counter to Locke's, which argues for "the need for a suprarational, gratuitous, *Biblical,* morality."[28] Sullivan similarly believes Toland rejects the novelty of Scripture by his construal of faith as knowledge and points to the exact same passage as does Leask as evidence. Sullivan concludes, "There were no exceptions to Toland's notion of faith as a form of knowledge."[29] Both Sullivan and Leask reference the said passage as backing up their claims but do not quote from it or demonstrate any attempt at its exposition. The passage they reference is as follows:

> From all these Observations, and what went before, it evidently follows that *Faith* is so far from being an implicit Assent to any thing above Reason, that this Notion directly contradicts the Ends of Religion, the Nature of Man, and the Goodness and Wisdom of God. But at this rate, some will be apt to say, *Faith* is no longer *Faith* but *Knowledg.* I answer, that if *Knowledg* be taken for a present and immediate View of things, I have no where affirm'd any thing like it, but the contrary in many Places. But if by *Knowledg* be meant understanding what is believ'd, then I stand by it that *Faith* is *Knowledg:* I have all along maintain'd it, and the very Words are promiscuously us'd for one another in the *Gospel* (139).[30]

Toland is saying that right assent or faith concerns only that which we comprehend, understand, or perceive. This does not make faith a species of knowledge, as Sullivan claims, nor does it entail a rejection of things without an evidentiary basis founded upon our own life experience, as Leask

---

28. Leask, "Personation and Imminent Undermining," 245; cf. Marko, "Promulgation of Right Morals."

29. Sullivan, *John Toland,* 126.

30. Leask references 3.4.65 of the 1st ed. of *CNM,* which is 3.4.66 or p. 139 of the second edition of *CNM.*

claims.[31] Toland has argued against that. But faith is knowledge in the sense that one comprehends, or "knows," the idea that one believes. This agrees with what Toland says throughout *CNM*. For instance, earlier he writes: "Rightly speaking then, we are accounted to *comprehend* any thing when its chief Properties and their several Uses are known to us: for *to comprehend* in all correct Authors is nothing else but *to know*; and as *of what is not knowable we can have no Idea, so it is nothing to us*" (76–77).

Beiser is another scholar who misunderstands what Toland is intending when Toland allows matters of faith to be referred to as knowledge. Beiser asserts that Toland gives two criteria for belief: propositions must be clear and distinct and they must be empirically verifiable.[32] Referencing the last quote above from Toland, Beiser remarks: "It is unclear, however, whether Toland was always so strict as to demand clarity and distinctness as a *condition of belief*. In some passages he appears to change his tune and to insist upon it only as a *condition of knowledge*."[33] In a prior part of his treatment of *CNM*, Beiser insists, "Toland employs the traditional distinction between clear, distinct, and adequate ideas."[34] So, Beiser interprets Toland as saying, in the last *CNM* excerpt given above, that we can know things without adequate ideas, and that we only need clear and distinct ideas for knowledge. If that is true, then clear and distinct ideas would seem, according to Beiser, to be too strict of a requirement for belief. Therefore, he thinks Toland changes his position part way through *CNM* as evidenced by the second to last excerpt from *CNM*, thus jettisoning the first criterion.[35] In said passage, however, and as already stated, Toland is actually saying that comprehending an idea or proposition can be in a sense knowing that idea or proposition. That one must know or comprehend the proposition in the described sense in order to be believed is mentioned throughout *CNM*, even toward the beginning. Early on, Toland writes, "But God . . . has also endu'd us with the Power of *suspending our Judgments about whatever is uncertain, and of never assenting but to clear Perceptions*" (22). That is, one cannot rightly assent to something one cannot comprehend. In other words, Toland does not feign or think that all theological doctrines must be clear

---

31. Again, it is not clear that Leask sees a difference between the novelty restriction and the verifiability criterion that he interprets Toland as promulgating.

32. Beiser, *The Sovereignty of Reason*, 251. Beiser is using the first edition and the page numbers he references are 77–78. Both editions read exactly the same on this passage.

33. Ibid., 252.

34. Ibid., 250n77.

35. Ibid., 252.

and distinct, or even empirically verifiable, but rather if they are to be considered they must be comprehensible. Again, this is a message throughout *CNM*.

Moreover, there are other aspects of Toland's teachings on knowledge, namely degrees of knowledge, that comport with Locke's. First, what Locke calls intuitive knowledge, Toland calls immediate knowledge. Toland defines immediate knowledge as the following: "*When the Mind, without the Assistance of any other Idea, immediately perceives the Agreement or Disagreement of two or more Ideas*" (12). He notes that it cannot be called reason even though it is the highest degree of evidence. This knowledge is self-evident. Furthermore this knowledge automatically creates axioms and maxims: "Propositions so clear of themselves as to want no Proofs, their Terms being once understood, are commonly known by the Names of *Axioms* and *Maxims*" (12).

Leask believes that Toland, in his description of immediate knowledge, is diverging greatly from Locke by conflating innate ideas and intuitive ideas. He argues that Toland's mention of maxims and axioms, which Locke attacks in his argument against innate ideas, and the use of an "innate idea" example—the whole is great than any part—shows a subtle yet profound divergence from Locke.[36] Leask is mistaken in thinking Toland is incorporating innate ideas with this scanty evidence. The passage where Leask believes Toland adopts innate ideas includes Toland's definition of immediate knowledge:

> First [degree of knowledge], When the Mind, without the Assistance of any other Idea, immediately perceives the Agreement or Disagreement of two or more Ideas, as that Two and Two is Four, that Red is not Blew; it cannot be call'd Reason, tho it be the highest Degree of Evidence: For here's no need of Discourse or Probation, *Self-evidence* excluding all manner of Doubt and Darkness. Propositions so clear of themselves as to want no Proofs, their Terms being once understood, are commonly known by the Names of *Axioms* and *Maxims*. And it is visible that their Number is indefinite, and not confin'd only to two or three abstracted Propositions made (as all *Axioms* are) from the Observation of particular Instances; as, that *the Whole is greater than any Part*, that *Nothing can have no Properties* (12–13).

Toland is saying that self-evident propositions could be called maxims or axioms. Axioms and maxims, therefore, ought not to be limited to the small number they otherwise would be if they were limited to those abstractions

---

36. Leask, "Personation and Imminent Undermining," 251–55.

from particular propositions and instances, such as "the Whole is greater than any Part." Toland is doing nothing more than offering an abridged form of Locke's argument in *Essay* IV.vii. There, Locke argues that some consider maxims or axioms innate because self-evident (IV.vii.1); but there is immediate knowledge that is self-evident that does not require the intervention of other ideas (IV.vii.2). Locke then considers whether self-evidence is peculiar to these so-called maxims and answers "that several other Truths, not allow'd to be Axioms, partake equally with them in this *Self-evidence*" (IV.vii.3). Many so-called Maxims are self-evident but so are "even an almost infinite number of *other Propositions*" (IV.vii.3); every idea we have from knowledge of identity gives self-evident propositions (IV.vii.4) as do some from the co-existence sort of knowledge (IV.vii.5) and from modes (IV.vii.6). He argues that the mind proceeds from particular propositions to associated general and abstracted propositions or maxims (IV.vii.9–11). Toland has not conflated innate and intuitive ideas as Leask thinks, but in fact goes so far, perhaps in a sense farther than Locke, as to appropriate the terminology of those who believe in innate ideas.

Turning to Toland's other degree of knowledge, it is clear that what he calls mediate knowledge is what Locke calls demonstrative knowledge. Toland gives the definition of mediate knowledge and illustrates it as follows:

> *when the Mind cannot immediately perceive the Agreement or Disagreement of any Ideas, because they cannot be brought near enough together, and so compar'd, it applies one or more intermediate Ideas to discover it*: as, when by the successive Application of a Line to two distant Houses, I find how far they agree or disagree in Length, which I could not effect with my Eye" (13).

This is akin to Locke's general description of ratiocination: "Yet the principle Act of Ratiocination is the finding Agreement, or Disagreement of two *Ideas* one with another, by the intervention of a third. As a Man, by a Yard, finds two Houses to be of the same length, which could not be brought together to measure their Equality by *juxta*-position" (IV.xvii.18). Such is Toland's dependence on Locke that he even uses Locke's analogy of comparing the length of two houses with a measuring stick (13). What is more, Toland, like Locke, explicitly distinguishes between the method and the resultant type of knowledge. He writes, "This Method of Knowledg is properly call'd *Reason* or *Demonstration*, (as the former *Self-evidence* or *Intuition*); and it may be defin'd, *That Faculty of the Soul which discovers the Certainty of any thing dubious or obscure, by comparing it with something evidently known*" (14). Furthermore, Locke also calls demonstration reason (IV.iii.2; cf. IV.ii.2; IV.xi.1). Moreover, Toland continues on in the next section saying that the parts of the demonstration must be indubitable: "So tho *Self-evidence* excludes *Reason*, yet all *Demonstration* becomes at length *self-evident*" (14).

It is in the context of his discussion of immediate and mediate knowledge that he distinguishes between certainty and probability: "It is yet plainer, that *when we have no Notions or Ideas of a thing, we cannot reason about it at all; and where we have Ideas, if intermediate ones, to shew their constant and necessary Agreement or Disagreement, fail us, we can never go beyond* Probability (14–15)." In other words, immediate knowledge and mediate knowledge have certainty. All else is simply probable. Again, this is akin to Locke. Toland adds: "When I have arriv'd at *Knowledg*, I enjoy all the Satisfaction that attends it; where I have only *Probability*, there I suspend my Judgment, or, if it be worth the Pains, I search after Certainty" (15). He tempers this slight overstatement of never admitting probable things by conceding shortly afterwards that they must be admitted (21).

Moreover, while Toland discusses a two-fold knowledge, Locke discusses a three-fold knowledge. Locke says that the assurance of the existence of the external objects we are observing *deserves* the name knowledge (IV.ii.14). Regarding the idea of a rose that appears in his mind, Toland says:

> And I cannot doubt of this, because the Properties must belong to the exemplary Cause, or to Nothing, or be the Figments of my own Brain; But *Nothing can have no Properties,* and *I cannot make one single Idea at my Pleasure,* nor *avoid receiving Ideas when Objects work on my Senses:* Therefore I conclude the Properties of the Rose are not the Creatures of my Fancy, but belong to the exemplary Cause, that is, the Object (20).

Toland thus reasons that the only conclusion to make when something *appears* to be working on one's senses is that the thing actually exists and *is* working on one's senses. So while he does not call the conclusion of the existence of external objects sensitive knowledge as does Locke, the conceptual and functional results are equivalent.

In sum, this chapter has so far shown that *CNM*'s teaching on ideas, knowledge, and certainty are less detailed than the *Essay*'s corresponding treatments, but they agree with them. It is evident that Toland, at times, is applying categories or concepts found in the *Essay* without explanation or simply rewording some Lockean concepts. Our focus will turn in the next section to Stillingfleet's reading of the *Essay* and *CNM* regarding the topics discussed in the last two sections.

Stillingfleet's Interpretation of *CNM*'s and the *Essay*'s Treatments of Ideas, Knowledge, Certainty, and Reason from the *Discourse*

The goals of Stillingfleet's final chapter in the *Discourse* and the reasons he draws in *CNM* are explicit in the opening pages. There are two objections that he wants to tend to, only the first of which concerns us here: "1. That this Doctrine [of the Trinity] is said to be a *Mystery*, and therefore *above Reason*, and we cannot in reason be obliged to believe any such thing." There are obvious verbal similarities between this statement and the full title of Toland's *CNM*: *Christianity Not Mysterious: or, A Treatise Shewing, That There Is Nothing in the Gospel Contrary to Reason, Nor Above It: and That No Christian Doctrine Can Be Properly Call'd a Mystery*. It ought to be said from the beginning that Toland mentions the doctrine of the Trinity only once and does so with an indeterminate air, but Stillingfleet believes the work is an attack on the doctrine (27).[37] Nevertheless, Stillingfleet begins the chapter rightly explaining that one must understand what reason is and "What ground in Reason there is, to reject any Doctrine that is above it."[38] He feels that the so-called Unitarians have not explained reason adequately: "I do not find the *Unitarians* have explained the *Nature* and *Bounds* of *Reason* in such manner, as those ought to have done, who make it the Rule and Standard of what they are to believe. But sometimes they speak of *clear* and *distinct Perceptions*, sometimes of *natural Ideas*, sometimes of *congenit Notions, etc*." But, he believes Toland has tried to clarify the Unitarian position: "But a late Author hath endeavour'd to make amends for this, and takes upon him to make this matter clear."[39]

Although this portion of the chapter focuses on Stillingfleet's interpretations of Toland and Locke on ideas, knowledge, certainty, and reason, laying out his attack on *CNM* will likely prove helpful as it gives an argumentative framework that shows the logic and reveals what, in Stillingfleet's

---

37. The reference to the doctrine of the Trinity comes in a chapter entitled, "The Absurdity and Effects of Admitting Any Real or Seeming Contradictions in Religion." Toland does not, however, explicitly attack the Trinity here or in any other part of *CNM*. When he mentions the Trinity this one time it is in the context of different views of Holy Communion. He chides those who hold to transubstantiation and impanation. The subsequent sentence, which ends the paragraph, reads: "And tho the *Socinians* disown this Practice, I am mistaken if either they or the *Arians* can make their Notions of a *dignifi'd and Creature-God capable of Divine Worship*, appear more reasonable than the Extravagancies of other Sects touching the Article of the *Trinity*" (27). Some might be suspicious of him for mentioning the Trinity in this chapter, but that is really all that one can do up to this point in this book's exploration of Toland.

38. Stillingfleet, *Discourse*, 230.

39. Ibid., 231.

view, is at stake. The first part of his argument against *CNM*'s teachings, and in defense of the doctrine of the Trinity, attempts to establish a sound basis for accepting substance, nature, and person as concepts with which the reason can work and make distinctions. In doing this he articulates his understanding of Toland's definition of reason, shows that it deals only in certainties and works only with clear and distinct ideas, points out where in Locke's *Essay* Toland bases his reasoning for this last point, and argues that the defended terms—substance, nature, and person—are truly reasonable, according to his sense of the term. The second part of his argument against Toland is built upon Toland's alleged inconsistencies. Toland clearly names one mystery: real essence. If Toland will allow mysteries from nature, why not from religion? Also, Toland is ready to accept God's eternity, of which one cannot have a clear and distinct idea. If he rejects the doctrine of the Trinity on grounds of incomprehensibility he must also reject the doctrine of God's eternity as it is incomprehensible as well, neither being a clear and distinct idea, at least according to *CNM*.

Stillingfleet thus begins his critique of *CNM* by exploring what it has to say about reason. He starts at the opening of *CNM*'s section I, chapter 1, "What Reason Is Not." He proceeds as if he is taking notes, offering brief comments along the way. He thus indicates a few things that Toland claims should not be considered reason and that which might be labeled reason. He then runs together a number of quotes from *CNM*. He thinks he is summarizing *CNM*'s explanation of reason but rather he is horribly distorting it. He begins this distortion by quoting, with liberties, from *CNM*'s attempted clarification of what reason[40] is: "*Every one experiences in himself a Power, or Faculty of forming various Ideas, or Perceptions of things: of affirming, or denying according as he sees them to agree or disagree, and this is Reason in General.*"[41] This is, however, not all that Toland writes. The full quote is:

> Every one experiences in himself a Power or Faculty of forming various Ideas or Perceptions of Things: Of affirming or denying, according as he sees them to agree or disagree: And so of loving and desiring what seems good unto him; and of hating and avoiding what he thinks evil. The right use of all these Faculties is what we call Common Sense, or *Reason* in general (9).[42]

Stillingfleet has pulled out two faculties or powers—of forming ideas or perceptions and of affirming and denying what one sees to agree or disagree—and made those alone the powers of reason in general.

40. It seems as though Stillingfleet identifies Toland's reason and reason in general.
41. Stillingfleet, *Discourse*, 231–32.
42. This quote verbatim is also on page 9 of the first edition of *CNM*.

This is not the end of Stillingfleet's problems. He continues the quote, this time giving *CNM*'s definition of knowledge—knowledge in the sense of a result of a power—as an extended definition of reason—the faculty or power: "*It is not the bare receiving Ideas into the Mind, that is strictly Reason,* (who ever thought it was?) *but the Perception of the Agreement, or Disagreement of our Ideas in a greater or lesser Number; wherein soever this Agreement or Disagreement may consist.*"[43] His mistake in cutting short the first definition of reason, or reason in general, apparently makes him think that "knowledge" and "reason" are interchangeable in *CNM*. He also apparently fails to distinguish between the powers or faculties, the results of those powers, and the associated methods. Whatever the case, once he limits reason to knowledge, reason then will only consist of immediate and intermediate knowledge in some sense (the methods or associated powers or the result), which is precisely what Stillingfleet does in the tail end of his lengthy quote of run-together *CNM* snippets:

> *If the Perception be immediate without the Assistance of any other Idea, this is not call'd Reason, but Self-Evidence: but when the mind makes use of intermediate Idea's to discover that Agreement or Disagreement, this method of Knowledge is properly call'd Reason or Demonstration. And so Reason is defined to be that Faculty of the Soul, which discovers the certainty of any thing dubious or obscure, by comparing it with something evidently known.*[44]

In short, Stillingfleet does not follow *CNM*'s punctuation and sees reason, in one sense, as being knowledge, apparently in a not too repugnant way, but reason, "properly" speaking, being limited to demonstration. This is reinforced by Toland's calling demonstration "reason," just as Locke does (cf. IV.ii.2; IV.iii.2; IV.xi.1). But Toland, like Locke, goes on to incorporate assent to probable things or things not *known* as being within the compass of reason (16–24). Regardless, it is evident how Stillingfleet concludes that reason deals only with certainty according to *CNM*: from Stillingfleet's erroneous reading, the faculty of reason, properly speaking, is the faculty of demonstration!

Stillingfleet reveals something of his train of thought why he believes *CNM* teaches that certainty can only be had with clear and distinct ideas, too. Directly after the lengthy, piecemeal quoting from *CNM*, Stillingfleet writes:

---

43. Stillingfleet, *Discourse*, 232.
44. Ibid., 232.

> This is offer'd to the World, as an Account of Reason; but to shew how very loose, and unsatisfactory it is, I desire it may be consider'd that this Doctrine supposes, that we must have *clear and distinct Ideas* of whatever we pretend to any certainty of in our Minds, and that the only Way to attain certainty, is by comparing these *Ideas* together. Which excludes all certainty of Faith or Reason, where we cannot have such *clear and distinct Ideas*.[45]

He argues that since reason involves comparing ideas, they must be clear and distinct so that they can be compared. In other words, and if Stillingfleet follows what Toland is saying about demonstration, since reason is demonstration (according to Stillingfleet's reading of *CNM*) one must be able to make the necessary connections and to do that one must have clear and distinct ideas.

He then reveals what the ultimate origin of clear and distinct ideas is according to *CNM*: sensation and reflection. But he does not mean this in the same sense that Toland (and Locke) means it. Stillingfleet mistakes "simple and distinct ideas," which Toland notes are the matter and foundation of reasoning, as being identical to clear and distinct ideas that are complex. And when Toland says that simple and distinct ideas come *only* from sensation and the simple operations of the mind (reflection), Stillingfleet concludes that clear and distinct ideas come *initially* from sensation and reflection. Thus, following Stillingfleet's line of reasoning, clear and distinct ideas originally come by sensation and reflection and subsequently by one's reasoning (or demonstration if Stillingfleet is consistent with his earlier errors) about those original complex ideas that results in other clear and distinct ideas.[46]

It becomes apparent that his understanding of the creation of clear and distinct ideas significantly narrows what can be subject to reason. Again, Stillingfleet thinks that Toland's foundations of reasoning are clear and distinct ideas that are sensed or in some way depend on reflections on the operations of the mind. He writes, "Then it follows, That we can have *no Foundation of Reasoning*, where there can be no such *Ideas* from *Sensation, or Reflection*."[47] He continues: "Now this is the case of *Substance*; it is not *intromitted by the Senses*, nor depends *upon the Operations of the Mind*; and so it cannot be within the compass of our Reason. And therefore I do not wonder, that the Gentlemen of this new way of reasoning, have almost

---

45. Ibid., 232–33.
46. Ibid., 234.
47. Ibid., 234. Stillingfleet is still referring to section I, chapter 1 of *CNM*.

discarded *Substance* out of the reasonable part of the World."[48] What he is saying is more lucid a few paragraphs later where he argues that although we cannot have a clear idea of substance,[49] we can reason about it without deriving the idea of it from sensation or reflection, despite what *CNM* says.[50] After making that assertion, he continues: "we find that we can have no true Conceptions of any *Modes* or *Accidents* (no matter which) but we must conceive a *Substratum*, or Subject wherein they are. Since it is a Repugnancy to our first Conceptions of things, that *Modes* or *Accidents* should subsist by themselves."[51] In short, Stillingfleet thinks that *CNM* promotes the notion that although we can have clear and distinct ideas of the accidents of a substance, we can have no idea of the substance itself or at least no clear and distinct idea because we cannot sense it beyond its accidents. Once he notes that Toland thinks we can have no clear idea and at another that we can have no idea.[52] (Even though the former argument would make more sense because Toland discusses nominal essences and inadequate ideas of substance, Locke also thinks that Stillingfleet can be read on a few occasions as conceiving of reason as being able to operate without ideas.[53]) Either because we have no idea or because we have no clear and distinct idea, substance cannot be certain or the subject of reasoning according to *CNM*. Whichever way he thinks Toland is arguing, they both give the same results. Stillingfleet argues that this is foolhardy because it is reasonable and certain, according to *his* senses of the terms, to conclude a substratum despite the fact that one cannot have a mental representation of it at all, or at least one that cannot be subject to further thought. Part of his confusion, as will be pointed out later, is based on the fact that he misses that ideas can be clear and distinct in part.

It is in the discussion of sensations and reflections being the sole matter of reasoning that Locke is implicated. Immediately after Stillingfleet includes Toland and Locke in a group designated the "Gentlemen of this new way of reasoning," he starts paraphrasing from the *Essay*: "For they not only tell us, *That we can have no Idea of it by Sensation or Reflection*; but that *nothing is signified by it, only an uncertain Supposition of we know not what.*"[54] In the paraphrased passage of the *Essay*, Locke does say that sensation and reflection cannot give us an idea of substance and since ideas of

---

48. Ibid., 234.
49. That is, at least according to *CNM's* definition.
50. Stillingfleet, *Discourse*, 235.
51. Ibid., 236.
52. Ibid., 234.
53. Locke, *Letter to Edward*, 156–61.
54. Stillingfleet, *Discourse*, 234–35.

substance do not come in through our own faculties, "We have no such *clear Idea* at all, and therefore signifie nothing by the word *Substance*, but only an uncertain supposition of we know not what; *i.e.* of something whereof we have no *Idea*, which we take to be the *substratum*, or support, of those *Ideas* we do know" (I.iv.18). Locke's alteration of his statement of our inability to have any idea of Substance—or "no *Idea*"—in the third edition (1695) to our inability to have any "particular distinct positive *Idea*" in the fourth edition (1700) is perhaps an acknowledgement that this section has the potential to be misleading in some way.⁵⁵ Stillingfleet apparently believes that Toland and Locke are working with the same notion of reason within the same parameters. After again paraphrasing from the *Essay*, Stillingfleet responds: "If it be grounded on plain and evident Reason, then we must allow an *Idea* of *Substance*, which comes not in by *Sensation* or *Reflection*; and so we may be certain of some things which we have not by those *Ideas*."⁵⁶

Stillingfleet mollifies his censure of Locke, however, in pointing out that while the *Essay* does promulgate what amounts to a rejection of substance from reasoning, Locke did not intend it to do so. He points out that Locke admits in the *Essay* I.xxiii.5 "*that we have as clear a Notion of a Spirit, as we have of a Body. . . . And that it is as rational to affirm, there is no Body, because we cannot know its Essence, as 'tis called, or have no Idea of the Substance of Matter; as to say, there is no Spirit, because we know not its Essence, or have no Idea of a Spiritual Substance.*"⁵⁷ Stillingfleet takes Locke's statement as Locke's admission that we can have certainty of spiritual and corporeal substances. But, for Stillingfleet, therein lies Locke's inconsistency:

> From hence it follows, That we may be certain, that there are both *Spiritual and Bodily Substances*, although we can have *no clear and distinct Ideas of them*. But, if our Reason depend upon our *clear and distinct Idea's*; how is this possible? We cannot reason without *clear Idea's* and yet we may be certain without them: Can we be certain without Reason? Or doth our Reason give us true Notions of things, without these *Idea's*? If it be so, this new *Hypothesis* about Reason must appear to be very unreasonable.⁵⁸

---

55. Nidditch's critical edition of the *Essay* replaces "*i.e.* of something whereof we have no *Idea*" with "(*i.e.* of something whereof we have no particular distinct positive) *Idea*." This change occurs after the debate with Stillingfleet in the fourth edition (1700). Note Toland's use of similar terminology: Toland, *CNM*, 29.

56. Stillingfleet, *Discourse*, 237.

57. Ibid., 239.

58. Ibid., 239–40.

In short, Stillingfleet believes Locke thinks we can only reason about and thus be certain about clear and distinct ideas. However, he thinks Locke elsewhere in the *Essay* says that we can be certain about things for which we have no clear and distinct ideas.

Stillingfleet thinks that Toland, however, has sinister intent in using the *Essay's* foundational principles. This becomes increasingly apparent in the second part of Stillingfleet's argument against *CNM*, after Stillingfleet makes his case for the reasonableness of substance, nature, and person in defense of the doctrine of the Trinity. Prior to indexing Toland's inconsistencies, Stillingfleet comments on a few passages from *CNM* to show, no doubt, the outrageousness of *CNM*. Stillingfleet notes that anything about which we have no clear and distinct idea is *"above our Reason"* according to Toland. Although he doesn't mention Locke in this context it is important to realize that Locke is likely not brought in at this point as Stillingfleet is probably aware that Locke affirms "above reason" things in the *Essay*, even though, again, that is inconsistent with the *Essay's* foundational principles. Besides, Stillingfleet thinks Locke admits certainty of material and immaterial substances. Moreover, on the same page of the *Discourse*, referencing a passage from *CNM* where Toland is simply following Locke in noting that we cannot receive new ideas without new organs or powers, Stillingfleet wrongly understands Toland to claim that we would need supernatural mental or sensory organs to reason about mysteries of the faith.[59] As a case in point, he offers Toland's taxonomy of so-called above reason things: 1) something unintelligible because veiled with figurative words, and 2) *"For a thing in its own Nature inconceivable, and not to be judged by our Faculties, tho' it be never so clearly revealed."* Stillingfleet incorrectly takes *"and not to be judged by our Faculties"* as a prescriptive interjection from Toland amidst *CNM's* description of the second sense of "above reason."[60] Based on Stillingfleet's reading of Toland's notions of ideas, knowledge, certainty, and reason, for Christianity to dismiss anything that is "above reason," or, equally, not clear and distinct, would be a dismissal of many important doctrines.[61]

Stillingfleet then proceeds to show the inconsistencies within *CNM*. Stillingfleet lays out a few propositions that he has gleaned from *CNM*, shows their logical conclusion when tied together, and points out a present inconsistency in *CNM*. Regarding the said propositions, Stillingfleet brings the reader to the same passage that has given present-day scholars trouble, the passage that states that faith is not an implicit assent but knowledge in

---

59. Ibid., 262.
60. Ibid., 263.
61. Ibid., 266.

one sense of the word (139–40).[62] Stillingfleet quotes Toland: "*That Faith is so far from being an implicit Assent to any thing above Reason, that this Notion directly contradicts the end of Religion, the Nature of Man, and the Goodness and Wisdom of God.*"[63] Stillingfleet then reminds the reader of his reading of *CNM*, which asserts that reason is only concerned with clear and distinct ideas. He then reiterates that *CNM* calls its "simple" ideas (by which he means clear and distinct ideas) from sensation adequate but all ideas of substances inadequate.[64] He then gives a conclusion, where it is important to note that he wrongly identifies the categories of clear and distinct ideas with adequate ideas. He writes: "But let us lay these things together. Whatever we can have no *adequate Idea* of is *above our Knowledge*, and consequently *above our Reason*; and so all *Substances* are *above our Reason*."[65] Stillingfleet notes that Toland, however, tries to brush this natural mystery aside by claiming something is not mysterious for lack of an adequate idea, but then slips up in noting that we are completely ignorant of real essences. Thus, according to Stillingfleet, Toland is truly allowing what Toland considers mysteries from nature but not from religion.[66] It is in this context that Stillingfleet mentions in passing that *CNM* is attacking the Trinity as being absurd and contradictory.[67] He explains that there is a difference between gross contradictions and not having a distinct conception of the nature of a thing or equally something "barely" being above reason (reason in Toland's sense). The bishop then points out a similar inconsistency in Toland's assertion that eternity is not mysterious even though we have no adequate, or clear and distinct, idea of it: Toland thinks that the Trinity is mysterious and above our reason and thus is to be rejected from the Christian faith for lack of a clear and distinct idea.[68]

It is within the context of the discussion over *CNM*'s alleged inconsistencies that Stillingfleet reveals more of his interpretation of Toland's and presumably Locke's ideas. Stillingfleet comments on what he thinks is an inconsistent acceptance of eternity by Toland based on *CNM*'s premises:

---

62. P.145 in the first edition of *CNM*.
63. Stillingfleet, *Discourse*, 266.
64. Ibid., 266–67.
65. Ibid., 268.
66. Ibid., 271–72.
67. Ibid., 272.
68. Ibid., 274–76. It is likely that Stillingfleet believes Toland's treatment of eternity is his attempt to enter the discussion Stillingfleet was having with the Unitarians over the same topic: Stillingfleet, *Discourse*, 284–88.

> But can you have a clear and distinct Idea of what you cannot comprehend? *A clear Idea, is that whereof the mind hath a full and evident Perception. A distinct Idea, is that whereby the mind perceives the difference of it from all others.* Is this right? Yes. But can you have a full evident Perception of a thing, so as to difference it from all others, when you grant it to be *Incomprehensible*? If you have a *full Perception* of it, you comprehend its Nature, and especially if you can *difference* it from all other things; but when you say, *its Nature is Incomprehensible,* and yet *believe it,* you must deny it to be necessary to Faith, to have *a clear and distinct Idea* of the thing proposed.[69]

As already mentioned he thinks adequate ideas are clear and distinct and inadequate ideas are not so. Also, he apparently thinks that certainty and reason do not concern ideas that are not in every part clear and distinct. This is a major misreading of Locke and Toland who is parroting him.

Regarding Locke's denial of the necessity of clear and distinct ideas for knowledge and certainty, a few things can be said. Locke asks the following question in the *Essay*: "But since our Knowledge is founded on, and employ'd about our *Ideas* only, Will it not follow from thence, that it is conformable to our *Ideas*; and that where our *Ideas* are clear and distinct, or obscure and confused, our Knowledge will be so too?" His answer is: "No: For our Knowledge consisting in the perception of the agreement, or disagreement of any two *Ideas*, its clearness, or obscurity, consists in the clearness or obscurity of that Perception, and not in the clearness or obscurity of the *Ideas* themselves" (IV.ii.15). Hence, one can understand and know, by virtue of the number of sides that one counts or according to the mathematical formulae, that a 1,000-sided polygon differs from a 999-sided polygon of a similar size, even though it is not evident by looking at their figures side by side.

If there is any doubt that Toland follows Locke in dismissing clear and distinct ideas as necessary to certainty all that must be done is, again, to juxtapose their definitions of knowledge. Locke's definition of knowledge is: "*Knowledge* then seems to me to be nothing but the *perception of the connection and agreement, or disagreement and repugnancy of any of our Ideas*" (IV.i.2). Toland defines knowledge as: "nothing else but *the Perception of the Agreement or Disagreement of our Ideas in a greater or lesser Number, whereinsoever this Agreement or Disagreement may consist*" (12). Like Locke, nothing is said about clear and distinct ideas. In both, knowledge

---

69. Ibid., 276.

is the perception of the agreement or disagreement of *any* ideas. And, for both Locke and Toland, certainty supervenes only and necessarily upon knowledge.

Taking into consideration all that has been explored in the *Discourse*, a few things might be said about it in conclusion. Stillingfleet misunderstands what Toland and Locke teach about ideas and reason. Most importantly, he thinks that according to the foundational premises of *CNM* and the *Essay* reason contemplates only clear and distinct ideas and thus ideas that are clear and distinct in every aspect, and reason is demonstration and thus gives certainty. As between Toland and Locke, Toland is the one who is more consistent in the application of these principles, according to the *Discourse*. Doctrines that are not clear and distinct in every part, since they cannot be the subject of reason, are above reason and therefore must be rejected as being unreasonable. And, when one considers the sheer number of doctrines that would have to be rejected, Stillingfleet is understandably perturbed. In the end, he makes some interesting counter-arguments against arguments that neither Toland nor Locke employ.

Regarding the entirety of part III of this chapter, it can be said that Stillingfleet is correct in asserting agreement between Locke's and Toland's notions of ideas and certainty, but misinterprets what both thinkers are conveying about these notions when he treats them in the *Discourse*, which is the first part of this chapter's thesis. Those who find Stillingfleet correct in his notion that Toland requires clear and distinct ideas for certainty cannot be right. This casts a shadow of doubt on their understandings of reason, as well, simply by the fact that ideas are a concept foundational to reason. The exploration of reason in Toland must wait until chapter four.

PART IV: RESPONSES AND RECEPTIONS

Responses from Locke on Ideas

The exploration of these responses will be limited even though Locke's responses to Stillingfleet are lengthy and important. This section of part IV is only concerned with Locke's corrections of Stillingfleet's interpretations of the *Essay*'s ideas as they relate to certainty, knowledge, and reason. What he relays in the debate in these regards are essentially clarifications and reinforcements of what he teaches in the *Essay*. Little is new, but it is helpful. All of what is said could be reasoned out of the *Essay*, but with no little expenditure of time and energy.

First, Locke corrects Stillingfleet on a few points concerning ideas and reason. He notes that it is simple ideas that originate in sensation and reflection. Also, he points out that it appears that Stillingfleet is charging him with conceiving of reason as only operating rightly with ideas of things that are sensed and the simple operations of the mind. This is a ridiculous conclusion, for then Locke would then have rejected "the Ideas of simple and mix'd Modes and Relations, and the complex Ideas of the Species of Substances, about which he has spent so many Chapters." If Stillingfleet were right, Locke would also be denying that these complex ideas are "the Objects of Mens Thoughts or Reasonings, which he is far enough from."[70] The *simple ideas* are the raw materials with which the reason and other faculties of the mind work and they are the ideas that come from only sensation and reflection.[71]

Perhaps the most important clarification Locke makes pertains to his correction of Stillingfleet's confusion arising from what clear and distinct ideas are and their connections with knowledge and certainty. In *L1*, Locke points out a few places in the *Essay*, as this chapter has already done above, where certainty of knowledge is found in the "clear and visible" connections or perceptions of agreement or disagreement between ideas in a proposition.[72] In short, Locke does "not limit Certainty to *clear* and *distinct Ideas* only, since there may be Certainty from Ideas that are not in all their parts perfectly *clear* and *distinct*."[73] He is adamant about this point and reiterates it a number of times in *L1*, *L2*, and *L4*.[74] In *L4*, he explains that any obscure and confused idea is not wholly indistinguishable from all other ideas.[75] "There is no object which the Eye sees, that can be said to be perfectly obscure, for then it would not be seen at all; nor perfectly confused; for then

---

70. Locke, *Letter to Edward*, 17. Here, Locke does not fully tend to Stillingfleet's concern with reflection and sensation and ideas about substance. Stillingfleet is perplexed because it seems that an implication of all ideas originating in sensation and reflection is that the thing reasoned about and contemplated upon must be detectable by the senses. Thus, accidents we can detect, but we cannot see the substratum in which the accidents abide. Locke comments further on Stillingfleet's concerns later in the text (156–61).

71. Ibid., 17–18, 157–58.

72. Ibid., 56–57; cf. Locke, *Mr. Locke's Reply ... Answer to His Letter*, 9, 23. On these pages he explicitly states that he does not place certainty only in clear and distinct ideas.

73. Locke, *Letter to Edward*, 122.

74. Ibid., 56–57, 88–91; Locke, *Mr. Locke's Reply ... Answer to His Letter*, 9, 23; Locke, *Mr. Locke's Reply ... Answer to His Second Letter*, 21–22, 41–52, 53, 67, 70–77, 277–80, 293.

75. Locke, *Mr. Locke's Reply ... Answer to His Second Letter*, 43.

it could not be distinguished from any other, no not from a clearer."[76] "For every Idea in the Mind, clear or obscure, distinct or confused, is but that one Idea, that it is, and not another Idea, that it is not; and the Mind perceives it to be the Idea, that it is, and not another Idea that it is different from."[77] Hence, every idea that is not perfectly clear in all its parts still has parts that are clear; it is these clear parts that may be perceived to agree or disagree with the clear parts of another idea and thus be known to be distinct: "an Idea that cannot be well compared with some Ideas, from which it is not clearly and sufficiently distinguishable, is yet capable of having its agreement or disagreement perceived with some other Idea, with which it is not so confounded, but that it may be compared."[78] And therein lies the ability to have knowledge and certainty in putting these obscure and confused ideas in propositions:

> ... because an Idea that is not in all its parts perfectly clear and distinct, and is therefore an obscure and confused Idea; may yet with those Ideas, with which, by any obscurity it has, it is not confounded, be capable to produce Knowledge by the perception of its agreement or disagreement with them. And yet it will hold true, that in that part wherein it is imperfect, obscure and confused, we cannot expect to have certain, perfect or clear knowledge.[79]

So, although some ideas are not perfectly clear, they will be distinct from others and thus can be placed in a proposition that is certain. Reflecting on this point, it should be noted that many ideas are thus assumed to be clear and distinct until a desired comparison brings one's attention to points of obscurity and reveals confusion.

Locke uses several helpful examples to illustrate his point that knowledge and certainty do not require clear and distinct ideas or ideas that are clear and distinct in all parts. The first example involves the observation of "two Things standing upright, near the size and shape of an ordinary Man; but in so dim a Light, or at such a distance, that they appeared very much alike." They are thus obscure and also confused relative to one another. Yet one could be certain about a proposition about either of them, such as they are something and they do exist. Locke explains that this is similar to our situation with an idea of a substratum. It is obscure and confused, but some things may be said about it with certainty and it is very much within the

---

76. Ibid., 73.
77. Ibid., 43.
78. Ibid., 73.
79. Ibid., 76; cf. 293.

compass of reason.[80] The second example that will be given here builds upon the first one. Locke presents a scenario where one observes something in a dim light that is similar in size and shape to a man. He cannot determine whether it is a man or a statue. But he can say with certainty, and thus knows, it is not a steeple or a star.[81]

Another very important point that Locke clarifies several times in this debate is what an idea is. Locke appears perplexed by Stillingfleet's description of the *Essay* as Locke's "new way by ideas." Locke writes:

> *My new way by Ideas*, or *my way by Ideas*, which often occurs in your Lordships Letter, is, I confess, a very large and doubtful Expression; and may, in the full Latitude, comprehend my whole *Essay*; because treating in it of the *Understanding*, which is nothing but the Faculty of Thinking, I could not well treat of that Faculty of the Mind, which consists in Thinking, without considering the immediate Objects of the Mind in Thinking, which I call *Ideas*: And therefore in treating of the Understanding, I guess it will not be thought strange, that the greatest part of my Book has been taken up, in considering what these Objects of the Mind, in Thinking are. . . . And this, in short, is *my way by Ideas*, that which your Lordship calls *my new way by Ideas*: Which, my Lord, if it be *new*, it is but a new History of an old Thing, For I think it will not be doubted, that Men always perform'd the Actions of Thinking, Reasoning, Believing, and Knowing, just after the same way that they do now . . . .[82]

Two important things can be gleaned here. First, ideas are the immediate objects of the mind when thinking. That is, there is always something present in the mind.[83] So, for instance, when someone attempts to envision a particular substance or substratum distinct from its accidents something is pictured. The mind cannot suspend itself from picturing something. That something might be revised by the mind, but there will always be something envisioned. This is also an important response to Stillingfleet who might be read, according to Locke, as taking Locke's claim how we have no idea of substance literally.[84] Second, Locke believes he is simply *describing* the pro-

---

80. Ibid., 43–44.
81. Ibid., 73.
82. Locke, *Mr. Locke's Reply . . . Answer to His Letter*, 72–73. Cf. Locke, *Letter to Edward*, 157–61; Locke, *Mr. Locke's Reply . . . Answer to His Second Letter*, 252–53.
83. Cf. Locke, *Letter to Edward*, 157, 160; Locke, *Mr. Locke's Reply . . . Answer to His Second Letter*, 60, 328.
84. Locke, *Letter to Edward*, 156–61. Locke appears to think that this is *possibly* what Stillingfleet is asserting.

cess of understanding that we all attempt to use rightly. He does not pretend to be conveying anything new. There are definitely prescriptive elements in the proper description but the main point of the *Essay* is the description.

It is important to note, again, that what this debate has to say more pointedly about reason will be dealt with in the next two chapters. The debate began, however, with a misunderstanding of reason, certainty, and ideas, but certainty and ideas were more often the focus in the course of the debate. As will be evident in the next two chapters, the treatments of reason and its interrelated topics in the *Essay* and *CNM* are far more complex than what little is said of the same in the Locke-Stillingfleet debate.

Locke's Regard for Stillingfleet's Treatment of *CNM*

As mentioned before, Toland's notoriety comes from the belief that he somehow employs Locke's foundational principles of the *Essay* and yet greatly deviates from Locke as is apparent in his rejection of above reason things. The question that will concern us here is: What does Locke, himself, actually say about Stillingfleet's treatment and interpretation of *CNM*?

Locke appears frustrated and amazed how Stillingfleet pulled him into the on-going Trinitarian debates in which Stillingfleet was involved. It is clear to Locke that Stillingfleet's line of reasoning for doing so is apparent but contorted:

> To take now a right View of this Matter, it is fit to consider, the beginning and progress of it: Your Lordship had a Controversie with the *Unitarians*; they, in their Answer to your Lordships Sermons, and elsewhere, *talk of Ideas*; the Author of *Christianity not Mysterious*, whether a *Unitarian* or no, your Lordship says not, neither do I enquire, gives *an account of Reason*, which, as your Lordship says, *supposes* Certainty to consist only in *clear and distinct Ideas*; and because he expresses himself in some other Things, conformable to what I had said in my Book, my Book is brought into the Controversie, though there be no such Opinion in it, as your Lordship opposed.[85]

---

85. Locke, *Mr. Locke's Reply . . . Answer to His Letter*, 56. The narrative continues on, but what is set down above suffices for the chapter's current purposes. Another issue involving reason that would be brought up if the quote were to continue is whether certainty can be had in matters of faith. For other accounts of Locke's narrative of how Stillingfleet resolved to bring him into the controversy: Locke, *Mr. Locke's Reply . . . Answer to His Letter*, 9–20; Locke, *Mr. Locke's Reply . . . Answer to His Second Letter*, 10–21.

And already, this chapter has shown that neither Toland nor Locke place certainty in only clear and distinct ideas.

While Locke defends himself from erroneous charges, he makes numerous comments on Stillingfleet's treatment of *CNM*. Locke notes throughout his responses that Stillingfleet attacks *CNM*'s account of reason because it makes clear and distinct ideas necessary for certainty. But, the biggest problem Locke notices in this regard is that Stillingfleet has not proven that *CNM*'s account of reason or any other part of the work confines certainty to clear and distinct ideas.[86] Locke goes even so far as to defend Toland and the Unitarians from Stillingfleet's charges:

> My Lord, when I writ my Book, I could not design *to distinguish my self from the Gentlemen of the new way of Reasoning*, who were not then in being, nor are, that I see, yet: Since I find nothing produced out of the *Unitarians*, nor the Author of *Christianity not Mysterious*, to shew, That they make clear and distinct Ideas necessary to Certainty.[87]

He even pleads with Stillingfleet throughout the discourse to show how the author of *CNM* built upon him.[88]

Another important point is that at no time in the debate does Locke distance his *Essay* from *CNM* or say that *CNM* does not agree with his *Essay* on the issue of ideas.[89] Although every single time he could appear at first glance to be writing against *CNM* on this issue, nevertheless, with a more careful look it becomes apparent that he is writing against Stillingfleet's *reading* of the author of *CNM* and not the author of *CNM*.[90] Besides, if he

---

86. Locke, *Mr. Locke's Reply . . . Answer to His Letter*, 9, 11–15; Locke, *Mr. Locke's Reply . . . Answer to His Second Letter*, 25, 32, 106.

87. Locke, *Mr. Locke's Reply . . . Answer to His Second Letter*, 52–53.

88. Locke, *Mr. Locke's Reply . . . Answer to His Letter*, 28–30, 32–41; Locke, *Mr. Locke's Reply . . . Answer to His Second Letter*, 24–26, 101–13, especially 106.

89. William Molyneux, "L2269: William Molyneux to Locke," 132–35. Some may think that Locke distanced his *Essay* from *CNM* on intellectual grounds from a letter to Locke where Molyneux, in discussing some problematic points about Toland's personality and conduct and Toland's public declarations of Locke's patronage and friendship, writes, "I believe you will not approve of this, as far as I am able to Judge by your shaking him off in your Letter to the Bishop of Worcester" (133). Molyneux is not saying that but simply remarking that Locke did not show his personal intimacy or acquaintanceship with Toland. Locke does not say anything against the content of *CNM* in any of his letters to Molyneux that touch on Toland, although both express well wishes for him and concern for his raw character: Locke, "L2243: Locke to William Molyneux"; Locke, "L2254: Locke to William Molyneux"; Locke, "L2277: Locke to William Molyneux."

90. E.g., Locke, *Mr. Locke's Reply . . . Answer to His Letter*, 9–20; Locke, *Mr. Locke's Reply . . . Answer to His Second Letter*, 22–23.

were arguing against the author of *CNM*, what was discussed directly above would not make sense, especially his defense of *CNM*. This is contrary to Toland's celebrated biography by Sullivan that claims: "He [Locke] had one aim, to dissociate himself from them [Toland and the Socinians], and he pursued it doggedly."[91]

There is one passage in particular from *L1* that might constitute an objection to what has just been argued. Locke writes to Stillingfleet: "For how can my using an *Argument*, whose *Certainty is not placed upon clear and distinct Ideas*, prove any thing against another Man who says, That *clear and distinct Ideas are the sole Matter and Foundation of all our Reasoning?* This proves only against him that uses the Argument."[92] To many this might sound like an implicit acceptance of Stillingfleet's reading of Toland. Toland, however, said *simple* and distinct ideas are the foundation of all our reasoning (11–12), which Stillingfleet somehow misses.[93] Locke likely realizes this which explains the rest of the quote which many have apparently missed: "... and therefore either I must be supposed here to hold, that clear and distinct Ideas are the sole Matter and Foundation of all our Reasoning, (which I do not remember that I ever said) or else that your Lordship here proves against no Body."[94]

Responses from Toland

John Toland's published responses to Stillingfleet about his mishandling of the *CNM* are shorter than Locke's on the same issue! Toland has three works that serve as vindications of *CNM*: *Apology*, *Defence*, and *Vindicius*. In two places he merely lists "Worcester" among those who have attacked him, once in the *Defence* and once in *Vindicius*.[95] Both times where he offers more space to the attack he does not attempt to personally respond to Stillingfleet but merely gives a lengthy quote from *The Agreement of the Unitarians with the Catholick Church*, a work that was penned by celebrated Unitarian and Worcester opponent Stephen Nye. A fair share of that book is an attack on Stillingfleet's *Discourse*. While Toland's *Vindicius* prints a quote from page 55 of the Unitarian work that takes up the final three pages of that

91. Sullivan, *John Toland*, 77; cf. Yolton, *John Locke*, 125–26.
92. Locke, *Letter to Edward*, 89.
93. Stillingfleet, *Discourse*, 233.
94. Locke, *Letter to Edward*, 89. Locke points out on the next page that simple ideas are the foundations of our knowledge. He does not say foundation of reason because Stillingfleet is concerned with certainty.
95. Toland, *Defence*, 13; Toland, *Vindicius*, 37.

vindication, his *Apology* incorporates a longer version of the quote, adding on a few lines from the previous page:

> I know not what it was to his Lordship's Purpose, to fall upon Mr. *Toland's* Book. But if he would needs attack the Book; he should have dealt fairly; he should have discussed the main Argument in it; and not carpt only at a few Passages, and those too, so mangled and deformed by his Representation of them, that I dare to affirm, Mr. *Toland* does not know his own Book in the Bishop's Representation of it. I do not perceive, to speak truly, but that the Book still stands in its full Strength; if it hath not also acquired a farther Reputation, by occasion of this (so) unsuccessful nibling at it. But suppose *the Bishop* had disarmed *the Gentleman*; what is that to *us*? Do we offer this Book, against *the Trinity of the Realists*; was it written with intention to serve *us*; doth it contain any of our Allegations from *Reason*, against the Trinity of *Philoponus*, *Joachim*, and *Gentilis*? We desire him to answer to the *Reasons* in our Books, against *the Trinity of the Tritheists*; but to these, he saith not a Word, but only falls upon Mr. *Toland's* Book: in which, or for which, we are not in the least concerned; nor do I think the (Learned and Ingenious) Author will hold himself to be interested to defend that *Christianity not mysterious*, which his Lordship presents us with.[96]

In the *Apology*, he explicitly uses the quote as evidence that even the Unitarians do not consider it Unitarian. There are other points made in the quote by Nye, however, that are obviously advantageous to Toland. Stillingfleet is said to mishandle *CNM*, mangle it, and treat Toland unfairly.

The most obvious possible reason that Toland said little in his own defense against Stillingfleet's charges, taking into consideration what has already been said in this chapter, is the involvement of more prominent thinkers who were attacking Stillingfleet's *Discourse*. Both Nye and Locke point out Stillingfleet's distortion of *CNM*. And, Locke even goes so far as to say Stillingfleet's reading of *CNM* on ideas and reason is incorrect. Toland perhaps thought he would be doing Locke, at least, a discourtesy in responding to Stillingfleet when Locke wants the bishop's full attention and has already dealt with Toland fairly.

Written admission from Toland that Locke managed Toland and *CNM* fairly does come about, but not until 1720, some twenty years after the debate. In response to a scholar, Dr. Hare, who mentions in passing that *CNM* misconstrues Locke's *Essay* with quotes from it, Toland quotes from Locke's

---

96. Nye, *Agreement of the Unitarians*, 55; cf. Toland, *Apology*, 42–43; Toland, *Vindicius*, 164–66.

L4 three times to show that Locke admits that Toland never quotes the *Essay* and to show that Stillingfleet misrepresented both himself and Locke in the debate. Toland first quotes, in a compressed form, Locke's synopsis of Stillingfleet's contorted line of reasoning where the bishop moves from interpreting *CNM* as requiring clear and distinct ideas for certainty to arguing against the *Essay*. Toland then includes a quote where Locke chides Stillingfleet for not quoting one sentence of Toland where "certainty by Ideas" is mentioned. He then recounts Locke's witty rehearsal of Stillingfleet's change of mind where he admits Locke went upon different grounds than certainty by ideas, but then to Locke's surprise says he prefers the view that he originally thought Locke held! Toland concludes by saying, in sum, that Locke shows that they were both misrepresented by Stillingfleet and that Stillingfleet never actually produced parallel places between himself and Locke, thereby showing Toland never quoted from the *Essay*. The upshot for Toland was that Dr. Hare changed his assertion that Toland misconstrues the *Essay* with quotes from it to the assertion that he "makes great use of Mr. Locke's Principles." The upshot for the history of the debate is that Toland affirms that Locke gives him a fair reading.[97]

Another reason that possibly accounts for his brief response is that Toland had to direct his attention elsewhere. His book created such a stir with numerous respondents that he had problems with various governments. The full title of his *Apology* reveals his more pressing needs: *An Apology for Mr. Toland, in a Letter from Himself to a Member of the House of Commons in Ireland; Written the Day Before His Book Was Resolv'd to Be Burnt by the Committee of Religion. To Which Is Prefix'd a Narrative Containing the Occasion of the Said Letter.* And the book was indeed burned in public at two separate places on September 11, 1697.[98] He had similar potential legal issues in England, which prompted *Vindicius Liberius: or M. Toland's Defence of Himself, Against the Late Lower House of Convocation, and Others, etc.*

Considering Toland's defense of *CNM* in addition to Locke's regard for Stillingfleet's interpretations of *CNM*, Locke and Toland leave us with little more than pointing out Stillingfleet's faulty interpretations and what Toland did not argue. Toland follows the same cautious approach twenty years later when he is slighted for misconstruing Locke with quotes from the *Essay*.

---

97. Toland, *Collection of Several Pieces*, 1:lxxiii–lxxvi. Toland quotes from pp. 438, 440, & 443 of Locke's *1714 Works*. Page 438 is erroneously printed as 138 on lxxiv. Interestingly, there is a *possible* sensitivity to being under the shadow of John Locke in Lockeans like Toland and Anthony Collins. Collins pays homage to Tillotson instead of Locke as being the most virtuous free-thinker of his age. Collins, *Discourse of Free-Thinking*, vi, 171–75.

98. Toland, *Apology*, 24.

The debate itself leaves little resolved regarding a comparison of Locke's and Toland's epistemologies. Had Toland known that this debate would forever tether him to Locke and would result in so many *CNM* misreadings that are not apparently questioned in the secondary literature on him, perhaps he would have responded more vigorously. In his defense, how could he have guessed?

Receptions

While Locke's and Toland's responses to Stillingfleet amidst the debate leave us with little in the way of a comparison regarding Locke's and Toland's epistemologies, a popular synoptic statement of Toland's epistemology in Toland scholarship is gleaned from the debate but is no more than what is *thought* to be Stillingfleet's reading of Toland's *CNM* on reason and revelation. Just as it seems very likely that those who agree with Stillingfleet that Toland requires clear and distinct ideas for certainty simply assume it to be true, it appears, due to lack of evidence of the pertinent analysis of *CNM*, that those who agree with the popular synoptic statement are assuming it to be true.

This chapter's contentions from the beginning have been that significant scholarship that comments on Toland assumes that Stillingfleet correctly interprets Toland on ideas and reason, and presumably all things related. Hopefully this chapter has cleared away all doubts to its initial claims, at least regarding ideas, knowledge, and certainty. Those familiar with the secondary literature might quickly point out, seemingly contrary to this chapter's claims, that many Toland scholars or commentators often assert that revelation is not subordinate to demonstration, as Stillingfleet understands *CNM* to assert, but is subordinate to reasonable probability. That is, revelation cannot be accepted as such if it gives novelty. Toland biographer, Sullivan, is a case in point: "Any assertion of revelation would have to be judged by the same tests of disinterestedness and probability as applied to data received on human authority."[99] Again, considering Sullivan, like many others, analyzes neither what Toland means by reason, nor what Locke means by reason, though he differentiates the two by claiming Locke accepts things that are above reason while Toland rejects them, Sullivan and others most likely get their reading that revelation is subordinate to human or natural probability from the same place that Roger Woolhouse gets the very same interpretation of Toland's understanding of reason versus

---

99. Sullivan, *John Toland*, 125.

revelation: a particular charge of logical inconsistency made by Locke against Stillingfleet in *L4*.

Over a number of pages near the end of *L4*, Locke charges Stillingfleet with using an argument which he "highly condemned in others."[100] Locke asserts that regarding the doctrine of the immortality of the soul Stillingfleet essentially argues that "it [the doctrine] is not so credible as if it *were easie to give an account* by Natural Reason."[101] Still on the topic of the immortality of the soul and Stillingfleet's argument for it and his well-known dismissal of Locke's claims of assigning different bases to assurance of faith and certainty, Locke fires off a series of questions:

> For if in this present Case, the credibility of this Proposition, The Souls of Men shall live for ever, revealed in the Scripture, be lessened by confessing it cannot be demonstratively proved from Reason; though it be asserted to be most highly probable: Must not by the same Rule its credibility dwindle away to nothing, if natural Reason should not be able to make it out to be so much as probable; or should place the probability from natural Principles on the other side? For if meer want of Demonstration *lessens the credibilty* of any Proposition divinely revealed, must not want of probability, or contrary probability from natural Reason, quite take away its *credibility*?[102]

Therefore, Stillingfleet's demand for the corroboration of natural reason for support of a revealed doctrine—in this case, the immortality of the soul—gives natural reason all of the power and makes natural reason the true authority over Scripture. Thus, if a particular claim made by a revelation seemed improbable it would be rejected as revelation!

This position on revelation and reason just articulated, which Stillingfleet is accused of holding but condemns in others, is precisely the position John Toland is often thought to hold. Woolhouse, treating the same pages from *L4* in his biography of Locke, writes: "Locke pointed out that Stillingfleet was here accepting precisely what he had begun by arguing against—Toland's principle of rejecting mysteries of the faith which are above reason. He was maintaining that 'divine revelation abates of its credibility' in proportion as human reason fails to support it."[103] In other words, Woolhouse takes Locke's argument that Stillingfleet adopts a position he argues against as thus being Toland's position. The obvious problem, other than the lack

---

100. Locke, *Mr. Locke's Reply . . . Answer to His Second Letter*, 425–26.
101. Ibid., 426.
102. Ibid., 428–29.
103. Woolhouse, *Locke: A Biography*, 408–9 (quotation, 408).

of analysis of Toland, is that Stillingfleet understands above reason things in Toland to be that which is not completely clear and distinct, which has nothing to do with probability. That is beside the point; the point being that Sullivan and Woolhouse, not to mention all of the yet-to-be-named commentators of Toland, who assign him this position, most likely receive it from the passages outlined above or they at least confirm the commentators' conclusions that were wrought in other ways.[104] Again, they do no analyses of reason and ideas and their interconnections, and, as will be shown in chapter 4, it is an unsupportable conclusion from *CNM*. They do give, at least, a more palatable interpretation of Toland, as it acknowledges that Toland's reason concerns probability in *CNM*, than Stillingfleet's thought that Toland accepted only that which could be demonstrated as reasonable. Regarding Locke scholarship, interestingly enough there are some prominent Locke scholars who actually think the position often ascribed to Toland is actually that of John Locke.[105] They will be discussed in chapter 3.

Many incorrect interpretations of reason or reason versus faith or reason versus revelation could have been avoided pertaining to Locke and Toland if scholarship had paid closer attention to the Locke-Stillingfleet debate. But again, it is understandable, considering its length, truncation, and so on, that few would want to get into the debate to challenge Stillingfleet's reading of *CNM*, the correctness of which has apparently become a matter of fact. The debate tells us better what Locke and Toland do not teach on said issues, however, than what they do teach.

CONCLUSION

This chapter made a case for the claim that Stillingfleet is correct in asserting agreement between Locke's and Toland's notions of ideas and certainty but misinterprets what both thinkers are conveying about these notions when he comments on them in the *Discourse*. While the clarifications on ideas and certainty Locke makes in the course of the debate are helpful, the controversy as a whole and its reception leaves little resolved regarding a comparison of Locke's and Toland's respective epistemologies. So, now that we have investigated Locke and Toland on the issues of ideas, knowledge, and certainty from the *Essay*, *CNM*, and related works, this book will investigate

---

104. This point will be further discussed in chapter 4, part V.

105. Helm, "Faith and Knowledge." Helm is one among a few prominent Locke scholars that hold this position. Helm surprisingly interacts with the debate throughout his essay. It is possible that Helm is tripped up by relying too heavily upon the index of the 1823 *Works of John Locke*.

these works on the issues of reason, faith, and revelation. And, while we leave the thoughts and interpretations of Edward Stillingfleet behind, we will still tend to one of his enduring legacies: his tethering, however obscure it has been, of John Toland to John Locke. In the end, it will be shown that John Toland followed the epistemological paths of Locke's *Essay* far closer than anyone, even Stillingfleet himself, has realized.

3

Locke's Incorporation of Faith and Revelation within Reason

INTRODUCTION

WHILE CHAPTER 2 DESCRIBES Locke's and Toland's notions of ideas, certainty, and knowledge (and shows them to be compatible), chapter 3 will focus solely on the thought of John Locke, namely his descriptions of the faculty of reason, its subordinate and related faculties, and reason's relationships to faith and revelation. As indicated earlier, this will enable a point-for-point comparison with Toland on the same notions in the next chapter.

Thus this chapter will answer the following questions: 1) According to Locke, what is reason?; 2) What is its relationship to faith?; and 3) What is its relationship to revelation? In so doing, this chapter will argue that to understand Locke's description of reason, and thus the relationships between reason and faith and reason and revelation, one must acknowledge that in the *Essay* Locke primarily conceives of the mind or agent employing the faculty of reason working in reason's proper office or scope, which entails the considerations of natural as well as supernatural sources of information, and a corresponding proper faith that pertains to probable (uncertain) propositions from the same sources. He asserts that divinely revealed propositions trump the propositions supported by the probability from purely natural sources. In *Essay* IV.xviii, however, he conceives of the mind employing reason in a diminished office, or concerning only natural sources, and a corresponding faith, concerned with only supernatural sources; but he does this partly, at least, to show that such an antithetical framing of the two fails to maintain definitive boundaries. As a result, faith in or assent to a proposition from *any* source and the determination of divine revelation as such morally *ought* to be the result of the mind employing its power of reason in its full scope or office.

What follows is an expanded explanation of the above thesis with additional details for clarity's sake. In Locke's consideration of the faculty of reason in the *Essay*, he acknowledges various renderings of the term but conceptually builds his idea of reason in its fullest sense. Reason as a faculty is a tool or power of the mind or agent. Its employment gives the mind knowledge and probability, the latter being that upon which the mind *should* base its judgments. Reason's proper office encompasses notices and propositions from natural sources of information and supernatural sources. Reason must assess whether or not something is revealed and in so doing determine how the revealed proposition or propositions should be interpreted. While a revealed proposition cannot overturn intuitive or demonstrative knowledge to be considered divine, it can overturn propositions that are probable based upon purely non-revelatory considerations or divinely unassisted reason.[1] The faculty of reason considered operating in its full scope or proper office will be called proper reason in this book. Assent, faith, opinion, or belief in natural *or* divine revelatory matters are not necessarily subordinate to proper reason, but morally they ought to be, especially regarding important issues, such as religion and morality; otherwise the mind's belief and assent are irrational, not properly heeding and utilizing its God-given guide. So, if the mind is acting reasonably in assent, an act done by the mind's power of judgment, it heeds the recommendations issued from reason employed in its proper office, or proper reason, and will thus have what this book will call proper faith or proper belief. What is more, the natural faculties or powers can be considered, for all intents and purposes, as reason when the mind or agent acts reasonably—reasonably in the sense of dictated by proper reason and in the sense of corresponding to the appropriate thoroughness that the circumstance warrants.

Near the end of *Essay* IV.xvii, "Of Reason," and in *Essay* IV.xviii, "Of Faith and Reason, and Their Distinct Provinces," Locke conceives of the faculty of reason operating in a diminished office, what this book will call vulgar reason. This is done by Locke so that vulgar reason can be

---

1. One might, through analogy and observation, assent to propositions regarding the supernatural realm through divinely unassisted reasoning. For instance, it is possible some have reasoned that it is likely that there are ranks of intelligent beings, some of which are immaterial, that reach up to the infinite perfection of God (*Essay* IV.xvi.12).

conceptually distinguished as much as possible from assent, faith, or belief in only divinely revealed matters, what this chapter will call vulgar faith. In other words, vulgar reason is the faculty of reason considered operating in an office without the assistance or propositions of revelation.

The use of the label "vulgar" that Locke does not use warrants some explanation. First, Locke referred to both considerations of reason as "reason," and both considerations of faith as "faith." Not differentiating them in the *Essay* has led to confusion in reading it, as will be argued in this chapter, and would likely lead to confusion in reading this chapter. Second, it is my desire to couple the two considerations of reason with each one's corresponding consideration of faith to avoid undue confusion. Locke does not make provision for this. Vulgar reason could have been called natural or unassisted or human reason in this book, which Locke actually does call it in places, but then this book would have to replace the efficient, coupling labels of *vulgar* reason and *vulgar* faith with the less economical and disconnected labels of *natural* or *unassisted* or *human* reason and *vulgar* (or some other adjective) faith; the labels natural or unassisted or human faith are not optional replacements for vulgar faith because natural faith or unassisted faith are more appropriate terms for faith in natural sources of information, which is ideally a function of the mind employing its natural or unassisted reason.[2] Labeling them as common also has too much room for misunderstanding, as referring to "common faith" seems more appropriate to describing a faith that is uniform to everyone or most. Other prefixes such as "chapter xviii" seem too clumsy. Vulgar was chosen because it was a term commonly used in Locke's day that could be interchanged with the adjective common.

Moreover, this distinguishing of faith and reason in a vulgar understanding is done simply as a concession since Locke believes that such an attempted distinction and opposition is too ingrained in the common or vulgar vernacular to dislodge it. This vulgar conception of reason is what allows Locke to concede to a category of propositions "above reason." That is, above reason propositions are intelligible or reconcilable propositions and *above natural or vulgar* reason in the sense that they are novel and would typically not be the subject of one's perception without being divinely revealed; but in the cases that they become the subject of one's fanciful perception, there would be no reason to assent to them outside of the fact that they are divinely revealed. Moreover, as the mind *ought* to listen to revelation

---

2. Examples of Locke employing "natural reason": Locke, *ROC*, 268, 278; Locke, *Mr. Locke's Reply . . . Answer to his Second Letter*, 418, 421, 423, 426, 427, 428, 429, 439. Examples of "unassisted reason": Locke, *ROC*, 268, 270. Examples of "human reason": Locke, *Mr. Locke's Reply . . . Answer to his Second Letter*, 418–19; Locke, *Second Vindication*, xvi.

and, in its absence, vulgar reason in their recommendations involving probability, it might not. Nevertheless, Locke shows that such an antithetical framing of faith and reason ultimately cannot be maintained in IV.xviii.

Owing to the considerations of reason operating in different offices, multiple considerations of faith have come to the fore. Proper faith refers to faith in propositions from natural or allegedly supernatural sources reasonably assessed. Vulgar faith refers to faith in propositions from only divine revelation reasonably assessed. Finally, irrational faith is the result of the mind not heeding the recommendations derived from proper reason and assenting otherwise or the result of the mind under- or over-employing reason in its endeavor according to the thoroughness that the circumstance warrants.[3]

By the end of the *Essay*, Locke's understanding of the relationship of proper reason and (special) revelation is evident, too. Revelation—original or immediate and traditional or recorded original revelation—must have the appropriate external and internal marks which reason must judge to be affirmed as revelation. The appropriate external mark for an original revelation is a clear miracle or miracles and for traditional revelation is accompanying fair testimonies of a clear miracle or miracles.[4] The appropriate internal marks of traditional or original divine revelation are that the interpretation of the revealed proposition is neither contrary to knowledge, both in the sense of contrary to knowledge where the proposition contradicts certain truths (i.e., is false) or is inherently contradictory (also, false) and in the sense that it is mentally irreconcilable,[5] nor definitively contrary to other

---

3. The mind may, despite its insufficient employment of reason, conclude correctly, but Locke is not sure how God assesses that (IV.xvii.24). Also, an over-employment of reason on a menial mental task is poor stewardship and thus irrational in the corresponding sense (IV.xix.16).

4. John Tillotson and John Locke were friends and were in dialogue. It is possible that Locke shared some of Tillotson's more specific views regarding miraculous confirmation of revelation. John Tillotson, *Fifteen Sermons*, especially "Sermon XI: Of the Miracles," "Sermon XII: Of the Miracles," and "Sermon XIII: Of the Miracles."

5. Something that is contrary to knowledge in the first sense will often be contrary to knowledge in the second sense. For instance, the purported revelation, "God has produced a square circle," is contrary to knowledge in both senses: a square circle cannot be imagined (the second sense) and God being illogical is a logical contradiction (first sense). There is a distinction one can make within the first sense, too. For instance, if one allows sensitive knowledge and that of memory to count as certain knowledge, then a proposition such as, "There are only flying pigs alive today," while not inherently contradictory, is certainly contrary to known truths (i.e., false) when visiting a pig farm and witnessing wingless pigs alive and well. Whatever the case, something is contrary to knowledge in the first sense if a contradiction or, more generally, something false undergirds a doctrine or proposition. Moreover, the proposition, "God occasionally sins," is arguably mentally reconcilable or envisionable though contrary to knowledge

accepted and assured revelation. One would not expect it to be contrary to knowledge in the first stated sense, at least, because if revelation could contradict knowledge—the goal and highest achievement of reason and the foundation of our further reasoning—it would be undercutting its source of validation that it is revelation. Also, God does not contradict Himself. Furthermore, it is evident from the *Essay* that Locke thinks that the Bible fits these criteria. Locke does admit, however, of unattested, extra-Biblical original revelation. Although such alleged revelations do not have the accompanying external marks, the internal marks are that the allegedly revealed propositions are not contrary to knowledge in either of the aforementioned senses and comport with either reasoned conclusions from purely natural considerations where assured revelation (in Locke's mind, Scripture) does not speak or assured revelation.

All of these conclusions considered, the guidelines of subordination and authority become clear. Locke subordinates attested revelation to proper reason regarding its external marks and internal marks or interpretation. Perhaps it is better to assert that Locke thinks God subordinates revelation to proper reason. Natural probability is subordinate to attested revelation. As alluded to already, Locke conceives of unattested original revelation as being subordinate to, or consistent with, Scripture, attested revelation, or else it must be subordinate to natural or vulgar reason. Finally, faith, the vulgar or proper considerations, should always be subordinate to proper reason as the mind ought to assent reasonably—reasonably, as qualified above.

This chapter will be divided into several parts. Part I will serve as the state of the question. Part II will touch on preliminary issues. It will build upon the treatment of knowledge and certainty from chapter 2 with an expositional explanation of the faculties of knowledge and judgment often associated with reason. Part III will describe Locke's primary conception of reason or proper reason. Part IV will describe the relationship between reason and faith. An explanation of what above reason propositions are will be offered in part V. Part VI will describe the relationship of reason and revelation. Finally, the chapter will end with its stated conclusions.

---

in the first sense. While the doctrine of the Holy Trinity or the doctrine of human freedom in light of God's absolute sovereignty are contrary to knowledge in the second sense, innumerable orthodox theologians have denied for millennia that they are contrary to knowledge in the first and more crucial sense. They do not expect to picture spiritual truths beyond their physical, empirical faculties, but they do expect God not to be illogical.

PART I: STATE OF THE QUESTION

There are numerous commentators on Locke. Some offer a rather brief treatment of Locke, especially those works surveying the history of philosophy over a long period of time and not isolated to the British Isles. And since they are not always concentrating just on his epistemology their comments on it are understandably few and important terms such as reason, above reason, and mystery are taken for granted and not expounded upon. Such are the important works of James Livingston, Claude Welch, Robert E. Sullivan, Frederick Copleston, John Herman Randall, Jr., James O'Higgins, William Uzgalis, and Manfred Kuehn.[6] At times desired answers the commentators

6. Livingston, *Modern Christian Thought*, 1:18–21. Livingston is very brief in his treatment of Locke. He says that Locke believes in that which is above and not contrary to reason. He does not explain what he means by this phrase (18). He vaguely uses the term "mystery" to denote that which is saved by Locke's above but not contrary to reason category (20–21). In describing a primary difference, however, between Locke and Toland—Locke's acceptance of mystery and Toland's rejection of mystery—mystery appears to mean doctrines beyond our full understanding or that which cannot be mentally pictured but does not offend the principles of logic (21). There is no evidence that he notices Locke uses two senses of the word reason (18). Welch, *Protestant Thought* 1:35–36. Welch groups Wolff and Locke together as understanding Christianity to transcend natural religion. This transcendence includes some "mystery." He offers what mysteries revelation would supply for Wolff—Trinity, Christology, grace, and atonement—but unfortunately not for Locke. Sullivan, *John Toland*, 79. Sullivan simply claims Locke believes in ideas above, but not contrary to reason, "for retention of the articles of faith." As pointed out in chapter 2, there is little evidence that Sullivan grasps the notions of Locke's ideas and reason. Cragg, *Church and the Age of Reason*, 13. Cragg writes, "Locke did not challenge the *need* or the value of revelation, but the relative position he assigned it implies that it *confirms what can be appropriated in other ways*" (emphasis mine). It is possible that Cragg means to say that Locke did not explicitly deny the need of revelation but implicitly did so; otherwise he would appear to be contradictory. Copleston, *History of Philosophy*, 5:69–70. Copleston claims that above reason propositions "may" include revelations not fully understandable. Randall, Jr. *Making of the Modern Mind*, 285–89. Randall believes that Locke's three categories, according to reason, contrary to reason, and above reason propositions, represent natural religion, superstition, and revelation, respectively. "Locke's disciple John Toland, in his *Christianity not Mysterious*, further pointed out that the first and last formed really but one class..." (289). There is no attempt to clarify important terms such as reason or superstition, the latter being Randall's term and not Locke's. O'Higgins, *Anthony Collins*, 52. O'Higgins writes this single cryptic statement on Locke: "Locke, however, admitted verbally at least, the existence of truths above reason" (52). From the surrounding context of this quotation, this chapter takes O'Higgins to mean Locke allows that there are some truths that should be believed but when put together cannot be reconciled or imagined. Uzgalis, "Anthony Collins," 13–14. Uzgalis appears admittedly uncertain exactly what is being said by Locke and others regarding what it means that things are above reason. Kuehn, "Reason and Understanding," 169–70. Kuehn calls Locke's category of propositions—above, according to, and contrary to reason—as "most interesting," but does not seriously attempt to explain these important labels (170). He

might have regarding important questions can be inferred, but frequently this is impossible. Sometimes they make claims with important implications that they do not have time to explain more thoroughly. In short, these accomplished commentators leave the reader wanting more!

Some scholars go beyond the role of general commentator and could be classified as critics. But sometimes these critical treatments are too brief to offer supporting explanations. One scholar, John C. Biddle (aka John C. Higgins-Biddle), claims that Locke's treatment of reason and revelation is "by no means thorough, clear, or consistent," while offering no evidence why he concludes this.[7] Although not explicitly charging Locke with contradictions or inconsistencies, Ian Leask notices vaguely that whereas Locke seemed to embark on a critique of faith by reason—the independence of reason and the weakness of faith—he in the end makes room for instances where faith overcomes reason.[8]

What is more, many who comment *at length* on Locke's views on reason and revelation or reason and faith strive to reconcile statements Locke makes that seem inconsistent or even contradictory or at least point out

---

also appears to maintain, as do some other scholars whom will shortly be discussed, that faith and revelation are subordinate to natural probability: "Locke also rejected the usage of 'reason' as the opposite of 'faith.' This usage may be common, but it is improper. Faith cannot be 'opposite' to good reason for him. In fact, Locke was convinced that reason is a kind of 'natural revelation'" (169).

7. Biddle, "Locke's Critique of Innate Principles," 415–22 (quotation, 415). What Biddle writes regarding Locke's understanding of the relationship of revelation and reason is helpful. He does seem surprised how we could have *assurance* in revelation when it is only a matter of probability (416). He also, with no evidence of doubt, claims the Trinity would fit into the category of above reason things (422).

8. Leask, "Personation and Immanent Undermining," 241–52. Leask also gives no evidence that he realizes the distinction between propositions that are above reason and propositions that are contrary to natural probability (243). That is, above reason propositions are propositions that we would not be expected to think of on our own, but if we did, we would not have any grounds for assenting to them, or, equally, not be able to arrive at probabilities on purely natural considerations that are for or against them. But there are other propositions that are also from revelation but are not above reason, or at least not so in the most basic sense; they are simply contrary to natural probability (*Essay* IV.xviii.7–8). He also thinks that Locke's ideas of substance would fit into the above reason category (251–52). Moreover, Leask indirectly calls Locke inconsistent since he claims Toland applied Locke's principles to revelation more consistently than did Locke: "Rather, the distinction between them was far more to do with Toland's greater consistency in applying Lockean principles to the questions of revealed mystery—the results of which consistency were now horribly evident" (247). Leask does not appear to have followed the Locke-Stillingfleet debate very closely. It seems, though, that he is trying to prove Stillingfleet's original charge that Toland was more consistent with the *Essay's* foundational epistemological principles than was Locke.

the seeming incongruities.⁹ A subset of this group are those that rightly acknowledge that faith regarding divinely revealed propositions can overturn reasonable probability, and thus, on the one hand, reason is subordinate to faith in such instances. But they become perplexed by virtue of the duties that are ascribed to reason—duties that this chapter ascribes to the proper office of reason, or proper reason—that, on the other hand, seem to make faith regarding divine revelation subordinate to reason. Richard Ashcraft and Alan P. F. Sell fall into this subset.[10]

Wioletta Polinska reads Locke similar to the way that Sell and Ashcraft read him. She acknowledges, like Sell and Ashcraft, that Locke asserts that revelation can overturn the dictates of reasonable probability made apart from revelation. She also acknowledges some seemingly incongruous Lockean statements on faith and reason and reason and revelation as Ashcraft and Sell do, but thinks that faith and reason are not to be placed in a hierarchical relationship. In other words, while Polinska acknowledges that there are aspects of Locke's teaching where reason appears to be authoritative—reason must identify revelation as being revealed, reason must interpret revelation, and revelation cannot contradict knowledge (or things of which we are certain)—faith and reason are to be understood as compatible

---

9. Chapter 3 will argue that the source of these inconsistent or seemingly contradictory statements is the multiple considerations of faith and reason Locke employs in the *Essay*.

10. Ashcraft, "Faith and Knowledge," 215–23. Ashcraft struggles to define the correct relationship between faith and reason. He notices rightly that there is an unexpected shift in the description of faith in chapter xviii of book IV of the *Essay*. Whereas faith and opinion were once identified prior to IV.xviii, that changes. He calls Locke's treatment of the relationship of faith and reason in the *Essay* unclear, inconsistent, and contradictory (215-16). After assessing the implications of the *Essay* and *ROC*, Ashcraft remarks, "If, ultimately, the epistemological views of Locke, the Christian, cannot be satisfactorily reconciled with those of Locke, the philosopher, it is the faith of the former which ensures the salvation of the latter." In other words, Ashcraft is saying that the inconsistencies in the *Essay* are not reconciled by what is found elsewhere in Locke other than the fact that he believes Locke's goal was to emphasize and legitimize the importance of faith over reason in his overall program (223). Sell, *John Locke*, 97. Sell seems likewise concerned: "It is hardly surprising that, given Locke's oscillation between the view that reason judges Scripture and is therefore in some sense above Scripture, and his less frequently expressed opinion that God can give a revelation which goes 'against the probable conjectures of reason,' some divines should emphasize the former position and others the latter." Sell is sensing rightly the tensions inherent in the vulgar faith and vulgar reason contradistinction that Locke shows to be ultimately untenable. That is, vulgar reason is forced to assist vulgar faith as vulgar faith must rely on vulgar reason for the identification of revelation as such and the interpretations of revelation. In my mind this subset is the best of those operating with a notion of reason simpliciter as they see the resulting inconsistencies and hold them in tension, as opposed to distorting the *Essay* as some do.

because faith can overturn divinely unassisted reasonable probability. When Locke writes, "Reason must be the last Guide and Judge in every Thing," in his chapter "Of Enthusiasm," what he really intends to convey is the rule that reason must be utilized to reject revelations that are contrary to knowledge and to Scripture.[11]

Furthermore, another subset of thinkers shares the common general assertion that if reason and revelation are ever in conflict, Locke assumes that revelation must submit: Paul Helm, David C. Snyder, and R. S. Woolhouse. Helm believes that according to Locke revelation cannot be allowed to overturn reasonable probability.[12] Helm's reading of Locke, as pointed out in chapter 2, is actually the rule Locke charges Stillingfleet with logically holding in the bishop's defense of the immortality of the soul. David C. Snyder and R. S. Woolhouse show no evidence that they think that reason has anything to do with probability or opinion.[13] Interestingly, this is similar

---

11. Polinska, "Faith and Reason," 305. Some might interpret her as saying that faith and reason are complimentary in that when they are identified with divine and natural revelation they will not, if viewed *correctly*, contradict one another. However, this goes without saying in Locke scholarship. That is, of course Locke would assert that general and special revelation should agree. Also, while not referencing Sell, she is tending to one of Locke's statements that gives him pause. Sell, *John Locke*, 93. Her express primary interlocutors are Snyder and Woolhouse, who will be discussed below.

Another scholar who does not express perplexity and whose argument is very much like Polinska's is: Losonsky, "Locke and Leibniz," 704–5. He also thinks that faith in revelation, while not capable of overruling or trumping knowledge, trumps that which is probable upon purely natural grounds. Their respective articles, in respect to Locke (Losonsky also treats faith and reason in the thought of Leibniz in his article), cover much of the same ground. Due to the earlier publication of Polinska's work, certain interesting subtleties of it, and for considerations of space, Polinska's article will be the one of the two that receives direct comment in the main text of this chapter.

12. Helm, "Locke on Faith and Knowledge." Near the beginning of the article in discussing the role that reason has in interpretation, he believes that Locke is asserting that an internal mark of a revelation is that it is possible to be interpreted not contrary to knowledge or probability when Locke writes: "Nothing that is contrary to, and inconsistent with, the clear and self-evident dictates of reason has a right to be urged or assented to as a matter of faith, wherein reason has nothing to do" (*Essay* IV.18.10). He fails to pay attention to the "clear and self-evident" that precedes "dictates of reason." This is a roundabout way of saying certain knowledge; reasonable probability is not self-evident. Also, Helm creatively comes up with a reading that frames Locke working simultaneously with two theses in the *Essay* that appears rather convincing if it were not for his subordination of revelation to natural or vulgar reason. In the end he is unable to fully reconcile Locke's various statements based on his two theses theory. That is no surprise due to his conceiving of reason simpliciter and his other mentioned misreading.

13. Snyder, "Faith and Reason." He is clearly operating with a faith-versus-reason distinction such that reason has nothing to do with probable belief, not even in nondivine revelation matters. In other words, Snyder thinks Locke's reason only gives knowledge, when in truth it gives probability and thus, if the mind is being rational,

at one point to Stillingfleet's reading of Locke, simply in that reason results in only certain knowledge.

Moreover, few scholars to my knowledge recognize that Locke is working with multiple senses of the term reason: one is Nicholas Jolley.[14] His work is worthy of a few initial comments. First, and generally speaking, he is primarily interested in making the distinction between two different senses of reason known and the immediate consequences of it, but does not venture into clearing up the many places in the *Essay* that trouble scholars. He is clear that anything beyond that goes beyond the goal of his study. Second, Jolley thinks that Locke is trying to be deceptive with the sense of reason he focuses on in *Essay* IV.xviii.

There are a few other related issues upon which scholars take different stances, one being the size of the compass of the faculty called reason. From some of the scholars listed above, one might reasonably infer what they might say on the matter. However, of those that comment specifically on the question, Michael Ayers believes reason is the natural faculties in general.[15] Nicholas Jolley points out that the narrow sense or discovery sense of reason has to do with finding out probability as well as the certainty of propositions and it is the broader sense of reason that Locke equates to the natural faculties in general.[16] Nicholas Wolterstorff, unlike Jolley, does not read Locke

---

belief as well. This allows him to make the incorrect conclusion faith cannot contradict reason, the correct statement being faith (proper *or* vulgar) cannot contradict knowledge (if the mind is operating rationally). Woolhouse, *Locke*, 140–43. Woolhouse has the same faith-versus-reason distinction. The idea that Locke's reason results only in knowledge was also held by Stillingfleet as discussed in chapter 2.

14. Jolley, "Locke on Faith and Reason."

15. Ayers, *Locke*, 1:121. Ayers believes that Locke's "[e]vident purpose in the chapters 'Of Faith and Reason' and 'Of Enthusiasm' was to clip the wings of revelation by subordinating it to 'reason', i.e., to the natural faculties in general." His comments on ulterior motives by Locke regarding revelation aside, Ayers is correct in what he affirms about the relationship between reason and revelation. However, his comments, though correct, are too general and unsupported to be of interest.

16. Jolley, "Locke on Faith and Reason," 442. Jolley cites *Essay* IV.xviii.3 for his support. A recent acknowledgement of Locke's utilization of two senses of reason that closely matches the thought of Jolley: LoLordo, *Locke's Moral Man*. She argues that Locke has a broad and narrow sense of reason: in the former "reason is simply the understanding," and in the latter, "reason is reasoning—inference." She rightly points to *Essay* IV.xviii.2 as containing the definition of this latter sense. She is not, however, as interested in the faith and reason question as Jolley is but rather Locke's distinction of the senses of reason. She does, however, say something about IV.xviii.2's definition of faith; but she misreads the way in which Locke differentiates the narrow sense of reason and its corresponding faith. That is, she thinks that the narrow sense of reason has to do with probability (as well as demonstration), while faith is " 'Assent to any Proposition . . . upon the Credit of the Proposer' (4.18.2)" (105). She stops short of adding the rest

as operating with the double sense of the term reason, and thus understands the *Essay* IV.xviii's definition of reason as Locke's official one. He believes reason to be "specifically, that faculty whereby we discover arguments and 'perceive' their logical force, thereby also forming beliefs as to the cogency of the inferences of which those arguments are the content." Wolterstorff takes issue with readings of Locke that make out all psychological faculties to be reason because Locke acknowledges that we hold and even assent to *irrational* beliefs.[17]

Still there is another important issue, and it deals with the question: What does Locke say regarding reason and the Bible? Helm argues that it doesn't make sense for Locke to call the Bible "infallibly true" (*Essay* III. iii.23) when believing the Bible to be true is based on testimony and thus only probable; in other words, "'it is probable that p is infallibly true' reduces to 'p is probably true.'"[18] Snyder, responding to Helm's concerns, explains that Locke "is simply asserting either that their source, God, is infallible, and so they [revelation propositions] in fact provide an unshakable foundation for morality and religion, or that they could afford us full assurance of faith if we *could* certainly know that they are revealed."[19] Other than that, he has his own concerns about Locke. Snyder's biggest issues derive from the fact that Locke understands belief and knowing to be two distinct acts. First, considering that faith involves doubt in the revelation being revealed and knowledge comes only by natural means, one cannot properly categorize the Biblical writers who were *certain* the revelation came from God.[20] Snyder believes this problem is compounded when one considers that a teaching of Scripture is that through faith one can have knowledge (Heb 11:8–19).[21] Second, Snyder acknowledges that Locke conceives of a distinction between certainty and assurance, but "he is being less than honest [with

---

of the definition: "as coming from GOD, in some extraordinary way of Communication." Although, again, not her main concern, this truncation of the definition of faith relegates the assent to testimonies on any matter to faith.

17. Wolterstorff, *John Locke and the Ethics of Belief*, 87–89 (quotation, 87). Wolterstorff is working from IV.xviii's definition of reason as Locke's official definition, but he does quote and build upon the definition of reason from *Essay* IV.xvii (88). I believe he thinks Locke is mistaken when in IV.xvii.2 Locke makes reasoning or illation or inference a part of reason (88n75, 89). Wolterstorff believes that illation or inference assents to opinion; and if this is allowed to be part of reason, we would contradictorily admit that our faculty of reason that does not err makes bad judgments at times. This work of Wolterstorff finds its start in: Wolterstorff, "John Locke's Epistemological Piety."

18. Helm, "Locke on Faith and Knowledge," 57–58.

19. Snyder, "Faith and Reason," 206.

20. Ibid., 207.

21. Ibid., 210.

Stillingfleet] when he concludes that as a result he never says or implies that therefore we cannot have full assurance of faith."[22] Moreover, Wolterstorff points out issues involving miracles as external indicators of revelation that are problematic, namely, "how much of a biblical writer's book is confirmed by a particular miracle?"[23] Polinska responds to some of these challenges. She argues that faith is based on probability and has only fallible interpretations, whereas the infallibility attributed to Scripture is based on the divine character of God, the one believed to have given it. She also argues that certainty is ascribed to knowledge and its analogue of sorts, or highest degree of reasonable conviction, in the act of believing, is assurance.[24]

Another issue that deserves mention is the question of whether Locke is a necessitarian or libertarian. One of the largest sticking points in the discussion is how the suspension of judgment is to be understood. Locke's younger friend and necessitarian, Anthony Collins, criticizes Locke either for admitting of occasions of liberty or because his discussions of the suspension of the judgment can be read that way.[25] This is important as Collins was proclaimed by Locke to understand the *Essay* better than anyone he knew.[26] Libertarian Samuel Clarke, in his comments on Locke's suspension, called Locke "much perplexed." From the context, it is not clear if he means that he thinks Locke was confused and did not know it or he was confused and did know it.[27] In short, from the generation coming after Locke, some were not pleased with his lack of clarity or consistency. The libertarian versus necessitarian interpretation of Locke continues today but this chapter will not enter the lists with contemporary scholarship on this issue; I have

22. Ibid., 211.

23. Wolterstorff, *John Locke and the Ethics of Belief*, 132.

24. Polinska, "Faith and Reason," 291–97. Cf. Losonsky, "Locke and Lebniz," 705, 706. In opposition to the stance of those like Polinska in her marked distinction between certainty and assurance, Losonsky surprisingly maintains that "While faith also involves certainty, albeit a different kind of certainty, and it can *equal* the certainty of rational knowledge, the certainty of faith cannot *exceed* rational certainty" (705). He cites IV.xviii.5 as support. There Locke writes, "For since no evidence of our Faculties, by which we receive such *Revelations*, can exceed, if equal, the certainty of our intuitive Knowledge, we can never receive for a Truth any thing, that is directly contrary to our clear and distinct Knowledge." Losonsky evidently misreads Locke, thinking (rightly) that the "no" applies to the "exceed" but (wrongly) not to the "equal." It is questionable if it can even make sense for the conviction of faith to be able to equal that of rational knowledge when it is the latter that Locke says (and Losonsky admits) that cannot, or at least should not be, overturned by the former. Regardless, as this chapter will show, assurance is not certainty and is a lesser degree of conviction.

25. Collins, *Philosophical Inquiry*, 39–40; cf. Marko, "Revisiting the Question."

26. O'Higgins, *Determinism and Freewill*, 12.

27. Clarke, *Remarks upon a Book*, 23; cf. Marko, "Revisiting the Question," 81.

done that elsewhere.[28] It will suffice to point out the problematic nature of the suspension of judgment when pertinent.

PART II: PRELIMINARIES

Before extrapolating on reason, there are several preliminary concepts to cover, some more or less in detail depending on what the later sections in this chapter require. In other words, a few concepts will be treated here, and will be built upon later on in the chapter. These notions bear directly upon this chapter's discussion of reason and are, in fact, addressed by Locke in building up to his discussion on reason. The terms that will be briefly discussed here are: knowledge, judgment, and assent.

Chapter 2 already revealed a few things related to Locke's use of the term knowledge. There it was specifically discussed as the result of the employment of powers by the mind. "*Knowledge* then seems to me to be nothing but *the perception of the connection and agreement, or disagreement and repugnancy of any of our Ideas*" (IV.i.2). Chapter 2 discussed the four sorts of knowledge in the resultant sense (identity and diversity, relation in general, co-existence or necessary connection, and real existence) (IV.i) and that with such knowledge comes certainty.[29] Also discussed were the three routes or methods by which the mind comes to have knowledge and be certain in degrees: intuition, demonstration, and sensation (IV.ii).[30] What is more, it was noted that simply to perceive or understand or frame an idea is to *know* that idea in a qualified sense (IV.i.4). But there is another important sense of the term knowledge inherent in the definition above: the faculty or power sense. Knowledge, in this sense, is one of two faculties Locke affords a certain pre-eminence. Locke writes, "Thus the Mind has two Faculties, conversant about Truth and Falsehood. *First, Knowledge*, whereby it [the Mind] certainly perceives, and is undoubtedly satisfied of the agreement or disagreement of any *Ideas*" (IV.xiv.4).

---

28. O'Higgins, *Determinism and Freewill*, 11–12. O'Higgins thinks it likely that Locke is a necessitarian but realizes one could make a case for libertarianism. Cf. Marko, "Revisiting the Question," 100n17. For other interesting recent discussions on the matter: Harris, *Of Liberty and Necessity*, 19–40; Rowe, "Causality and Free Will"; Marko, "Why Locke's 'Of Power' Is Not a Metaphysical Pronouncement." My article that weighs in on the debate has a survey of the scholarship on the issue.

29. Cf. Locke, *Mr. Locke's Reply . . . Answer to his Second Letter*, 70–71.

30. Cf. Ayers, *Locke*, 1:95. Moreover, recall from chapter 2 that intuition, demonstration, and sensation can be understood as methods, powers, or results of those powers.

The second faculty, "conversant about Truth and Falsehood," is judgment (IV.xiv.4). This is what we must rely on in issues where (certain) knowledge cannot be had, and what we do rely on sometimes out of laziness, unskillfulness, or haste, where knowledge could be had. Judgment is the faculty "whereby the Mind takes its *Ideas* to agree, or disagree; or, which is the same, any Proposition to be true, or false, without perceiving a demonstrative Evidence in the Proofs" (IV.xiv.3). He expands further:

> As Demonstration is the shewing the agreement, or disagreement of two *Ideas*, by the intervention of one or more Proofs, which have a constant, immutable, and visible connexion one with another; so *Probability* is nothing but the appearance of such an agreement, or disagreement, by the intervention of Proofs, whose connexion is not constant and immutable, or at least not perceived to be so, but is, or appears for the most part to be so, and is enough to induce the Mind to *judge* the Proposition to be true, or false, rather than the contrary (IV.xv.1).

In other words, in demonstration the yield is knowledge by the linking together of intuitive connections; and probability is the appearance of agreement or disagreement that is sufficient for the mind to judge accordingly, but without the certainty that accompanies the former. Whereas indubitable proofs are required for demonstrative knowledge, probability, "likeliness to be true," is what is required for faith, belief, assent, or opinion (IV.xv.3). All of the grounds of probability are what *ought* to be considered by the mind in judgment when conditions warrant it (IV.xv.5).

Probability supplies the defect in our knowledge and helps to guide us where it fails (IV.xv.4). Again, when our mind judges a proposition true based on probability, this is not knowledge, but something else: belief, faith, assent, or opinion (IV.xv.2–3). Moreover, probability is grounded by "*First*, The conformity of any thing with our own Knowledge, Observation, and Experience," and "*Secondly*, the Testimony of others, couching their Observation and Experience" (IV.xv.4). "In the Testimony of others, is to be considered, 1. The Number. 2. The Integrity. 3. The Skill of the Witnesses. 4. The Design of the Author . . . 5. The Consistency of the Parts, and Circumstances of the Relation. 6. Contrary Testimonies" (IV.xv.4). The mind "*ought to examine all grounds of Probability*" and see how each makes the proposition more or less probable. Upon a due balancing by the mind, which occurs "*if it will proceed rationally*," the proposition will, or at least should, be rejected or received with more or less assent "proportionably to the preponderancy of the greater grounds of Probability on one side or the other" (IV.xv.5). There is another ground of assent, other than conformity and testimony that is not legitimate, and that is authority, or taking a proposition that is merely one's opinion to be true on that person's say-so. In other words, one must be convinced from their own reasoning and study into a particular matter, or from the veracity of the claims of another's knowledge, and not to be influenced by the respect of or deference to an esteemed person's or group's opinion (IV.xv.6; IV.xix.18).

Locke finds the implicit faith corresponding to authority as a basis of assent especially dangerous in religion (IV.xv.6).[31] For one, each person rationally ought to be exceedingly concerned about the eternal state of his or her soul (IV.xix.3-6). And for any doubtful of his natural, rational argument of this intellectual burden each of us carries (or the intellectual abilities God has given us to assent rationally in matters of religion, and therefore the obligation to do so), despite our own low estimation of our mental abilities, he argues the same in discussing the nature of Scripture and the Christian's corresponding individual and obligatory response to it in his theological treatise, *ROC*, and its two vindications. It is one's individual duty as a kingdom member to understand the duties and doctrines for one's self.[32] He writes:

> That every Man should receive from others, or make to himself such a System of Christianity as he found most conformable to the Word of God, according to the best of his understanding, is what I never spake against, but think it every one's Duty to Labour for, and to take all opportunities as long as he lives, by Studying the Scriptures every day, to perfect.[33]

In fact, while God forbids that we treat anyone as our infallible interpreter, we can and must rely on the Spirit of God.[34] He believes that Christendom would have more Christians if "reading and study of the Scripture were more pressed" and people were sent to the Bible for religion as opposed to having it "put into their hands only to find the Opinions of their peculiar Sect or Party."[35]

---

31. This arises in *ROC* as well. E.g., Locke, *ROC*, 306.
32. Locke, *Second Vindication*, 410.
33. Ibid., 401–2.
34. Ibid., 340–41. "For whether by *men* he here means those on whom the Holy Ghost was so eminently poured out, *Acts. II*. Or whether he means by these Words, that special Assistance of the Holy Ghost, whereby particular men to the end of the World, are to be lead into the Truth, by opening their understandings, that they may understand the Scriptures (for he always loves to speak doubtfully and indefinitely) I know no other infallible guide, but the Spirit of God in the Scriptures."
35. Ibid., 211.

There are several degrees of assent. These "are, or ought to be regulated" by the grounds of probability (IV.xvi.1). Due diligence in this area should be increased based on the gravity of the issues at hand (IV.xvi.3, IV.xix.2–3[36]). There are two types of propositions "we receive upon Inducements of *Probability*": matters of fact or that which are capable of human testimony and speculation or that which are beyond our senses (IV.xvi.5).[37] Locke starts discussion with the matters of fact or that which is capable of human testimony. The first and highest degree of assent is assurance. This occurs when propositions testified of by fair witnesses are supported by our never-failing experience. Examples of these are properties of bodies and proceedings of causes and effects in the course of nature. "These *Probabilities* rise so *near* to *Certainty*, that they govern our Thoughts as absolutely, and influence all our Actions as fully, as the most evident demonstration; and in what concerns us, we make little or no difference between them and certain Knowledge" (IV.xv.6). The next degree is confidence and it is produced in two different scenarios. The first scenario is when a fact is attested by numerous, undoubted witnesses and conforms to one's own occasional experiences (IV.xvi.7). The second scenario that produces confidence is when the truth of a proposition could not benefit anyone and it is attested by many unsuspected witnesses and contradicted by none (IV.xvi.8).[38] The above propositions and described contexts "leaves us as little at liberty to believe, or disbelieve, as Demonstration does."[39] This is not the case when experience contradicts testimony and/or testimony contradicts testimony. In any of these instances, judging rightly requires diligence. There are so many factors and issues to consider that Locke does not attempt to describe the situations associated with subsequent levels of assent. He remarks:

> This only may be said in general, That as the Arguments and Proofs, *pro* and *con*, upon due examination, nicely weighing every particular Circumstance, shall to any one appear, upon the whole matter, in a greater or less degree, to preponderate on either side, so they are fitted to produce in the Mind such

---

36. In the fourth edition (1700) (and all subsequent editions) of the *Essay*, IV.xix became IV.xx.

37. "Speculation" is a term used in the margin, but not in the text of IV.xvi.5. Interestingly in his final reply to Bishop Stillingfleet, Locke speaks of "Matters of Speculation" in juxtaposition to "Matters of Fact." Locke, *Mr. Locke's Reply . . . Answer to his Second Letter*, 265–66.

38. The text does not say that this is a description of a scenario that leads to confidence. The margin states that the scenario gives confidence.

39. This is an enigmatical statement by Locke. One could read it literally and thus as allowing for liberty.

Entertainment, as we call *Belief, Conjecture, Guess, Doubt, Wavering, Distrust, Disbelief,* etc. (IV.xvi.9).

Thus, instead of going through the lengthy descriptions of the situations and scenarios that induce the mind to varying degrees of assent commonly called conjecture, guess, doubt, etc., he simply reiterates the point that every pertinent matter must be weighed and considered.

Locke then turns his focus to assent in matters where human testimony cannot be had. These matters include finite immaterial beings, material things too small to be observed with our bare senses, material things too far away to be observed with our bare senses (extraterrestrials, distant planets, etc.), and the causes of the sensible effects that we experience in nature. Locke says very little regarding assent in these matters. He only relays that analogy is the only help that we have. We typically observe gradual connections throughout nature that leave no discernible gap. So, for instance, just as we see a gradual connection, or chain of life, moving from humans downward, it would appear likely that there are a ranks of beings between humans and God. Hence, we can interpolate and extrapolate based on our sensible observations in the areas of natural philosophy. Other than that, he says little other than that we draw all our grounds of probability from analogy in these instances. But it is "This sort of Probability, which is the best Conduct of rational Experiments, and the Rise of Hypothesis has also its Use and Influence: and a wary Reasoning from Analogy leads us often into the discovery of Truths, and useful Productions, which would otherwise lie concealed" (IV.xvi.12).

In this discussion of judgment and degrees of assent, Locke also discusses miracles and revelation. Whereas assurance is produced by the ordinary course of things and fair testimony, there is one case—namely miracles—where the strangeness, or contrariety to the ordinary course of things, with fair witnesses are sufficient to produce assent. Miracles should be considered possible as God is able to change the course of nature. Moreover, just as the greater number of fair witnesses will tend to increase the firmness of assent, so will the greater the outlandishness of the event. In short, these miracles are used by God to give credit to God's revelation (IV.xvi.13). This comports with what Locke says in *ROC* regarding revelation and miracles:

> For though it be as easie to Omnipotent Power to do all things by an immediate over-ruling Will; and so to make any Instruments work, even contrary to their Nature, in Subserviency to his ends; Yet his Wisdom is not usually at the expence of Miracles (if I may so say) but only in cases that require them, for the

> evidencing of some Revelation or Mission to be from him. He does constantly (unless where the confirmation of some Truth requires it otherwise) bring about his Purposes by means operating according to their Natures. If it were not so, the course and evidence of things would be confounded: Miracles would lose their name and force, and there could be no distinction between Natural and Supernatural.[40]

In short, God uses miracles sparingly, as it would seem, and uses them as external indicators or marks that a message or mission is from Him.

The section following the aforementioned IV.xvi.13 is extremely dense and will not be treated fully here. For accuracy purposes it will be treated later in this chapter, once the relationship between reason and revelation has been discussed more extensively, as Locke might recommend. Locke writes this ending to the section: "But of Faith [faith in divinely revealed propositions], and the Precedency it ought to have before other Arguments of Persuasion, I shall speak more hereafter, where I treat of it, as it is ordinarily placed, in contradistinction to Reason: though in Truth, it be nothing else but an Assent founded on the highest Reason." There are two important things to notice. First, and most importantly, Locke says that at a later time he will set faith in divine revelation in contrast to reason, although it is really assent or the result of the act of rationally assenting.[41] That is why revelation is included in the chapter on assent, chapter xvi. Second, it appears, at least some propositions that one assents to as being divinely revealed will have a precedence or priority over all other persuasions, a thing that Paul Helm and others deny.[42]

PART III: REASON

It is not until chapter xvii, "Of Reason," that Locke formally begins his discussion on reason. After giving several senses in which others use the term reason, Locke gives his lengthy definition. Reason is needed for the enlargement of our knowledge, as was indicated earlier by its role in demonstration, and for "regulating our Assent." The extended definition of reason is crucial

---

40. Locke, *ROC*, 161; cf. 191.

41. There is not only a different understanding of faith put forth here, but there are two considerations of reason intimated here as well. There is the reason that will be put in contradistinction to faith and there is the "highest Reason" that truly governs all assent.

42. Helm, "Locke on Faith and Knowledge," 56. But evidence in a much clearer context is forthcoming, so Paul Helm will be responded to more extensively later.

for understanding what he really intends by the term reason throughout most of the *Essay*. This definition is also important for understanding the disagreements that have arisen regarding the interpretation of reason. Thus, the lengthy definition will be given in full, but segmented by numbers in brackets inserted into the text of the definition.

> [1] What need is there of Reason? Very much; both for the Enlargement of our Knowledge, and regulating our Assent: For it hath to do, both in Knowledge and Opinion, and is [2] necessary and assisting to all our other intellectual Faculties, and indeed *contains* two of them, [3] *viz. Sagacity and Illation*: By the one, it finds out, and by the other, it so orders the intermediate *Ideas*, as to discover the connexion there is in each Link of the Chain, whereby the Extremes are held together; and thereby, as it were, to draw into view the Truth sought for, which is that we call Illation or Inference, and consists in nothing but the Perception of the connexion there is between the *Ideas*, in each step of the deduction, whereby the Mind comes to see, either the certain agreement or disagreement of any two *Ideas*, as in Demonstration, in which it arrives at Knowledge; or their probable connexion, on which it gives or with-holds its Assent, as in Opinion . . . [4] And in those Cases, where we are fain to substitute Assent instead of Knowledge, and take Propositions for true, without being certain they are so, we have need to find out, examine, and compare the grounds of their Probability. [5] In both these Cases, the Faculty which finds out the Means, and rightly applies them to discover Certainty in the one, and Probability in the other, is that which we call Reason. [6] For as Reason perceives the necessary, and indubitable connexion of all the *Ideas* or Proofs one to another, in each step of any Demonstration that produces Knowledge: [7] so it likewise perceives the probable connexion all the *Ideas* or Proofs one to another, in every step of a Discourse, to which it will think Assent due. [8] This is the lowest degree of that, which can be truly called Reason: For where the Mind does not perceive this probable connexion; where it does not discern, whether there be any such connexion, or no, there Men's Opinions are not the product of Judgment, or the consequence of Reason; but the effects of Chance and Hazard, of a Mind floating at all Adventures, without choice, and without direction (IV.xvii.2).

In summary, [1] the faculty of reason has functions pertaining to knowledge and assent and [2] it contains (at least) two other faculties: sagacity and illation. [3] Sagacity here, as in the description of the demonstrative process described earlier, finds the intermediate ideas, and illation indicates the surety (certainty or degree of confidence) two ideas have. In the end reason displays to the mind either certainty—and the mind has knowledge—or the probability of a proposition. [4] When we do not have certainty but are only able to assent or dissent we must consider and weigh the related factors and their associated probabilities. [5] Reason is the faculty that obtains knowledge and probability. [6] It obtains knowledge through indubitable demonstration and [7] determines and assesses probabilities. Regarding probability, reason gives the mind a *recommendation* for assenting or dissenting. [8] The lowest type of reasoning we have is that which ascertains probability. But if we didn't have that, decisions and beliefs would be given to chance.

This interpretation of reason runs counter to important scholarship on the issue. While the above interpretation claims that reason offers [7] *recommendations* to the mind in instances where only probability can be had, Jolley's and Ayers's interpretations rule this out as they indicate from clear textual evidence that reason is the natural faculties in general.[43] In other words, this claim that reason comprises the natural faculties in general appears to make the mind interchangeable with reason.[44] Jolley references a quote subsequent to the one above from the *Essay* in this regard: "For our simple *Ideas* then, which are the Foundation, and sole Matter of all our Notions, and Knowledge, we must depend wholly on our *Reason, I mean, our natural Faculties*" (emphasis mine) (IV.xviii.3; cf. IV.xviii.2).[45] To allow reason to be the sum total of our natural faculties would include the faculty of knowledge and the faculty of judgment, the faculty through which the mind assents, or takes something only probable to be true (IV.xiv.3). Against the position held by Ayers and Jolley that reason is the totality of the natural faculties, as it appears to be in the quote from IV.xviii above, one could argue a separation between reason and the "distinguishing faculty" that perceives agreement or disagreement of two ideas in intuition. That is, one could argue that intuition has no need of reasoning and thus this distinguishing faculty is likely conceived of by Locke as being separate from

---

43. Jolley, "Locke on Faith and Reason," 442; Ayers, *Locke*, 1:121.

44. It is surprising that Jolley and Ayers would concede to Locke making the mind and reason interchangeable, but this is the result of their statements. Nevertheless, if all the powers of the mind are called reason, the mind is essentially reason. Locke says as much in IV.xviii.3 and they both note it, but it simply seems that neither has followed the implications of Locke's assertion, or at least do not care to do so. Locke uses the mind and reason interchangeably elsewhere, too. E.g., Locke, *Letter to Edward*, 137.

45. Jolley, "Locke on Faith and Reason," 442. Jolley is quoting from the critical edition of the *Essay*.

reason (IV.i.1; IV.xiii.1). But it is possible that that distinguishing faculty (or faculty of distinct perception) is the very same faculty used by reason to acknowledge the indubitable connection between two steps in a proof (IV.ii.5–6). In fact it is likely as Locke does not find it helpful to talk about faculties as if they were agents but rather faculties as being the powers or abilities the body and mind have (II.xxi.20). In other words, the power to perceive agreement or disagreement immediately in intuition is the same power to perceive agreement or disagreement or identity and diversity immediately in a step in a demonstrative proof. So, the distinguishing faculty is likely a part of the whole called reason, which comports with reason being all the natural faculties in the quote pointed out by Jolley. What is more, it appears that the faculty of knowledge is subsumed entirely under the faculty of reason as reason can result in knowledge.

This likelihood that knowledge is part of reason, however, does not fully explain the aforementioned distinction between reason and the mind in Locke's definition of reason. The mind has the powers or faculties of understanding or perceiving and willing or preferring (II.xxi.6). Presumably the mind has all of the intellectual faculties or powers. In [2] reason is said to assist our other powers or faculties, while reason contains two faculties itself. Presumably all faculties discussed in the definition of reason are mental. The part cannot be the whole so reason cannot be the total of the mind's faculties or powers. Furthermore, in [3] Locke says that the mind, and not reason, gives or withholds assent. Again, Locke appears to be proposing that reason *recommends* to the mind where it thinks assent due in [6] and [7]: "[6] For as Reason perceives the necessary, and indubitable connexion of all the *Ideas* or Proofs one to another, in each step of any Demonstration that produces Knowledge: [7] so it likewise perceives the probable connexion all the *Ideas* or Proofs one to another, in every step of a Discourse, to which it will think Assent due." As a result, the phrase at the end of [7] just quoted, "to which it will think Assent due," is better interpreted as "to which reason *recommends* Assent to the mind" as opposed to "to which reason assents for the mind." Further support for the former interpretation is that the latter interpretation effectively negates "think" in "think Assent," making think and assent the same action and thus a useless redundancy in the definition.

The question of how it is possible that the sum total of the mind's powers can be identified with reason in one sense by Locke, as pointed out by Jolley and Ayers, and distinguished in another by Locke, however, has not been answered. This recommendation function that reason might have is consistent with an "oughtness" that Locke associates often with judgment. For instance, where Locke is discussing the use of probability in assent, he notes that the grounds of probability, supplied by reason, are "the measure whereby its [Assent's] several degrees are, or *ought to be regulated*" [emphasis mine] (IV.xvi.1). Thus, this quote might be read as implying the mind's ability to avoid following the guidance of the probability supplied by reason. There is another location in the same general vicinity that appears to advance this same sense of oughtness in following reason. While Locke describes situations where sometimes the intermediate ideas are tied so tightly together with the extremes in a probable proof that assent necessarily follows, especially in indifferent matters (IV.xvi.6–9), and thus the recommendation would functionally be a determination, this might not always be the case based on a quote from the very next chapter: "The great Excellency and Use of the Judgment, is to observe Right, and take a true estimate of the force and weight of each Probability; and then casting them up all right together, chuse that side which has the overbalance" (IV.xvii.16). In other words this last citation might be read as saying we *should* judge reasonably or, equally, the proper "Use" of the judgment is to follow reason's findings on reasonable probability (cf. II.xxi.67), and not simply that we ought to employ reason, which results in the determination of our mind.

Regardless of whether this is the correct reading of this last quotation or not, there is support for this sentiment of "oughtness" elsewhere or, in other words, the implied ability of the mind not to follow its conclusions arrived at through the employment of reason. In the chapter of "Wrong Assent, or Error," Locke notes instances when judgment will actually take the less probable side. In one area he describes general ways in which the mind can avoid the most apparent probabilities: 1) ceasing the weighing of the evidence built and continually mounting, or at least rapidly building, in a particular proposition's favor, and not employing reason in examining the issue any further or thoroughly, and 2) suspending the assent to a proposition that is already due, and thus, by default, taking what is in fact the less probable side for the time-being (IV.xix.12–14).[46] Locke gives a somewhat amusing real-life scenario where one avoids the most apparent probabilities. He says, "Tell a Man, passionately in Love, that he is gilted; bring a score of Witnesses of the Falshood of his Mistress, 'tis ten to one but three kind Words of hers, shall invalidate all their Testimonies. . . . *What suits our Wishes, is forwardly believed*" (IV.xix.12). He subsequently describes the arguments in which such a one will likely attempt to alleviate some of the mental discomfort created by the preponderance of testimonies to the contrary side. One can console oneself by dismissing the disturbingly or

---

46. Regarding the two ways in which one avoids the most apparent probabilities, one refers to instances were individual probabilities or cumulating individual probabilities of various elements pertinent to an argument are avoided and the other refers to instances where the final cumulative probability is avoided.

uncomfortably reasonable argument by focusing on the fact that the argument might have a fallacy latent in it or that one does not know yet what is to be said on the contrary side (IV.xix.13–14).[47] Besides, "One does not want to act rashly!" is a true (and easily abused) life principle. Despite this ability to avoid obvious probabilities, Locke concludes that upon a full examination with reason, and thus an accompanying *willingness* to possibly greatly inconvenience oneself, judgment will always go to the most probable side (IV.xix.15–16). In short, Locke does conceive of instances where the mind will *not* follow reason's recommendation. But other than that, reason *is*, in a sense, the *natural faculties when the mind heeds reason's recommendations in operation*, which is most of the time.[48]

Although this explanation of in what sense reason can be the natural faculties is helpful, that the mind can suspend assent in some instances in which reason and probability are involved but is necessarily determined by reason's recommendations in another has been a source of no little controversy from the beginning.[49] It is possible that Locke intends for strong

47. It seems that it is possible that reason is used to find these alternatives. For instance, one might employ one's reason to follow the argument of someone on some issue. The reason understands the argument and finds it rather likely. The desire for the conclusion of this argument to be wrong, and thus not the case, prompts the mind to employ the reason to find possible bases upon which the disliked argument could, upon a fuller examination, prove to be incorrect. Reason, not having a will, is employed and finds one or two *more comfortable* possibilities. The mind and the corresponding desire being satisfied for now immediately suspend any further examination, possibly not even entertaining the following question: Which is more likely, the conclusions arrived at by reason in the disliked argument or the possible alternatives. The uneasiness of not heeding reason's conclusion based on its employment is, possibly, partly assuaged by heeding reason's conclusions on a related question. That is, perhaps, having a reason that *could* be right is enough to put oneself at ease so as to be able to move off of the topic.

48. Locke does discuss the problems of discoursing about the faculties as if they were agents, but the personification of reason just used above is consistent with the degree of personification, for facility's sake no doubt, that Locke employs in his chapter on reason.

49. Locke's younger friend, Anthony Collins, criticizes Locke either for admitting of occasions of liberty of the will or because his discussions of the suspension of the judgment can be read that way. Collins, *Philosophical Inquiry*, 39–40. This is important as Collins was proclaimed by Locke to understand the *Essay* better than anyone he knew. O'Higgins, *Determinism and Freewill*, 12. Samuel Clarke, in his comments on Locke's suspension, called Locke "much perplexed." From the context, it is not clear if he means that he thinks Locke was confused and did not know it or he did know it. Clarke, *Remarks*, 23. The discussion on whether or not Locke was a necessitarian or libertarian is ongoing despite Locke's possible attempts to side-step the question. The following have shorter but helpful discussions on the issue: Rowe, "Causality and Free Will"; O'Higgins, *Determinism and Freewill*, 12–13; Harris, *Of Liberty and Necessity*, 2–3; Marko, "Revisiting the Question," 80–82; Marko, "Why Locke's 'Of Power' Is Not

inclinations, just like false hypotheses, to be mistaken by the mind for knowledge, and thus it will be the case that a high probability given by the mind engaged in reasoning will be subordinated by the mind itself to something it mistakes as knowledge. And then a full examination prompted by a suspiciously high probability would entail the examination of proofs and the root of the so-called knowledge and thus a suspension of judgment until all is settled. In short, in this general scenario, the mind realized it may have employed reason properly but from incorrect premises and then corrects for it. But that does not seem what he is attempting to convey when discussing the mind judging irrationally and the nature of suspense in IV.xix.12–16, referenced above. In Locke's descriptions found there, it appears as though the mind has a nagging suspicion or uneasiness supplied from reason that it (the mind) might not be judging correctly or at least it is doing so without sufficient information, as in the case of the jilted lover. The mind can stop rational inquiries and avoid a thorough examination of a situation that at first glance appears likely to yield an unfavorable answer.

What is more, the suggestion made here, that the mind can avoid being guided by reason, has support through an analogue in the area of knowledge. Locke notes instances where the mind actually decides against what knowledge would say is certain![50] The Roman Catholics, for instance, believe that the bread in the Lord's Supper is the body, contrary to their sensitive knowledge and the intuitive knowledge that a body cannot be in two places at once and other like instances (IV.xix.10; IV.xviii.5). Nevertheless, either reason is the natural faculties or reason can be equated to the natural faculties when the mind is acting reasonably. The weight of the evidence tilts the scales in favor of the latter.

"Acting reasonably," in the statement, "reason can be equated to the natural faculties when the mind is acting reasonably," just made is deserving of a qualification. In the above discussion, acting reasonably was described regarding a specific case where one judged contrary to the most apparent probabilities—what we typically call lying to oneself. In other words it is unreasonable for the mind to believe or act against the dictates provided by reason. Locke would hardly think it *reasonable*, in a yet a different sense, to treat every instance of mental uneasiness with a full examination. Acting reasonably in general, then, does not encompass a full examination into *every* possible issue that arises—"The Conduct of our Lives, and the Management of our great Concerns, will not bear delay" (IV.xvi.3)—but only

---

a Metaphysical Pronouncement."

50. Cf. Locke, *Mr. Locke's Reply . . . Answer to His Second Letter*, 218–19. Here he says the mind is determined by certainty.

on issues that are of great concern to us such as morality or religion, or as Wolterstorff says, issues that are of "maximal concernment" (II.xxi.67–68).[51] Although appropriated here in a somewhat different context, C. S. Lewis's assessment of scruples is apt here: "And scruples are always a bad thing—if only because they distract us from real duties."[52] In short, acting or operating reasonably is when the mind is working reasonably—reasonably in the sense of dictated by reason *and* in the sense of corresponding to the appropriate thoroughness that the circumstance warrants.

So far in this part, there are a few conclusions that come from pondering an objection to this chapter's claims that Locke's definition of reason portrays reason as *recommending* to the mind what it should believe (*Essay* IV.xvii.2). The objection, again, is that this would make the sum total of the natural faculties distinct from the reason; and some interpret reason to be the sum total of all the natural faculties. Although understanding reason as all of the natural faculties has some warrant, it does not account for the instances where Locke acknowledges that sometimes people believe against their reason. So, it this chapter's conclusion that reason is taken as the natural faculties *when* the mind is acting reasonably. But even acting reasonably needs to be qualified. Acting reasonably has both to do with heeding reason *and* the examinational thoroughness required by the circumstance and importance of the issue at hand.

The other important scholarly assessment of Locke's reason to which this chapter objects is Nicholas Wolterstorff's. Wolterstorff interprets Locke's extended definition of reason somewhat differently and ultimately thinks Locke's prevailing view of reason is far narrower than this chapter's or Jolley's or Ayers's. He believes that the fundamental sense of reason that Locke operates with in the *Essay* is "the capacity to 'perceive' the logical force of arguments."[53] This corresponds, for Wolterstorff, to the third degree of reason spoken of in IV.xvii.3: "So that we may in *Reason* consider these *four degrees*; the first and highest, is the discovering, and finding out of Proofs; the second, the regular and methodical Disposition of them, and laying them in a clear and fit Order, to make their Connexion and Force be plainly and easily perceived; the third is perceiving their connexion; and the

---

51. Wolterstorff, "John Locke's Epistemological Piety," 581. I agree with Wolterstorff that there are instances where it seems like Locke could be advocating for a full examination by reason in all things (e.g., IV.xvii.24), but such a message would contradict other places in the *Essay*, one referenced above (IV.xvi.3). It is not the purpose of the chapter to attempt to go further in speculating guidelines for determining some sort of hierarchy of issues of maximal concernment and associated conditions.

52. Lewis, *Letters to Malcolm*, 33.

53. Wolterstorff, "John Locke's Epistemological Piety," 587.

fourth, the making a right conclusion."[54] Wolterstorff notes that "Locke's subsequent discussion leaves little doubt that he regards the third in the list as fundamental." Part of his textual support for this comes from IV.xvii.2's definition of reason that he believes is describing reason's capacity to perceive indubitable and probable connections: "[8] This is the lowest degree of that, which can be truly called Reason." Wolterstorff thus claims that the "lowest degree" means *fundamental degree*, as in the fundamental degree or aforementioned third degree in the *Essay* IV.xvii.3.[55]

That the working sense or predominant sense of reason's activity that Locke employs in the *Essay* is not described best by all four degrees in concert but rather the third degree alone is problematic for a few different reasons. First, it is unclear why Wolterstorff claims that Locke's "subsequent discussion leaves little doubt that he regards the third in the list as fundamental." The subsequent discussion is a lengthy discourse on syllogisms that is in turn followed by a discussion of explanations of why and when reason fails us. In this latter portion, Locke talks of reason "proceeding" (IV.xvii.12), being "puzzled" (IV.xvii.13), etc. These descriptions appear opposed to Wolterstorff's claims that Locke's further treatment of reason shows that he conceives of reason as merely perceiving connections or the logical force of an argument.

The second problem with Wolterstorff's minimalistic interpretation of Locke's understanding of reason is that he wrongly believes it is stated in the quotation from IV.xvii.2. That is, Wolterstorff thinks the following quotation from Locke's definition of reason shows that Locke primarily conceives of reason in a very narrow scope:

> [6] For as Reason perceives the necessary, and indubitable connexion of all the *Ideas* or Proofs one to another, in each step of any Demonstration that produces Knowledge: [7] so it likewise perceives the probable connexion all the *Ideas* or Proofs one to another, in every step of a Discourse, to which it will think Assent due. [8] This is the lowest degree of that, which can be truly called Reason (IV.xvii.2).

So Wolterstorff believes the "lowest degree" of reason refers to the perception of "indubitable" and "probable" connections. The quote above is, however, followed by more:

---

54. There are no notable differences between the third edition and the critical edition pertaining to this passage.

55. Wolterstorff, "John Locke's Epistemological Piety," 581.

> [8] ... For where the Mind does not perceive this probable connexion; where it does not discern, whether there be any such connexion, or no, there Men's Opinions are not the product of Judgment, or the consequence of Reason; but the effects of Chance and Hazard, of a Mind floating at all Adventures, without choice, and without direction (IV.xvii.2).

Thus, the "lowest degree," taken in its right context, is not in relation to the perception of indubitable *and* probable connections, but rather pertains to the probable connection alone. That is, if we had no abilities to construct probable proofs, we would act in a random fashion in most circumstances where we did not have knowledge. So Locke is not drawing boundaries around what Wolterstorff thinks is his fundamental and working sense of reason in the main definition of reason. In other words, the "lowest degree" of reason in IV.xvii.2 is not equal to the third degree of reason in IV.xvii.3 as Wolterstorff thinks.

There is still more that witnesses against Wolterstorff's interpretation of reason and claim that it is the predominant sense. For instance, near the beginning of the *Essay*, Locke, in the context of deductions of our reason, writes, "For all Reasoning is search, and casting about, and requires Pains and Application" (I.ii.10). Similarly, sagacity, the faculty that discovers the middle terms, is part of reason in Locke's treatment of demonstration (IV.ii.3; IV.iii.2). These descriptions of reason are much more multi-dimensional and involved than Wolterstorff's description of reason as perception of logical force. These early utilizations of reason by Locke speak of reason searching and casting about for ideas and constructing arguments and not just perceiving. Besides, it does not seem likely that Locke would use a subordinate definition of reason in material occurring before IV.xvii, the chapter that finally describes the faculty of reason in detail. In the end, Locke might very well agree on some points with Wolterstorff, another brilliant and accomplished philosopher. The agreement, however, would be on what Locke should or could have said and not what he did say.

So far, in sum, reason is the faculty or power employed by the mind to obtain demonstrative knowledge and probability and generally to assess situations and problems. Reason is all of the natural faculties, for all intents and purposes, *when* the mind acts reasonably—reasonably in the sense of dictated by its employment of reason and in the sense of corresponding to the appropriate examinational thoroughness that the circumstance warrants. Only in cases of maximal concernment need the mind employ reason in a full examination to that which it would otherwise give a lesser exertion.

PART IV: REASON AND FAITH

The relationship between reason and faith and reason and revelation in Locke has been a significant point of perplexity for Locke scholars. The main reason is that IV.xviii's definitions of reason and faith are set in contrast to one another, while in IV.xv–xvi the judgment assents, believes, has faith in, or opines based on the probability provided by reason (at least ideally). In Locke's earlier treatment of assent, IV.xvi, he incorporates revelation and miracles, or, in short, discussions of assent to or faith in things divine. So, there are two major changes that take place in chapter xviii: 1) while there was no distinction between faith, assent, belief, and opinion prior to xviii, faith is separated from the rest and has only to do with revealed propositions in xviii; and 2) while faith (and equally assent, belief, and opinion) prior to xviii should be based on the probability supplied by reason, making faith a product of reason when the mind is acting reasonably, they are set in contrast in IV.xviii.

This has been the source of confusion for some well-known Locke scholars. Scholars such as Richard Ashcraft struggle to define the correct relationship between faith and reason. He notices rightly that there is an unexpected shift in the description of faith in chapter xviii of book IV of the *Essay*. Whereas faith and opinion were once identified, in IV.xviii that is no longer the case. He calls Locke's treatment of the relationship of faith and reason in the *Essay* unclear, inconsistent, and contradictory.[56] Also, there are scholars such as David C. Snyder and R. S. Woolhouse who show no evidence that they realize that reason has anything to do with probability or opinion. It appears that they somehow reconfigure what Locke had said about reason and faith prior to IV.xviii with the definitions of reason and faith he gives there.[57] Perhaps they have kept IV.xviii's contradistinction of faith and reason, but identified pre-IV.xviii faith and IV.xviii's faith. In other words, for them, reason produces knowledge and anything not certain is a

---

56. Ashcraft, "Faith and Knowledge," 215–16.

57. Snyder, "Faith and Reason." He is clearly operating with a faith-versus-reason distinction and as if reason has nothing to do with faith. For him, reason only gives knowledge, when in truth it gives probability and thus, if the mind is being rational, right belief as well. This allows him to make the incorrect conclusion that faith cannot contradict reason. Divine revelation, according to Locke, ought to trump any contrary probability of natural reason. Thus, Locke asserts that faith in things divine or naturally probable cannot contradict knowledge if the mind is operating rationally, but faith based on divine revelation should trump the contrary direction pointed to by probability based on wholly natural considerations. Cf. Woolhouse, *Locke*, 140–43.

matter of faith.[58] Whatever the case may be, the potential for confusion in understanding the *Essay* is rather high.

While IV.xviii's definitions of faith and reason are considered by nearly all of Locke scholarship as his *official* or intended definitions of faith and reason, this chapter argues that they are nothing more than concessions to "vulgar" or common ways of speaking. In chapter xviii, "Of Faith and Reason, and Their Distinct Provinces," Locke writes:

> *Reason* therefore here, as contradistinguished to *Faith*, I take to be the discovery of the Certainty or Probability of such Propositions or Truths, which the Mind arrives at by Deductions made from such *Ideas*, which it has got by the use of its natural Faculties, *viz*. by Sensation and Reflexion.
>
> *Faith*, on the other side, is the Assent to any Proposition, not thus made out by the Deductions of Reason, but upon the Credit of the Proposer, as coming immediately from GOD; which we call Revelation (IV.xviii.2).

Thus, Locke withholds the association of assent to divinely revealed propositions as such from this new definition of reason. The new definition of reason does incorporate assent to propositions that are only probable; but this probability is based on reason without the assistance or information provided by divine revelation.[59]

Contrary to Jolley, one of the few Locke scholar who notices that Locke uses two definitions of reason, Locke is not toying with the Christians by giving new definitions of faith and reason in IV.xviii wherein faith is still ultimately subordinated to its counterpart despite Locke's contradistinction of the two. Rather, Locke twice forewarns the reader of this alternative construal of the elements of the epistemological faculties with which he has been working. In Locke's earlier discussion of probability, chapter xv, he writes, "And herein lies the difference between *Probability and Certainty*,

---

58. This is ultimately what Stillingfleet does. Stillingfleet as discussed in chapter 2 read the *Essay* as framing reason such that it only concerns knowledge. It is possible, however, that Stillingfleet read his interpretation of Toland's *CNM* into the *Essay*.

59. Notice that Locke is express in making "Deductions" the concernment of IV.xviii's reason. It is not clear if he intends human testimony to be included into what this chapter will call vulgar reason. It is difficult to imagine that human testimony is not included as it is hardly natural to think of one person alone with no outside influences or information sources. On a related point, it might be the case that Locke does not consider intuition as a method of knowledge associated with vulgar reason, though it would still be employed in demonstration. Whatever the case may be, the answers to these questions are not crucial since IV.xviii's contradistinguished definitions of faith and reason, as will be argued, are concessionary.

Faith and Knowledge, that in all the parts of Knowledge, there is intuition; each immediate *Idea*, each step has its visible and certain connexion; in Belief not so" [emphasis mine] (IV.xv.3). There faith is nothing more than assent or belief. But, in the last section of chapter IV.xvi, "Of the Degrees of Assent," he refers to faith as the assent to divine revelation as such and its propositional content. The last sentence of that chapter demonstrates, however, what he is planning: "But of Faith, and the Precedency it ought to have before other Arguments of Persuasion, I shall speak more hereafter, where I treat of it, as it is ordinarily placed, in contradistinction to Reason: though in Truth, it be nothing else but an Assent founded on the highest Reason" (IV.xvi.14). In other words, faith is a function of reason (again, ideally), but Locke notifies the reader that he will treat it "in contradistinction" to reason as is frequently done. Also, this forthcoming contradistinction and the resulting new definitions of faith and reason would explain the difference between "Reason" and the "highest Reason" in the quote. That is, reason might refer to the IV.xviii version of reason and the highest reason could refer to the pre-IV.xviii version of reason.[60] All said, this is but the first indication of the future construal or shift in the definitions of "faith" and "reason." The second comes at the end of chapter xvii, before chapter xviii (where faith and reason are set in "contradistinction"):

> There is another use of the word *Reason*, wherein it is *opposed to Faith*: which though it be in it self a very improper way of speaking, yet common Use has so authorized it, that it would be folly either to oppose or hope to remedy it: Only I think it may not be amiss to take notice, that however *Faith* be opposed to Reason, *Faith* is nothing but a firm Assent of the Mind; which if it be regulated, as is our Duty, cannot be afforded to any thing, but upon good Reason; and so cannot be opposite to it (IV.xvii.24).

Locke states clearly above that faith and reason cannot be opposites, but speaking about them as opposing ideas is so prevalent that he cannot hope to remedy it.[61]

---

60. Of interest here is the idea of right reason. It pertains to the faculty of reason employing correct argumentation or simply proper argumentation. Often times in theology, the conclusions of right reason are delivered by Scripture. So although we might not expect certain conclusions to result from our employment of reason, Scripture can make up for the deficit and give us conclusions up to which we are able to correctly reason. One might think that Locke is referring to right reason when he mentions the "highest Reason." Based on the context, however, it would seem that he means proper reason.

61. It is also worthy to note that in this quote Locke says that it is our duty or moral obligation to have our assent regulated by reason, which possibly implies, as this

In sum, Locke isolates the mind's assent to divine revelation as such and thus the revelation's propositional content in IV.xviii and calls it faith. This faith is different from the faith of which he spoke in previous chapters. In the previous chapters faith was assent to any probable proposition, *including* divinely revealed ones. Both versions of faith, pre-IV.xviii and IV.xviii versions, are still a function of proper reason when the mind is acting reasonably.[62] Therefore Locke defines a new version of reason corresponding to his new version of faith in IV.xviii by re-marshalling the *Essay's* epistemological elements. This new version of reason corresponds with assent only to natural, probable propositions. In the end, Locke's IV.xviii version of reason concerns knowledge and judgment of natural, probable propositions and his new version of faith concerns assent to divinely revealed propositions.

It is not only in the *Essay* that Locke acknowledges a conception of reason without the assistance of divine revelation. Responding to Stillingfleet's concern that the immateriality of the soul cannot be demonstrated from Locke's principles, Locke writes:

> This your Accusation of my *lessening the Credibility* of these Articles of Faith is founded on this, That the Article of the Immortality of the Soul abates of its Credibility, if it be allowed, That its Immateriality (which is the supposed Proof from Reason and Philosophy of its Immortality) cannot be demonstrated from natural Reason: Which Argument of your Lordship's bottoms, as I humbly conceive, on this, That Divine Revelation abates of its *Credibility* in all those Articles it proposes proportionably as Humane Reason fails to support the Testimony of God . . . But if Humane Reason comes short in the Case, and cannot make it out, its *Credibility* is thereby *lessened*; which is in effect to say, That the Veracity of God is not a firm and sure foundation of Faith to rely upon, without the concurrent Testimony of Reason, *i.e.* with Reverence be it spoken, God is not to be believed on his own Word, unless what he reveals be in it self credible, and might be believed without him.[63]

---

chapter concluded above, that one has the ability to assent contrary to reason's recommendations. It could also mean that we ought to assent with thought and consideration and therefore not to assent lazily.

62. Locke uses the IV.xviii versions of faith and reason in his later chapter, "Of Enthusiasm," which becomes chapter xix from the fourth edition (1700) onwards.

63. Locke, *Mr. Locke's Reply . . . Answer to his Second Letter*, 418–19. Use of the terms natural reason or human reason that signify Locke's concept of reason without the assistance of divine revelation, which this chapter calls vulgar reason, continues throughout the rest of Locke's treatment on this point.

Thus, Locke refers to reason without the considerations and assistance of divine revelation as natural and human reason in the above quotation. He eventually uses the term natural reason in reference to his IV.xviii delimited reason in his chapter "Of Enthusiasm" that he adds to the *Essay* in 1700. There he speaks of three grounds of assent: faith, reason, and enthusiasm.[64] He rejects the third, but keeps the first two: "*Reason* is natural *Revelation* . . . *Revelation* is natural *Reason* enlarged."[65] In short, he is operating with the versions of faith and reason as described in IV.xviii in his 1700 chapter addition, "Of Enthusiasm," which allows him to call that version of reason natural reason.

From this point on special labels will be employed to distinguish between the two considerations of faith and reason. Proper reason and proper faith or assent will denote the conceptions of reason and faith or assent being utilized prior to IV.xviii.[66] They are labeled with "proper" because those are the definitions he builds throughout book IV and they are not concessionary. Thus, proper reason is reason employed or operating in its proper office or with its concernment with natural and divine sources of information. Proper faith is its corresponding faith that concerns assent to natural and divine probable propositions. Vulgar reason and vulgar faith will denote the considerations of reason and faith used as a concession to the vulgar or common manner of speaking in IV.xviii. Vulgar reason is reason employed or operating in its diminished office or concernment with only natural sources of information. Vulgar faith is its corresponding faith and concerns only assent to divine revelation as such and thus its propositional content.

The use of the label "vulgar" that Locke does not use warrants some explanation. First, Locke referred to both considerations of reason as "reason," and both considerations of faith as "faith." Not differentiating them in the *Essay* has led to confusion in reading it, as is argued in this chapter, and would likely lead to confusion in reading this chapter. Second, it is my desire to couple the two considerations of reason with each one's corresponding consideration of faith to avoid undue confusion. Locke does not make provision for this. Vulgar reason could have been called natural or unassisted

---

64. This is IV.xix.3 in the critical edition, the fourth edition (1700), and all subsequent editions.

65. This is IV.xix.4 in the critical edition, the fourth edition (1700), and all subsequent editions. Also, this is a standard view of at least part of the orthodox tradition going back to the medieval philosophers and theologians.

66. Locke uses assent and faith interchangeably. One could argue that this is not strictly correct as assent is something that is done and faith is something that one has. Nevertheless, this chapter will conform to Locke's practices. Perhaps he found the distinction too minor to mention.

or human reason in this book, which Locke actually does call it in places, as just shown, but then this book would have to replace the efficient, coupling labels of *vulgar* reason and *vulgar* faith with the less economical and disconnected labels of *natural* or *unassisted* or *human* reason and *vulgar* (or some other adjective) faith; the labels natural or unassisted or human faith are not optional replacements for vulgar faith because natural faith or unassisted faith or human faith are more appropriate terms for faith in natural sources of information, which is ideally a function of the mind employing its natural or unassisted reason.[67] Labeling them as common has too much room for misunderstanding too, as referring to "common faith" seems more appropriate to describing a faith that is uniform to everyone or most. Other prefixes such as "chapter xviii" seem too clumsy. Vulgar was chosen because it was a term commonly used in Locke's day that could be interchanged with the adjective common.

In sum, this section has argued that Locke makes a critical and (what should be considered an) unsurprising shift to new definitions of faith and reason in IV.xviii. The pre-IV.xviii proper reason, or reason employed in its proper office, concerns knowledge and certainty and the probabilities associated with natural and divine sources of information. The IV.xviii vulgar reason, or reason employed in its diminished office, concerns the same, but with the exception of divine sources of information. Proper faith corresponds to proper reason and it concerns assent to natural and divine probable propositions based on the assessment of proper reason. Vulgar faith concerns only assent regarding divine revelation. Giving attention to the previous section as well, we could add irrational faith to this short list of faiths. Irrational faith arises from two general situations: 1) the mind not heeding its own conclusions wrought from its employment of reason, or 2) the mind not employing reason appropriate to what the circumstance warrants. Enthusiasm would be an extreme case of the latter, where reason is underemployed.

PART V: "ABOVE REASON" PROPOSITIONS

The differences between proper reason and proper faith versus vulgar reason and vulgar faith help explain what Locke intends by labeling certain propositions as being "Above Reason." Many take this category of propositions as

---

67. Examples of "natural reason": Locke, *ROC*, 268, 278; Locke, *Mr. Locke's Reply . . . Answer to his Second Letter*, 418, 421, 423, 426, 427, 428, 429, 439. Examples of "unassisted reason": Locke, *ROC*, 268, 270. Examples of "human reason": Locke, *Mr. Locke's Reply . . . Answer to his Second Letter*, 418–19; Locke, *Second Vindication*, xvi.

being Locke's window for allowing doctrines that transcend the strictures and office of reason or that are *beyond* reason. But, in light of the previous sections, it is crucial to understand to which definition of reason Locke is referring when he labels things as being above reason. One might think that he is working with proper reason since this is prior to chapter xviii and its new consideration of reason, but this appears unlikely from what follows. Locke writes in chapter xvii:

> By what has been before said of *Reason*, we may be able to make some guess at the distinction of Things, into those according to, above, and contrary to Reason. 1. *According to Reason* are such Propositions, whose Truth we can discover, by the examining and tracing those *Ideas* we have from *Sensation* and *Reflexion*; and by natural deduction, finds to be true, or probable. 2. *Above Reason* are such Propositions, whose Truth or Probability we cannot by Reason derive from those Principles. 3. *Contrary to Reason* are such Propositions, as are inconsistent with, or irreconcilable to our clear and distinct *Ideas*. Thus the existence of one GOD is according to Reason; the Existence of more than one GOD, contrary to Reason; the Resurrection of the Body after death, above Reason. Above Reason also may be taken in a double sense, viz. above Probability, or above Certainty; and in that large sense also, Contrary to Reason, is, I suppose, sometimes taken (IV.xvii.23).[68]

In all three categories "reason" pertains to the human faculty involved in obtaining knowledge through indubitable demonstration and guiding the judgment through probability. The "natural deduction" corresponding to the "According to Reason" category is most likely taken in a sense that rules out supernatural assistance or divine revelation. Thus, according to reason propositions are any that come to us by natural means and, therefore, the reason being used here is vulgar reason. This is even more likely since "Above Reason" apparently denotes propositions that we would never be expected to come up with ourselves. That is, above reason propositions are those we would not have conceived of simply by the contemplation of the ideas that are naturally available to us. On the outside chance that we did conceive of such a true proposition and its ideas on our own we would have no basis to assent to it. In short, "Above Reason" is above vulgar reason. In addition,

---

68. The critical edition makes the last sentence clearer to the contemporary English reader. It is less compressed. The critical edition reads as follows: "Farther, as *Above Reason* may be taken in a double Sense, viz. either as signifying above Probability, or above Certainty: so in that large Sense also, Contrary to Reason, is, I suppose, sometimes taken."

above reason propositions are intelligible, conceivable, or imaginable-in-part because their examples are: the rebellion of the angels and resurrection of the dead (IV.xvii.23; IV.xviii.7). That means an above reason proposition's (or doctrine's) summative idea does not transcend our ideas, or, in other words, is reconcilable, and is thus still within the compass of our understanding and proper reason and is not beyond them, even if the proposition or doctrine comprises metaphorical or analogous language.[69] Finally, the propositions are supernatural in focus because all of their examples are.

Still more can be said about these three categories that points to vulgar reason being the reason incorporated into them. It appears that above reason propositions are judged to have been truly revealed. So propositions that are above reason are reasonable in the proper reason sense and true and propositions that are according to reason are true and reasonable in both the vulgar and proper sense. Interestingly enough, contrary to reason propositions are unreasonable because their acceptance would equate to the acceptance of falsehoods (contrarieties to known truths or logical contradictions) and, perhaps, they are simply irreconcilable or incomprehensible (the human mind is not able to arrive at a singular and summative complex idea for each one).

There are a few possible problems with the categories of propositions that are worthy of mention here that appear to show that they are concessionary. Where would one place a divinely revealed (presumably assured and intelligible) proposition that contradicts a probable proposition that one would assent to on purely natural considerations? Since the divinely revealed proposition was able to be reasonably assessed by divinely unassisted reason, albeit incorrectly, it seems it cannot qualify as being above reason. It does not fit into the according to reason category as that category is reserved for propositions deduced on wholly natural considerations or without the assistance of divine revelation. Contrary to reason is not fitting either (as will be shown) as the revealed proposition is intelligible and does not carry a contradiction or falsehood. Moreover, if a divinely revealed proposition, which presumably is assured, concurs with an according to reason category

---

69. A helpful taxonomy of "above reason" doctrines is given by Robert Boyle. He notes that there are comprehensible and incomprehensible above reason propositions and doctrines. Of the incomprehensible doctrines there are those that are: "not clearly *conceivable* by our Understanding, such as the Infiniteness and Perfections of the Divine Nature"; "*inexplicable* by us, such as the Manner, how God can create a rational Soul"; and "*asymmetrical*, or unsociable; that is, such, as we see not how to reconcile with other Things" like the divine prescience and human liberty. What Locke appears to reject (though, inconsistently, as this chapter will point out) is akin to this last category. E.g., Locke, *Second Vindication*, 93–101; Boyle, *Reflections upon a Theological Distinction*, 8–9; cf. Marko, "Above Reason Propositions," 231.

proposition, then the natural probability supporting the according to reason proposition becomes irrelevant. Into which category would this proposition be placed? In short, the set of divinely revealed propositions is not identical to, but larger than, the set of above reason propositions. The categories of propositions do not appear, based on their descriptions, to be able to accommodate to all divinely revealed propositions. Furthermore, does the source, natural or divine, necessarily attach to the proposition such that two propositions although verbally and conceptually the same cannot be considered identical based on the fact that God asserted one and a human asserted the other? These questions are not asked or entertained by Locke, but the categories are introduced without much comment.[70]

In short, the according to reason category of propositions appear to be those that are determined only through natural sources and are the concern of vulgar reason. The above reason category of propositions are, as a result, those that are determined through divine sources, are comprehensible or intelligible, are supernaturally focused, and are something that we would not determine on our own; but if we happened to conceive of something above reason without any revelation, we would have no basis to assent to it. And finally, the category of contrary to reason propositions involves only those propositions that are unacceptable because they produce a logical contradiction or falsity (i.e., contrary to knowledge) or perhaps their summative ideas are incomprehensible, or irreconcilable, but not definitively contrary to knowledge (i.e., they are not definitively contradictory or false, or, thus, not definitively contrary to the primary sense of knowledge, but presently contrary to knowledge in the sense that they cannot be mentally pictured or represented).[71]

That above reason propositions are within the compass of proper reason and thus consist of ideas capable of being held by humans is supported by other places in the works of Locke and elsewhere in the *Essay*.[72]

---

70. He could be assuming that all according to reason propositions are true and can be truly assessed with natural reason and that above reason propositions are ones that are true and could not be assessed based on experience or merely natural reasoning. This chapter will soon show that natural reason or vulgar reason does end up being forced into proper reason when confronted with revelation.

71. John Norris argues adamantly that contradictory propositions are clearly conceivable in the sense that they are clearly not true. For example, the falsity of the proposition "the number one is equal to two" is clear and conceivable and thus we should not speak of the said proposition being incomprehensible or above reason. In short, he was trying to maintain a clear distinction between the categories of above reason and contrary to reason. Norris, *Account of Reason and Faith*, 100–136.

72. This chapter makes no claims about Locke's stance on the doctrine of the Trinity other than the following. Any version or explanation that was not imaginable

In Locke's final reply to Bishop Stillingfleet, Locke explains that ideas are always the objects of our minds in thinking and further, "every thing which we either know or believe, is some Proposition. Now no Proposition can be framed as the Object of our Knowledge or Assent, where two Ideas are not joined to, or separated from one another."[73] That above reason propositions are graspable by the human mind also comports with Locke's insistence in *A Second Vindication of the Reasonableness of Christianity* that it is not possible to assent to doctrines that are unintelligible. There he defines "Mysteries" as "things *not plain, not clear, not intelligible to common apprehensions*," and writes that when those thinkers who claim it is necessary for people to assent to such mysteries, allegedly in Scripture, they are making a requirement out of "what is impossible for them to do."[74] Soon thereafter he writes, "For a Man cannot possibly give his assent to any Affirmation or Negation, unless he understand the terms as they are joyn'd in that Proposition, and has a Conception of the thing affirm'd or deny'd, and also a Conception of

---

or irreconcilable could not be assented to by a person according to the *Essay*. And a definitively incomprehensible status amounts to a rejection. Perhaps Locke had a version of the Trinity in mind that he accepted because it was supported by Scripture and was imaginable or perhaps he had suspended his judgment on the doctrine awaiting an imaginable version or explanation. It is noteworthy, however, that he apparently thought the ideas of human free will and God's omnipotence difficult to reconcile (IV. xvii.10), yet he still writes of a kind of free will and can be read as being a type of libertarian or non-necessitarian, though I do not think that is his goal in II.xxi, "Of Power" (cf. Marko, "Why Locke's 'Of Power' Is Not a Metaphysical Pronouncement"). If a libertarian, it would seem that in the case of libertarian free will he was satisfied with his understanding *that* we had the power of contrary choice regardless of *how* that understanding was reconcilable with God's omnipotence. The difference between his brand of libertarian free will and rejected versions of the Trinity, however, might be that we can visualize or remember our experience of free choice regardless of its reconciliation with God's power. Whatever the case may be, such exploration and speculation on the topic of Locke and the Trinity would take us too far afield.

Admittedly, it is hard to believe that Locke would be thorough-going in his reconcilability requirement. The issue of free will is already one area in which he balks. It would seem to cause needless rejections of theories in fields other than theology and metaphysics. Perhaps conundrums from general revelation are acceptable but they are not expected from Scripture and not accepted. So perhaps the doctrine of the Trinity is not acceptable but the naturally construed or construable notions of God's absolute sovereignty and human free choice, for instance, are acceptable even though together they are irreconcilable. Or perhaps since Locke thinks Scripture was written at the level of the uneducated God requires only belief in what is clear to the individual. While the above comments serve as a possible explanation, there is no textual evidence for it. Cf. Marko, "Justification, Ecumenism, and Heretical Red Herrings."

73. Locke, *Mr. Locke's Reply . . . Answer to His Second Letter*, 245.
74. Locke, *Second Vindication*, 95; cf. 337.

the thing concerning which it is affirm'd or deny'd."[75] Also, each proposition or doctrine that he labels as being "above reason" later on in the *Essay* is, as already mentioned, imaginable in some respect: rebellion of the angels and the resurrection of humans (IV.xviii.7). That means neither that every legitimate doctrine or idea is easy to conceive or determine (IV.xvii.10), nor that every legitimate doctrine's corresponding ideas are clear in all parts or distinct from every other idea.[76] But, again, they can be pictured or represented by a singular, summative, complex idea. Curtly stated, they are reconcilable.

Considering proper reason as the reason he is utilizing in the three categories of propositions proves to be even more evidence that vulgar reason is the sense of reason being used. Again, this limitation of reason to natural deductions, as is the case with the "According to Reason" category, does not square with the concept of proper reason developed prior to this point in IV.xvii, the conception of reason that incorporates divine testimony and revelation. And, if he were using his conception of proper reason, the category of "Above Reason" propositions would logically collapse into the category of "According to Reason" propositions because proper reason, which includes revelation, would make "Above Reason" propositions *properly* reasonable and, therefore, "According to Reason." Therefore it follows that Locke made an early shift to the vulgar conception of reason that he explains more thoroughly in chapter xviii and about which he gave two earlier forewarnings. In fact, one of the forewarnings is immediately after his discussion of the three categories of propositions (IV.xvii.24). Thus, vulgar reason is a theme and touch point of both sections 23 and 24 of IV.xvii. Again, this suggestion that vulgar reason is being used in the three categories of propositions is bolstered by the fact that vulgar reason in chapter xviii is in agreement with the restriction of "reason" to natural deductions offered in the "According to Reason" category. All of this illuminates why Locke notes that he is making "some guess" at the distinction of things into these three categories. In order to make accommodations to the masses' improper way of speaking without making any conceptual changes in his epistemology, he fashioned the three categories of propositions based on vulgar reason.

A very important conclusion is now evident: if Locke had chosen expressly to use a preferred categorization of propositions schema there would only be two categories, according to reason and contrary to reason.

---

75. Locke, Ibid., 99–100 (quotation, 99). Locke makes a helpful distinction regarding the *matter* of the fact versus the *manner* of the fact. One may be able to conceive the resurrection and believe it but need not understand the manner in which God executes it. Cf. Boyle, *Reflections upon a Theological Distinction*, 8–9; Marko, "Above Reason Propositions," 231.

76. E.g., Locke, *Mr. Locke's Reply . . . Answer to His Second Letter*, 73.

The reason associated with these two categories is proper reason. The three categories of propositions that have been discussed in this section and that were the focus of the block quote above are, again, based on vulgar reason; and since vulgar reason is a concession so is the associated categorization of propositions Locke gives in IV.xvii.23. Obviously, Locke is not explicit how he would draw the boundaries of these two categories. It would seem that he would simply combine the above reason and according to reason categories. The complications involved in clearly delimiting the lines perhaps took the *Essay* too far afield or perhaps was too liable to misunderstanding.

It is noteworthy to consider his mindset in accommodating his understanding of reason to vulgar, improper ways of speaking. Locke apparently does not think of himself as so much *constructing* or *prescribing* a better epistemology as he is *describing* how we operate at our best. He cannot simply describe anyone on any day, but rather describes the mind working with the principles of logic and with prudence. This is sometimes called experimental philosophy. Of Locke's experimental philosophy, James Harris writes:

> Experimental philosophy, is, simply, philosophy that aims to be true of the facts of experience, and the experience in question might well be that of everyday life. An important factor in Locke's success was the manner in which he succeeded in making it possible for his readers to think of themselves as practicing philosophy when they compared the description of the mind given in the *Essay* with their own experience of themselves, their acquaintances, and the world in general.[77]

He makes his descriptive designs of the *Essay* explicit in his response to Stillingfleet's labeling his treatment of the faculty of thinking "new": "my Lord, if it be *new*, it is but a new History of an old Thing, For I think it will not be doubted, that Men always perform'd the Actions of Thinking, Reasoning, Believing, and Knowing, just after the same way they do now . . . ."[78] So, assuming we all have similar mental equipment and fundamental mental processes, Locke does not simply disregard the opposition of faith and reason by some because they are technically wrong. Instead, he wants to figure out for himself why they are claiming what they are claiming and how might there be some truth in it. Thus, just as Locke is making "some guess" regarding the way some would categorize propositions based on a

---

77. Harris, *Of Liberty and Necessity*, 2.

78. Locke, *Mr. Locke's Reply . . . Answer to His Letter*, 72–73; cf. Locke, *Mr. Locke's Reply . . . Answer to His Letter*, 80–82, 87–89, 90–92; Locke, *Mr. Locke's Reply . . . Answer to His Second Letter*, 240, 286–93, 308–14.

contradistinguished faith and reason, he does not assert with confidence what vulgar reason is but instead writes, "*Reason* therefore here, as contradistinguished to *Faith*, *I take to be* . . ." (emphasis mine) (IV.xviii.2).

As an additional corrective to scholarship, Locke never claims that the "Above Reason" category is "Above and According to Reason" or "Above and not Contrary to Reason." John Toland shows his displeasure with the label "above and not contrary to reason" and what is meant by it in his book *CNM*. Since all think that he is attacking Locke's propositional category of above reason, Toland is *the* or *a* likely root for such augmented labels being applied by Locke and Toland scholars to John Locke's above reason category.[79]

Furthermore, the augmented labels applied in place of Locke's "Above Reason" simpliciter label are not appropriate. Due to the way that Locke has drawn the boundaries of the three categories of propositions, a proposition that is above reason cannot be according to reason as well. And to say that an above-reason proposition is not contrary to reason is a needless redundancy. That is, an above-reason proposition is by definition not according to reason and not contrary to reason. What is more, if any scholars are incorrectly operating with proper reason and using these augmented labels, they are equivocating in that they are saying some proposition or doctrine is above reason in the sense that human reason cannot mentally represent the doctrine but according to reason in the different sense that it does not defy logical principles.[80]

This chapter is now in the position to clarify the end of the block quotation describing the three categories of propositions: "Above Reason also may be taken in a double sense, *viz.* Above Probability, or above Certainty; and in that large sense also, Contrary to Reason, is, I suppose, sometimes taken" (IV.xvii.23).[81] Here Locke is giving—albeit in a compressed way—

---

79. John Toland and his thoughts on categories of propositions will be discussed in the next chapter.

80. O'Higgins, *Anthony Collins*, 52–53. A possible example of a scholar understanding above reason to be above proper reason is James O'Higgins. It appears that he believes Locke to be operating with proper reason as the reason of the three categories. He thinks that Locke admitted in writing that he believed in above reason things, but O'Higgins is nevertheless skeptical that he did believe in those things. From the context, it appears that O'Higgins believes that above reason, or that which is not "fully comprehensible" but "agreeable to reason" in the *Essay* refers to things that we cannot perceive or multiple claims that can be imagined separately but together are irreconcilable yet not logically contradictory. This, however, contradicts Locke's explicit comments quoted above from *A Second Vindication* that doctrines must be intelligible. Propositions cannot be untethered from proper reason. If they do, then they are contrary to reason in Locke.

81. Again, the critical edition makes the last few lines a bit clearer: "Farther, as *Above Reason* may be taken in a double Sense, *viz.* either as signifying above Probability, or

other manners in which he has heard the notion of "above reason" things identified. Above reason things are above or beyond probability or certainty because we could not demonstrate them or conceive of them with unaided or unassisted reason, and if we did conceive of them we would have no grounds to assent to them.[82] "Above" is apparently not intended to imply that above reason propositions can overturn divinely-unassisted or natural probability or knowledge, although later this chapter will discuss revealed propositions' abilities to overthrow propositions that are based on natural probability. Finally, Locke "supposes" some might say the above reason category is contrary to reason in the sense that it consists of propositions that divinely unassisted reason would not know through demonstration or believe through natural probable reasoning. Therefore, above reason refers to things known by a different means or source of information. Again, from the examples, these above reason propositions are divinely-revealed propositions of a *supernatural* nature of focus. In other words, they are about things we would have no good reason to affirm or deny if told to us by an ordinary, and even trusted, human.

Moreover, it is not completely clear if Locke has incorporated human testimony of non-revealed, non-supernatural propositions in his understanding of vulgar reason.[83] Again, from the examples he gives of above reason propositions, the above reason category of propositions are all supernaturally focused propositions directly from God or from a human intermediary, a distinction that will be discussed more in depth shortly. This question is pertinent here because it is argued above that vulgar reason corresponds

---

above Certainty: so in that large Sense also, Contrary to Reason, is, I suppose, sometimes taken."

82. It is possible that someone without any direct or indirect association with Scripture could conceive of God, whom she reasoned exists, making all humans rise from the dead at an end-times judgment. Locke would concede to this possibility as well. However, one would have no grounds to believe this idea that she invented in contemplation of death. This idea that one could conceive of something above reason but have no grounds to assent to it comports with Locke's later discussion of above reason propositions: "There being many Things, wherein we have very imperfect Notions, or none at all; and other Things, of whose past, present, or future Existence, by the natural Use of our Faculties, we can have no Knowledge at all; these, as being beyond the Discovery of our natural Faculties, and above Reason, are, when revealed, *the proper Matter of Faith*" (IV.xviii.7). Hence his description of above reason propositions does not rule out the possibility of one imagining a doctrine on one's own that is actually true.

83. Revealed propositions may pertain to natural or supernatural things. And, if human testimony is of something supernatural it counts as revelation. Moreover, it is difficult to say where Locke would place the biblical historical narratives. Some of the details could be determined through research and other details would be otherwise lost.

to the sense of reason utilized in the according to reason category. An argument for the inclusion of human testimony of non-supernaturally sourced propositions is that it is one of the grounds of our reasonable—reasonable pertaining to proper reason—probability, so it would be surprising if it were left out of consideration entirely. Furthermore, since Locke's examples of above reason things are supernatural in nature and source, it is likely that through his distinction of according to reason and above reason things he is making a naturally sourced versus supernaturally sourced distinction *as best as he can* as opposed to a demonstration-and-natural-probability-grounded-only-in-conformity (to experience and knowledge) versus *divine* testimony (including divine immediate revelation and testimony of it by a human intermediary) distinction. In short, although it is possible that human testimonies regarding non-supernaturally focused and issued propositions are not factored into vulgar reason, they at least would nicely fit into vulgar reason. Since Locke thinks this is an improper way of framing the elements of the discussion anyway, the matter will be left to rest.

The placing of the three categories of propositions, and thus the interjection of vulgar reason, into the chapter where proper reason is being explained has been the source of much mischief. This is likely why many think that vulgar reason, given in the *Essay*'s subsequent chapter, is the official definition of reason and that which Locke was *attempting* to clearly explain throughout IV.xvii. This perhaps imprudent interjection of vulgar reason into IV.xvii has assisted in compelling nearly all to try to reconcile with it all that had been said by Locke about reason prior to it. Furthermore, this might have something to do with Woolhouse's and Leask's reasoning that truths about the properties and powers of material substances and substances themselves are "above reason."[84] They both miss the point that the above reason category is reserved for propositions of a supernatural focus.

So far in this chapter, several conclusions have been presented. It has been concluded that Locke is operating with two considerations of reason and faith. There is proper reason and proper faith (or assent) that he is using throughout the bulk of the *Essay*. Reason operating or employed in its proper office or proper reason offers demonstration and probability working with ideas from knowledge, propositions from experience, and propositions from human and divine sources. The natural faculties can be considered reason when the mind acts reasonably—reasonably in the sense of dictated by proper reason and in the sense of corresponding to the appropriate thoroughness of engagement that the circumstance warrants. Reason

---

84. Woolhouse, *Locke*, 141–42; Leask, "Personation and Immanent Undermining," 251–52.

operating or employed in its diminished office or vulgar reason is the same with the exception of its exclusion of propositions that originally came from God. His vulgar conceptions of reason and faith, vulgar reason and vulgar faith, are concessions. Vulgar reason is incorporated into his well-known three categories of propositions.[85] This is thereby a concession as well. If Locke were to categorize propositions according to his preferred definition of reason, something it is doubtful he would want to do, the above reason category would disappear.

PART VI: REASON AND REVELATION

Locke offers his most thorough discussion of revelation in chapter xviii of book IV. This includes its relationship with reason, which this section will make explicit. Locke is working with vulgar reason throughout chapter xviii, but part of his plan is to show the insufficiency of such a vulgar distinction between faith and reason. That is, the nature of revelation as an accepted source of information makes the distinction between vulgar faith and reason ultimately untenable. His position on vulgar reason and vulgar faith and the relationship between revelation and reason that come to the fore in IV.xviii also help clarify the very dense section 14 of IV.xvi that this chapter touched on briefly in its discussion on judgment in the "Preliminaries" part.

Locke begins the discussion with a taxonomy of divine special revelation. First there is original revelation, impressions made by God on a human's mind "to which we cannot set any Bounds." There are two primary types of original revelation, incommunicable and communicable. Regarding the former, God may communicate to the human mind by new simple ideas and complex ideas made up of them. This type of original revelation is incommunicable to other humans by words or signs for there are no latent ideas in the minds of others of such new simple ideas; for words seen or heard recall to our thoughts ideas that already are in the mind and cannot introduce any new simple ideas into it. Natural human simple ideas come from natural human sensation and reflection. So, God can impress on the human's mind the ideas received by the sixth sense of an extraterrestrial, for instance, but these ideas would be as incommunicable to others as the simple ideas of colors would be to a person born blind. Locke claims that this is the type of revelation Paul received in the third heaven. This type of original revelation cannot be communicated to other humans unless God

85. Vulgar faith could include so-called pure matters of faith (See next part). But vulgar faith is not necessarily limited to those. Revelation, for instance, might correct a particular conclusion derived from the probability supplied by vulgar reason.

supernaturally equips a person with the faculty or faculties, not naturally found in humans, which can receive these new simple ideas and their complex counterparts. He does not, however, insist that all original revelation is in this incommunicable form. Original revelation may also be of the communicable sort. Thus it consists of impressions using our common, latent ideas. One who is given original revelation of this type can convey it to others.[86] Finally, traditional revelation is revelation conveyed from God to humans via a human intermediary "delivered over to others in Words, and the ordinary ways of conveying our Conceptions one to another." Therefore, traditional revelation is made possible by original revelation of the communicable sort (IV.xviii.3).

Locke proceeds to clarify a few issues that arise regarding revelation. First, there are some truths that can be conveyed to us by traditional revelation that are discoverable to us by vulgar reason, namely demonstration achieved by vulgar reason. There is little use for revelation in such instances as the assurance afforded by human testimony can never be as secure as the certainty afforded through our knowledge. Also, the "knowledge" we have that it is from God can never be as certain as intuition or demonstration.[87] Thus, Locke writes:

> As it were revealed some Ages since, That the three Angles of a Triangle, were equal to two right ones, I might assent to the Truth of that Proposition, upon the Credit of the Tradition that it was revealed: But that would never amount to so great a Certainty, as the Knowledge of it, upon the comparing and measuring my own clear *Ideas* of two right Angles, and the three Angles of a Triangle.

The same holds true for a matter of fact: the certainty of seeing the fact for oneself is more certain than hearing of it second hand (IV.xviii.4).[88]

---

86. Although Locke doesn't say the following it can be reasonably inferred. God can communicate through mental propositions or even images or words. Therefore, communicable original revelation might be images, mental propositions, images with verbal propositions, mental propositions with verbal propositions, just verbal propositions, etc. If original revelation of the incommunicable type he will equip them with the appropriate faculties as stated above. He might even assign words to the new simple ideas and their complex counterparts. Incommunicable revelation (revelation that incorporates new simple ideas) will have the same list as communicable original revelation with the exception of merely verbal propositions, as that would be useless. It should be noted, however, that Locke owns the infallibility of Scripture such that the original manuscripts are without error as can be seen from the pages that follow. So, however one might imagine God's revelation to the authors, the result for Locke is perfection.

87. Locke is using "knowledge" possibly in an off-handed way.

88. The description of knowledge versus traditional revelation is perhaps analogous

Locke then shifts a bit, turning the *Essay* to considerations of certainty and assurance regarding revelation. It is true that God never errs and our minds do. So, one might think, hypothetically, if we could *know* a proposition was from God and *know* its interpretation as well, both via original revelation, then that proposition's status and interpretation would have more certainty than our knowledge. That is, we would trust God over our finite (but God-given) faculties. But, since we have human faculties, the highest certainty we can have is human certainty. That is, in reality there is no higher certainty than intuitive knowledge. This has a few important implications. For instance, it is reason that must determine if a given proposition is revealed. Reason concerns identification of a miracle in original revelation or probability in traditional revelation. So if the foundation of reason—our intuitive knowledge—were contradicted by a revealed proposition, the revealed proposition would be undercutting the source that gives it authority, or deems it divinely revealed. And if revelation, therefore, cannot overturn intuitive knowledge, it cannot overturn or contradict demonstrative knowledge either (IV.xviii.5–6).

Some may object to one of the above assertions because in these passages Locke says nothing explicitly about revelation's inability to contradict demonstrative knowledge. If that were an option—that is, revelation could overturn demonstrative knowledge—he would not need to reiterate the point that revelation can overturn a proposition based on natural probability. Besides, demonstration is less liable to error than our senses, which helps identify miraculous phenomena. In the case of traditional revelation, revelation's status as such is only probable. In the case of original revelation, one is always certain that something is being revealed. Putting aside the issues of certainty and probability regarding revelation's divine *origin*, one still has to wrestle with the fact that *interpretations* of the revelation are often uncertain. Thus, there is some level of probability, at least with one aspect of an allegedly, originally revealed proposition. All of this points toward revelation not being able to overturn a demonstration. There is one case, however, in which a revelation could contradict a "demonstrative proposition": a revealed proof that provides one with a demonstrative proof that serves as a correction to an erroneous proof that was thought to be demonstrative. In Locke's economy the revealed proof would be demonstrative knowledge and not probable, even though its status of being a divine revelation is but

---

to Locke's critiques of claims of innate principles. Seeing for Locke is better than believing something probable. That is, he can perceive how these so-called innate principles are actually not such but rather apprehended by the mind experientially (I.ii).

probable. In other words, the probable divinely revealed status of a demonstrative proof would not affect the fact that it is a demonstrative proof.[89]

It is in this immediate discussion that he starts his critique of vulgar reason. First, Locke indicates one important insufficiency of separating vulgar reason and vulgar faith: something needs to identify an originally revealed proposition as being such. That something is reason employed by the mind. So it is impossible to separate faith and reason (IV.xviii.5). Second, he follows this up with a similar critique of vulgar reason versus vulgar faith in a short discourse on traditional revelation: "But to all those who pretend not to immediate Revelation, but are required to pay Obedience, and to receive the Truths revealed to others, which, by the Tradition of Writings, or Word of Mouth, are conveyed down to them, Reason has a great deal more to do, and is that only which can induce us to receive them." He notes that the matter of vulgar faith, as he understands it, is only propositions that are supposedly divinely revealed. But, something has to identify the proposition as being revealed or not, and that thing would have to be our faculty of reason, which many try to restrict to vulgar reason. Locke does point out one scenario where vulgar faith in some proposition or propositions is based on vulgar faith in another proposition. That is the situation in which one receives an original revelation that a certain proposition or an entire book was divinely revealed. So, that book or proposition is thought to be revealed based on another revelation; but that latter revelation is still confirmed as such by reason (IV.xviii.6).[90] Again, it is impossible to separate faith and reason as those who ascribe to the vulgar notions of faith and reason suggest.

---

89. Locke does not believe that there is any sort of demonstrative proof that comes up against the acceptance of any Scriptural revelation, though it is likely that demonstration could be used as a check against other claimed divine revelations. Locke, *Mr. Locke's Reply . . . Answer to His Second Letter*, 230–31.

Locke would say revelation could not overturn sensitive knowledge to be considered such (IV.xix.10). That, like Scripture's conformance to logical principles, is a traditional stance for some Christian sects. Cf. Turretin, *Institutes of Elenctic Theology*, 1:34–37.

90. It is possible that he intends to put forth a scenario where an original revelation, unattested by a miracle, reveals a book or proposition to be divinely revealed. Nevertheless, according to the rules laid out earlier, since there is no corresponding external mark identified by reason, the said proposition or book could not be put on the same authoritative level as Scripture and thus must be subordinate to it and, as will be discussed, vulgar reason concluding upon an issue to which Scripture (or assured revelation) does not speak. Even with an external mark it could not contradict Scripture, which also is confirmed by external marks. And if it turns out that Scripture was that said to be divinely inspired in the revealed proposition, that original revelation is superfluous.

Directly after the sections referenced above, Locke specifically discusses propositions with which vulgar reason has "directly, nothing to do." These propositions correspond to a subset of propositions that would be found in Scripture. They are beyond the discovery of our natural faculties and consist of "many Things, wherein we have very imperfect Notions, or none at all; and other Things, of whose past, present, or future Existence, by the natural Use of our Faculties, we can have no knowledge at all." Examples are the rebellion of the angels and the resurrection. Locke calls these propositions "above Reason," "*the proper Matter of Faith*," and "purely Matters of Faith" (IV.xviii.7). Reason has nothing directly to do with them because propositions according to vulgar reason do not overlap with propositions that are above vulgar reason. If propositions that are above vulgar reason could be imagined by vulgar reason without any help from revelation, they would still have no grounding for assent. In other words, that one can imagine something is no basis for assent to it. Thus, to believe them would not be done according to vulgar reason.[91] So although vulgar reason has nothing directly to do with above vulgar reason propositions in the sense just outlined, vulgar reason would still have to determine whether or not something is a revealed proposition, even the divinely-revealed above reason propositions. Again, this is outside vulgar reason's office of operation as determined by the definitions Locke gives at the beginning of IV.xviii.[92]

Moreover, Locke provides the reader with another operative rule governing the relationship of revelation and reason that concurrently shows the insufficiency of the vulgar reason and vulgar faith paradigm. Anything with the character of divine revelation is a "Matter of Faith," although not necessarily a "*proper Matter of Faith*" or above vulgar reason. While divine revelation cannot contradict intuition and demonstration, it can tell us that which we could not have come up with on our own; or if we did come up with something above reason we would have a very imperfect idea of it, and would have no basis to judge that idea true. But, there are also divinely revealed propositions that come into the realm of the probability of vulgar reason. That is, there are some propositions that we could conceive of

---

91. The well-known description of the categories of propositions discussed above (IV.xvii.23) does not go this in depth. It is beyond doubt that Locke would not consider that something should be believed simply because it could be imagined (II.xxx). If an idea was contrived as a solution to a problem it might fall into the "according to reason" category depending upon a variety of factors such as, but not limited to, the variety of other possible solutions, analogies, and conformance to what we know about God by natural notices. These could not be informed by divine revelation in any way if they were to maintain their according to (vulgar) reason status.

92. Of the different senses of faith Locke uses in *ROC*, one is quite capable of construing faith as *fiducia* or trust. Locke, *Second Vindication*, 195–96.

without divine assistance to which we could rightly and (in a vulgar sense) reasonably assent that are confirmed or denied by a divinely revealed proposition. Responding to the scenario when an unassisted proposition contradicts a revealed proposition, Locke declares: "In these, *Revelation must carry it, against the probable Conjectures of Reason:* Because the Mind, not being certain of the Truth of that it does not evidently know, but is only probably convinced of, is bound to give up its Assent to such a Testimony, which, it is satisfied, comes from one, who cannot err, and will not deceive" (IV. xviii.7–8; cf. IV.xviii.9–10; IV.xvi.14). Nevertheless, Locke adds, reason must judge the truth of it being a revelation as well as interpreting it or judging "of the signification of the Words wherein it is delivered." The interpretation, although possibly contrary to vulgar reason's reasonably probable proposition, cannot be contrary to vulgar reason's knowledge (which is identical to the knowledge of proper reason) (IV.xviii.8). Therefore, and here is the rub, the vulgar reason and vulgar faith distinction falters not only because reason must determine whether or not a revelation is divine but also how it is to be interpreted. What is more, the interpretation made by vulgar reason might contradict the otherwise-probable proposition provided by natural or vulgar reason.

Although a brief aside, there is a related epistemological principle that Locke makes in his debate with Stillingfleet that further illuminates the relationship of revelation and vulgar reason: one that has already been discussed. Locke is adamant that a particular doctrine derived from Scripture is not to be thought more or less credible depending on the probability for or against it supplied by vulgar reason.[93] What can be inferred from that is that while vulgar reason (without Scripture's help) may provide us with a possible interpretation in a way, one should not be compelled in any sense to use or favor such an interpretation. So, an interpretation of a passage that is supported by a prevailing theory of natural science, for instance, is not because of that to be given more weight than an interpretation that does not seem as probable under only natural considerations or vulgar reason. When it comes to multiple, possible interpretations, the only advice Locke has is one proposition of Scripture cannot contradict another. If that cannot be done with two propositions, for instance, after "fair endeavours," one must suspend one's judgment.[94]

As said in the previous part, that a proposition deemed to have favorable probability by vulgar reason is subordinate to divine revelation

---

93. Locke, *Mr. Locke's Reply . . . Answer to His Second Letter*, 136–39, 418–29, 443–44.

94. Locke, *ROC*, 304.

speaking to the same issue is evidence against thinking Locke approves of the three categories of propositions, namely according to reason, above reason, and contrary to reason. How would one label an intelligible, revealed proposition that is identical to a proposition that was affirmed by the probability given to it by natural or vulgar reason? It seems that it could not be in the above reason category as the concern is sufficiently understood to the point where the proposition at hand can be reasonably judged without divine assistance. Locke's definition of above reason propositions is those propositions "whose Truth or Probability we cannot by Reason derive from those Principles." On the other hand, such a proposition made by divine revelation cannot be placed in the according to reason category because it did not issue forth from there. Besides, its credibility is higher than other probable propositions since it was revealed. And, since it is intelligible, it cannot be contrary to reason. So, apparently, such an intelligible, revealed proposition would technically not have a category into which it fits. The implication is that while Locke shows intentionally that the vulgar reason and vulgar faith distinction collapses, his discussion implicitly shows how the corresponding vulgar categories of propositions also fail.

The point made above, that a revealed proposition might overturn a proposition thought to be probable on purely natural considerations, is an important point. Some deny it and some do not understand its full import. Before concluding our discussion on Locke's explanation of the rules governing revelation and reason and his concurrent erosion of the vulgar faith and reason contradistinction, this chapter will point to how a few important scholarly works have responded to the seeming authority that revelation has over natural probability.

Paul Helm believes that revelation cannot overturn natural probability. He notes that there is a quote in IV.xviii.18 that sounds like it is the case, but the subsequent lines show otherwise. The following is Helm's quote of the *Essay* IV.xviii.18 with his emphasis in italics:

> Because the mind, not being certain of the truth of that it does not evidently know, but only yielding to the probability that appears in it, is bound to give up its assent to such a testimony which, it is satisfied, comes from one who cannot err, and will not deceive. *But yet, it still belongs to reason to judge of the truth of its being a revelation and of the signification of the words wherein it is delivered.*

Helm thinks that the first part seems to indicate that revelation can overturn probability but that the italicized line qualifies "it beyond recognition."[95]

---

95. Helm, "Locke on Faith and Knowledge," 62–63.

He unfortunately says nothing more. Contrary to Helm's assertion that revelation cannot overturn divinely unassisted probability, one section later there is a very clear quote to the effect that revelation can overturn probability:

> For where the Principles of Reason have not evidenced a Proposition to be certainly true or false, there clear Revelation, as another Principle of Truth, and Ground of Assent, may determine; and so it may be Matter of Faith, and be also above Reason. Because Reason, in that particular Matter, being able to reach no higher than Probability, Faith gave the Determination, where Reason came short; and Revelation discovered on which side the Truth lay [end of section] (IV.xviii.9).

In other words, natural probability is not certain and so can be overturned. God can, through his revelation, correct and inform our limited capacities that work with limited sources of information.

Some guess can be made regarding the root of Helm's misunderstanding. He rightly acknowledges that reason must identify a proposition as revealed and also interpret it. He also, as discussed, believes the interpretation must be thought probable on purely natural considerations to be considered valid. This chapter takes that to mean that the revealed proposition, if the proposition is truly from God, must not be definitively contrary to natural, unassisted probability. So, if an interpretation could not be derived from the alleged revelation that comports with natural, unassisted probability, the alleged revelation cannot be considered as divinely revealed. An interpretation can be contrary to natural probability, however, as long as it is accompanied by a supporting proof in the revelation with a higher natural probability than the natural probability that (originally) opposed the interpretation of the revelation. If this is what Helm is thinking, his reasoning does not square with the last quote from Locke given above. Helm is likely noticing how reason operating in its vulgar office keeps creeping into vulgar faith's province in IV.xviii; that reason must determine if a revelation is divine and must interpret the revelation is discussed after the defining of vulgar reason and faith in IV.xviii; but this encroachment, unbeknown to Helm, is because of the insufficiencies of such a conceived contradistinction. Helm thus misses Locke's critique on such a contradistinction. As a result, Helm thinks Locke subordinates faith to vulgar reason as opposed to subordinating it to proper reason. The same could be expected of any scholar who notices that Locke is clearly subordinating "faith" to "reason" prior to IV.xviii but then views those chapters retrospectively through the vulgar faith and vulgar reason lenses of chapter xviii. In short, subordinating vulgar faith to proper reason—as Locke does—allows revelation to overturn a proposition supported by natural, unassisted probability, whereas subordinating vulgar faith to vulgar reason—as Helm concludes that Locke does—subordinates revelation to propositions supported by natural, unassisted probability. Again, in Helm's view the interpretation of a revelation must comport to what is thought reasonable by purely natural considerations or deductions (one can have natural considerations or deductions pertaining to supernatural concerns); and if such an interpretation is not feasible, the alleged revelation cannot be considered as such. Again, part of Locke's plan in chapter xviii is to show how that chapter's definitions of vulgar reason and vulgar faith, or, more specifically the limitations of reason's vulgar office and the province of vulgar faith, therein breakdown. To miss this point is to miss a significant piece of the *Essay*.

On a related point, Polinska believes that Locke's rule that revelation is able to overturn reasonable probability shows that faith and reason are *compatible* and not in a hierarchical relationship. That is, while faith cannot overturn reason in the realm of knowledge, it can overturn reason in the area of probability. As true as that is in *Essay* IV.xviii, it seems as though she has not fully answered the concerns of other scholars like Ashcraft and Sell who see faith as subordinate to reason, at least, by the fact that reason sets the bounds to faith and identifies revelation as such.[96] It appears that she like Helm has not considered the steady deconstruction of the vulgar reason versus vulgar faith distinction made in chapter xviii. Had she interacted with Ashcraft's declarations of Locke's inconsistencies between chapter xviii and what preceded it, she may have concluded that although at first blush faith is portrayed as not being subordinate to vulgar reason, that relationship eventually erodes as the power of reason is forced back into its proper office. And when reason is in its proper office, assent, even pertaining to divine propositions, ought to be reasonable (according to the double sense of reasonable discussed earlier). Hence, faith in or assent to propositions from any source ought to be subordinate to proper reason and so is to be rational. The mind could assent irrationally, but assent or faith ought to be subordinate to the power of reason. For all intents and purposes Locke thinks we should operate as if faith and reason are not two powers, but rather that faith is a result of the mind acting reasonably.

Locke ends the discussion of revelation and reason with a brief explanation of rules governing the relationship of vulgar reason and revelation and vulgar reason and vulgar faith, which serves, perhaps, as a summary of

---

96. The vulgar reason and faith contradistinction is used also in "Of Enthusiasm," a new chapter added by Locke to the fourth edition of the *Essay*. It was inserted prior to what was previously IV.xix.

the chapter (IV.xviii.10–11). It also serves to summarize the argument that faith and reason cannot rightfully be separated. It is not clear however if he is treating traditional revelation or both original and traditional revelation in section IV.xviii.10. There he writes: "Whatever GOD hath revealed, is certainty true; no doubt can be made of it. This is the proper Object of Faith: But whether it be a Divine Revelation, or no, Reason must judge; which can never permit the Mind to reject a greater Evidence to embrace what is less evident, nor prefer less Certainty to the greater." What follows is a statement on traditional revelation. So he might be moving from a statement on divine revelation in general to one specifically on traditional revelation, or it might be a movement of original revelation to traditional revelation. The latter reading is possible because he has used "divine Revelation" specifically in regards to original revelation in IV.xviii.5–6. Either way, a basic principle that has been quite explicit throughout and is reiterated here is that reason must judge whether a divine revelation is such. So again, vulgar faith is not actually separable from reason, whatever strictures one puts on it.

Section IV.xviii.10 continues the explanation of principles undergirding the relationship of vulgar reason and vulgar faith that show they are inseparable. Immediately after the quote given above, is the following:

> There can be no Evidence, that any traditional Revelation is of divine Original, in the Words we receive it, and in the Sense we understand it, so clear, and so certain as those of the Principles of Reason: And therefore, *Nothing that is contrary to, and inconsistent with the clear and self-evident Dictates of Reason, has a Right to be urged, or assented to, as a Matter of Faith, wherein Reason hath nothing to do.* Whatsoever is divine Revelation, ought to over-rule our Opinions, Prejudices, and Interests, and hath a Right to be received with a full Assent: Such a Submission as this of our Reason to Faith, takes not away the Land-mark of Knowledge.

The first sentence alludes to the probability that is involved in two areas regarding traditional revelation. The status of a particular traditional revelation being from a divine original is probable, and thus not certain. And the interpretation is only probable as well, not because of its probable status as divine revelation, but because of the imperfect nature of communicating concepts with words. The second sentence says that a divine revelation and its interpretation cannot contradict the "*clear and self-evident Dictates of Reason.*" The clear and self-evident dictates means at least intuitive knowledge but could also refer to demonstration since it is comprised of intuitive links.⁹⁷ It evidently includes sensitive knowledge as well. At least Locke treats sensitive knowledge as being certain in his comments made regarding the Roman Catholic doctrine of transubstantiation (IV.xix.10).⁹⁸ And, as already established, something cannot be assented to unless it is intelligible or mentally reconcilable; in other words, one must be able to form a mental representation of it or else it is contrary to reason in a particular sense. Therefore, anything that is contrary to knowledge (logically contradictory or, more generally, false), as taken from the excerpt above, and anything that is not definitively contradictory or false but at least contrary to knowledge in the mentally irreconcilable sense, as previously discussed, are those propositions or doctrines to which one cannot assent. Moreover, the third sentence makes it clear that a divine revelation and its thoughtful interpretation should overturn unassisted, natural probability. Locke ends the chapter stating that if these rules governing reason and faith are not adhered to, there will be no room for reason. This would mean no one is culpable for taking the wrong way in religion (IV.xviii.11).

So, in the end, faith in divine matters is a function of proper reason. Belief in matters of divine faith, or assent to divinely revealed propositions, ought to follow proper reason. But this statement is mollified by considering John C. Biddle's assessment of Locke and traditional revelation: "Although the right and necessity that reason judge the content as well as the authenticity of revelation appears to be the height of religious rationalism, such an interpretation would grossly belie Locke's intentions . . . he sought in the *Essay* to establish traditional revelation as the primary guide in that proper science and business of mankind, morality and religion."⁹⁹ Locke says as much in *ROC*. In fact, he portrays Christ and the Scriptures as clarifying morality and religion for us and showing us what we should try to demonstrate. Thus, while monotheism and morals are demonstrable and certain now for Locke, we were guided there by divine revelation first. Nature gave sufficient evidence but the world did not appropriately employ its reason prior to Christ.¹⁰⁰

97. Again, revelation cannot have more certainty than demonstration unless a revelation showed how a supposed demonstration was actually not that. But again, the content of the revelation could give certainty (such as a demonstrative proof) but it might still be uncertain as to whether it was actually a revelation.

98. Sensitive knowledge is required to identify a miracle. Also, one would need to trust the senses to trust the words one is seeing on the pages of traditional revelation. Cf. Turretin, *Institutes of Elenctic Theology*, 1:35–36.

99. Biddle, "Locke's Critique," 417. Being that it is not completely evident from Biddle's essay what he means by "reason," the quote is appropriated for this chapter's designs and thus incorporates proper reason by virtue of the appropriation.

100. Locke, *ROC*, 255–93; cf. Marko, "Promulgation of Right Morals."

This chapter is now in a better position to revisit the last section, section 14, from the chapter "On Assent." As already discussed, IV.xvi.13, the preceding section of the same chapter, discusses a paradigmatic instance of miracles: great contrariety to the normal and observable course of nature and many fair witnesses. After this brief description of miracles and assenting to them as such, Locke begins section 14 as follows:

> Besides those we have hitherto mentioned, there is one sort of Propositions that challenge the highest degree of our Assent, upon bare Testimony, whether the thing proposed, agree or disagree with common Experience, and the ordinary course of Things, or no. The Reason whereof is, because the Testimony is of such an one, as cannot deceive, nor be deceived, and that is of God Himself. This carries with it Certainty beyond Doubt, Evidence beyond Exception. This is called by a peculiar Name, *Revelation*, and our Assent to it, *Faith*: which has as much Certainty[101] as our Knowledge it self; and we may as well doubt of our own Being, as we can, whether any Revelation from GOD be true. So that Faith is a setled and sure Principle of Assent and Assurance, and leaves no manner of room for Doubt or Hesitation.

First, in reference to the quote above, and as already discussed, the faith in the quote is vulgar faith. The quote, however, is primarily discussing the nature of communication from God, *objectively speaking*. God cannot be deceived or deceive so everything he says is true and we can rely on His testimony. This is obviously not the case with our other sources of information. Therefore, God's revelation can overturn propositions that would otherwise have been thought to be reasonable.

Locke then abruptly moves from a theoretical discussion of revelation into practical discussions related to divine revelation in general:

> Only we must be sure, that it be a divine Revelation, and that we understand it right; else we shall expose ourselves to all the Extravagancy of Enthusiasm, and all the Errour of wrong Principles, if we have Faith and Assurance in what is not divine Revelation. And therefore in those cases, our Assent can be rationally no higher than the Evidence of its being a Revelation, and that this is the meaning of the Expressions it is delivered in. If the Evidence of its being a Revelation, or that this its true Sense be only on probable Proofs, our Assent can reach no

---

101. Every edition published in Locke's lifetime reads "Certainty" here. The 1706 or fifth edition changes this "Certainty" to "Assurance."

higher than an Assurance or Diffidence, arising from the more, or less apparent Probability of the Proofs.

As already established, but indicated also in the excerpt above, reason in practice has a role not only in identifying a divine mark of the revelation (the miracle) or the probability of truthfulness of the human testimony that there was in fact a divine mark or marks, but further, reason must provide an interpretation. As already discussed, this interpretation would not contradict knowledge, in the two aforementioned senses, which, among other things, assures that one is not assenting (or, rather, not claiming to assent) to something for which they cannot concoct a summative, complex idea. And, although he does not say it here explicitly, if it is divine it would, at least, not definitively contradict other propositions one is convinced are divinely revealed.[102] In short, while God cannot deceive or be deceived and thus a revelation from Him would be truthful, we must use our reason in practice to ascertain whether or not a communication is from Him. Furthermore, our degree of assent should be proportional to the probability that the so-called divine revelation is such.

Finally, Locke has another subtle shift, focusing specifically on divinely revealed propositions, whose evidence of being divine is such that we have assurance, the highest degree of assent, that they are such: "But of Faith, and the Precedency it ought to have before other Arguments of Persuasion, I shall speak more hereafter, where I treat of it, as it is ordinarily placed, in contradistinction to Reason: though in Truth, it be nothing else but an Assent founded on the highest Reason." As discussed already, this is Locke's first explicit indication that he is conceiving of faith and reason in two senses in the *Essay*. That is, faith in this passage deviates from faith throughout the rest of the chapter since faith here pertains only to divine revelation; faith throughout the rest of the chapter pertains to any proposition that is probable. And, there is a distinction between the first mention of reason, which is contradistinguished to vulgar faith, and the "highest Reason," which is actually responsible for the assent to the revealed proposition. In other words, vulgar reason and proper reason are distinguished in the quote as well.

There are some very important implications that are worthy to make clear and explicit from our discussion focusing on IV.xvi.14. It is not just any allegedly revealed proposition that does not contradict knowledge in multiple senses and have associated claims of miraculous testimonies that will have the highest assurance. The more outlandish the miracle(s) and/or the greater the number of fair testimonies of the miracle(s), the more

---

102. Cf. Locke, *ROC*, 303–4.

convinced the mind will be that the associated proposition or revelation is divine. Scripture somehow meets these criteria and is deserving of the highest assent (cf. IV.xiv.13).

Having now looked at the dense section, IV.xvi.14, there are a few final points that are worthy of mention pertaining to revelation. They are prompted by our discussion on section 14. First, what additional evidence is there that Locke thinks the mind should be *assured* that the Bible is revealed? On a related note, and second, if the Bible has a paradigmatic status—Locke was professedly a Christian—what are the implications for alleged extra-biblical revelation? Third, how much of a divine revelation is confirmed by a miracle?

Pondering the first question, there is significant evidence for thinking that Locke has the Bible in mind as *the* paradigm of the traditional revelation that is a subject of his vulgar faith, the construal of faith discussed in IV.xvi.14 and more thoroughly in IV.xviii. It is that which qualifies for assurance, the highest degree of assent. First, all of the examples that he uses of above reason propositions are biblical. Second, he refers to the Old and New Testaments as infallibly true (III.ix.23). Contrary to Paul Helm, infallibly true refers not to the certainty of the truth of revelations, but rather that by assurance of it being God's word, we must take a hermeneutical stance that it cannot contradict itself.[103] Presumably Locke can say this in part because he has not found propositions in Scripture that are necessarily or definitively contradictory. In fact, he instructs his readers to suspend their judgment on two passages of Scripture that they cannot reconcile, offering no suggestion that one might be illegitimate.[104] Third, few Locke scholars deny his self-identification as a Christian and the divine status he ascribes to the Bible. Fourth, his later added chapter, "Of Enthusiasm," which appears in the fourth edition of the *Essay*, supports the Bible's paradigmatic status. There, Locke notes that God sends marks—miracles—which "reason" cannot be mistaken in to verify to the recipient that it is He who is giving the revealed propositions.[105] His examples are Gideon and Moses. Moses was also given the power to perform miracles in front of others to show that he was the emissary of God.[106] Furthermore, Locke does not deny that God might enlighten humans' minds today in apprehending certain truths and influence us to action by the immediate assistance and influence of the Holy

---

103. Helm, "Locke on Faith and Knowledge," 55–58.

104. Locke, *ROC*, 303–4.

105. This is from IV.xix.14 in the critical edition, the fourth edition (1700), and all subsequent editions.

106. This is from IV.xix.15 in the critical edition, the fourth edition (1700), and all subsequent editions.

Spirit without any sign. He notes that if such a proposition without an external mark is to be received as a divine revelation it must be consonant to reason or Scripture:

> Where the Truth imbraced is consonant to the *Revelation* in the written word of GOD; or the Action conformable to the dictates of right *Reason* or Holy Writ, we may be assured that we run no risque in entertaining it as such, because though perhaps it be not an immediate Revelation from GOD, extraordinarily operating on our Minds, yet we are sure it is warranted by that Revelation which he has given us of Truth.[107]

In the quotation above, right reason is a term that pertains to proper argumentation from the employment of human reason making correct reasonable connections and conclusions that it is possible for humans to make on our own, but, because of our weaknesses and limitations, not always likely. Revelation can be used as confirmation and guidance to this otherwise natural reasoning process of the employment of reason. In short, Scripture, for Locke's *Essay*, is a metric of sorts for all other alleged revelation.[108]

Focusing now on the second question, while the Bible is the paradigm for traditional revelation, it does not necessarily exhaust all traditional revelation, even though Locke might appear personally to think that it does.[109] First, he writes of traditional revelation, not Scripture, in chapter IV.xviii. Second, since he makes room for present-day original revelation, it only follows that he would make room for that conveyable type of original revelation with clear external marks or miracles to be set down in writing or passed on to others. And since he does not simply start with the infallibility and divinity of Scripture as givens and does not consider rejecting one or more of the biblical passages that he could not reconcile, perhaps he treats potential traditional and original revelation somewhat similarly. That is, an internal mark is not so much, generally stated, that it must agree with

---

107. This is from IV.xix.16 in the critical edition, the fourth edition (1700), and all subsequent editions.

108. So, practically speaking, when Christians dogmatically assert that the Bible clearly says something that is contrary to knowledge or produces a contradiction (i.e., logically contradictory or contradictory to certain truths), they make *it appear* unreasonable. When enthusiasts claim unattested divine revelation as such that does not correspond to vulgar reason's conclusions on issues to which Scripture does not speak or Scripture they make *themselves* unreasonable. This last assertion can be inferred in what is said in the earlier editions of the *Essay*, but it is made explicit in the fourth and later editions.

109. It appears as though Locke is often skeptical of those who claim to have been given original revelation. Cf. IV.xviii.6 and "Of Enthusiasm," which becomes IV.xix starting in the fourth edition of the *Essay*.

Scripture, but that it does not definitively contradict assured traditional revelation, which includes, at least, Scripture. Such revelation thus becomes "traditional revelation." So if a present day, alleged, traditional revelation has the clear external marks, miracles, and internal marks, an interpretation that is representatively reconcilable and non-contradictory (i.e., not contrary to knowledge in the senses discussed) and not definitively contrary to confirmed traditional revelation, it should be considered traditional revelation.

It might be the case, however, that he is so convinced by the divinity of Scripture that the alleged, traditional revelation with the association of miracles and which is itself representatively reconcilable and non-contradictory must also be reconcilable with the Bible. In other words, the final mark of such a revelation is that it is simply not contrary to Scripture; thus a person must be able to show that it is reconcilable with potentially contrary parts of Scripture prior to accepting it as a divine revelation.[110] And so, while alleged passages from the Bible might not be reconcilable for some though they keep their divine status in the minds of those people, purported, extrabiblical, traditional revelation might not be afforded the same privilege.

It is difficult to decide which of the above options is closer to Locke's intent for the *Essay*. But, thankfully, for this book's purposes, it does not significantly matter. As will be shown in the next chapter, where Toland's views on reason, faith, and revelation will be juxtaposed with those of Locke, Toland thinks that there is no further traditional revelation beyond Scripture. In fact, the divinity of Scripture is one of young Toland's givens. So, whichever of the above options one chooses, the *Essay* and *CNM* will be different. In the end, this chapter will take the stance that if a present day, alleged, traditional revelation has the clear external marks, miracles, and internal marks, an interpretation that is representatively reconcilable and does not produce a certain falsehood and is not definitively contrary to other confirmed or assured traditional revelation, it should be considered traditional revelation. Of the two options discussed, it is that which comports least closely with the classical position of Christianity that the canon is closed, since it is the less restrictive of the two options. But, it appears to

---

110. All of this brings up other questions that are beyond the concerns of this book. One such question is, assuming that a supposed revelation must be shown to be consonant to Scripture, might it be the case that it might simply need to be not definitively contrary to other accepted, extra-biblical revelation to be considered revelation. Another question is, might the seriousness of the action prompted, for instance, play into the thoroughness one would have to expend in making sure that a supposed original or traditional revelation with the association of miracles agrees with or at least does not definitively go against Scripture? In that case, however, one would probably expect God to use miracles in only situations of the highest gravity.

be consonant with the focus on the more general concepts of "traditional revelation" and "original revelation" in IV.xviii that becomes a bit lost in the chapter, "Of Enthusiasm," added in 1700. In the former chapter he appears to be writing as a philosopher using the Bible as the paradigm for traditional revelation, while in the latter, he seems to be writing more as a Christian theologian.[111]

Thirdly, the problems of miracles being evidence of divine revelation have been noted by Nicholas Wolterstorff. He communicates some of these problems with the following questions: "How much of what a person believes has been divinely revealed to him is *confirmed* as having been divinely revealed to him by the miraculous sign of which he is the recipient? Correspondingly, how much of what a person *claims* to have been divinely revealed to him is *confirmed* as having been divinely revealed to him by his performance of a miracle?"[112] Unfortunately, Locke does not answer these questions. Some have responded that a detailed treatment of these issues was not pressing for Locke since his targets in the *Essay* are Christians. Nonetheless, miracles were used by others as external indicators of divine revelation. For instance, Locke's friend, Archbishop Tillotson, extolled God's use of confirming revelation through miracles. For Tillotson, the number, greatness, surety, public nature, and the duration of miracles was important for Jesus', the apostles', and Moses' legitimacy as divine agents.[113] Perhaps for Locke, the association of great and numerous miracles with the group of apostles confirms their divine agent status and thus they are to be considered authoritative in anything that they wrote or affirmed that was written by another. Something similar could be the case for the Old Testament books. Any Old Testament books, however, without an association with a miracle or miracles or some likely affirmation by an Old Testament author who was indicated as a divine agent by a miracle or miracles could be viewed as affirmed by Jesus and the apostles as there is no historical evidence that they disputed with the Jewish leaders over the canon. Rather the apostles and Jesus quote from or allude to the Old Testament frequently.[114]

111. The most restrictive option would be that such a revelation must agree or be shown to agree with Scripture. Locke's rule for alleged original revelation without appropriate external marks requires that in some cases, however. Therefore, this chapter also reasoned that Locke would be less restrictive with alleged revelation with marks of miracles.

112. Wolterstorff, *John Locke and the Ethics of Belief*, 132. It is important to remember that David Hume had not yet treated miracles. Also, see Locke's *A Discourse of Miracles* in the collection of his *Posthumous Works*. Locke, *Posthumous Works*, 217-30.

113. Tilllotson, "Sermon XI: Of the Miracles," 325.

114. Moreover, regarding the evidence of a divine revelation being such, one probably should not rule out the role of the Holy Spirit—whom Christ promised would enlighten

In summary, there are a number of important principles and implications from the *Essay* regarding the relationship of revelation and reason. For one, alleged revelation must be confirmed or denied as being such by the mind employing the power of reason. Reason must judge through the external marks and internal marks whether a divine revelation is such. This relationship necessarily overturns any attempted separation of reason and faith in divine revelation into distinctive provinces or spheres. Otherwise, faith is irrational. In the end, the idea of reason operating in a restricted office or the idea of vulgar reason breaks down and reason is forced back into its proper office. Therefore, faith, understood as pertaining to just divine revelation (vulgar faith) or *any* proposition with only probabilities for and/or against it (proper faith), ought to be reasonable in the proper sense of the term. Furthermore, while Locke may be suspicious of the many claims to original revelation, he does not rule out all such claims. If an alleged original revelation with no association of miracles is reasonable on purely natural considerations where Scripture (or other assured revelation) does not speak or comports with Scripture (or other assured revelation) there is no harm in allowing one to consider it as divine. Moreover, while Scripture does not necessarily exhaust his category of traditional revelation, it is the paradigm of assured divine revelation that deserves the highest degree of assent. Such traditional revelation with proper external and internal marks can overturn any proposition to which one has assented on purely natural considerations.

CONCLUSION

This chapter has explained Locke's conception of reason and its relationships to faith and revelation. In Locke's consideration of the faculty of reason in his *Essay*, he acknowledges various renderings of the term but conceptually builds his idea of reason in its largest sense. Reason as a faculty is a tool of the mind or agent. It gives the mind knowledge and probability, the latter being that upon which the mind *should* base its judgments. Reason's proper office does not only deal with natural sources of information but also divine sources. The faculty of reason, then, considered operating in its full scope or proper office was called proper reason by this chapter. Proper reason's corresponding faith (or assent, opinion, or belief), what this chapter called proper faith, concerns natural and divine revelatory matters as well. While the mind's faith and the judgment that produces it morally ought to be

---

our minds and whom Locke calls an infallible guide and giver of assistance—in assuring one of the divinity of *all* Scripture. Locke, *ROC*, 292; Locke, *Second Vindication*, 340–41.

based on proper reason's recommendation and thus should be subordinate to it, especially in important areas such as religion and morality, the mind's assent might not follow proper reason. In that case the mind does not have proper faith but irrational faith as the mind is not heeding and utilizing properly its God-given guide. In short, proper faith, an act done by the mind from its judgment, if reasonable, heeds the recommendations issued from reason working in its proper office. What is more, the natural faculties can be considered, for all intents and purposes, as reason when the mind acts reasonably—reasonably in the sense of dictated by proper reason and in the sense of reason being utilized to the appropriate thoroughness that the circumstance warrants.

Near the end of *Essay* IV.xvii, "Of Reason," and in *Essay* IV.xviii, "Of Faith and Reason, and Their Distinct Provinces," he conceives of the faculty of reason operating in a diminished office, what this chapter called vulgar reason. This is done such that vulgar reason can be conceptually distinguished as much as possible from assent, faith, or belief in divinely revealed propositions as such and their content, what this chapter called vulgar faith. In other words, vulgar reason is the faculty of reason considered operating in an office without the assistance or propositions of divine revelation. This distinguishing of faith and reason in a vulgar understanding is done simply as a concession to the masses since Locke believes that such a distinction and opposition is too ingrained in the common vernacular to dislodge it. This vulgar conception of reason is what allows Locke to concede to a category of "above reason" propositions. If Locke were adhering to his preferred consideration of reason, proper reason, the three categories of propositions often associated with Locke—according to reason, contrary to reason, and above reason—would actually transmute into two categories—according to reason and contrary to reason.

By the end of the *Essay*, Locke's understanding of the relationship of reason and revelation becomes evident, as does its bearing on the relationship of reason and faith. Original and traditional revelation must have the appropriate external and internal marks which reason must identify to be affirmed as revelation. The appropriate external mark for original revelation is a clear miracle or miracles and for traditional revelation is accompanying fair testimonies of a clear miracle or miracles. The appropriate internal marks are that the interpretation of the revealed proposition is neither contrary to knowledge, both in the sense of contrary to knowledge where the proposition contradicts certain truths or is inherently contradictory and in the sense that it is mentally irreconcilable, nor definitively contrary to already accepted and assured divine revelation, especially Scripture. One would not expect divine revelation to be contrary to knowledge in the first sense, at least, because if revelation could contradict knowledge—the goal and highest achievement of reason and the foundation of our further reasoning—it would be undercutting its source of validation that it is revelation. One would not expect a divine revelation to contradict another revelation either; God does not oppose Himself. Moreover, this inseparable role reason has in vindicating faith in revelation as such and its interpretation of revelation makes a contradistinguishing of vulgar faith and vulgar reason into distinct provinces untenable. Thus, Locke subordinates revelation to proper reason with respect to external marks and internal marks or interpretation. And proper or vulgar faith should be subordinate to proper reason as the mind ought to believe rationally.

There are a few other important arguments Locke lays out pertaining to reason, faith, and revelation, or which could be inferred. First, when an attested and assured divine revelation stands in contradiction to a proposition supported not by reasonable certainty but natural probability, regardless of the subject matter, the revelation ought to trump the proposition that is probable on purely natural considerations. Second, while the Bible is the best example of traditional revelation and deserves the highest degree of assent, it does not necessarily exhaust traditional revelation or traditional revelation deserving of assurance. This is because Locke does not rule out God performing miracles and giving original revelation today that might be recorded. Third, if an alleged original revelation does not have external marks accompanying it, one can receive it as such as long as it is agrees with the conclusions of reason based upon purely natural considerations where Scripture (or other assured revelation) does not speak or Scripture (or other assured revelation). Fourth, it is possible that miracles associated with a person or persons mark them as divine agents. Thus, this divine agent status confirms that what they affirm in writing or confirm in the writing of another to be divine revelation is such. Of course, the so-called revelation must not contradict knowledge in any of the aforementioned senses and must not definitively contradict other assured revelation.

4

Toland's Incorporation of Faith and Revelation within Reason

INTRODUCTION

IF SIMPLY RECEIVING MUCH attention had been the goal of young John Toland when he published *CNM* he would have hit the mark. It is to this day the work for which he is best known and which continues, in some way, to fuel his public image of being mischievous. As already discussed, because of his heavy borrowing from John Locke's *Essay*, the two writers are paired together and critiqued by Bishop Edward Stillingfleet. Even though Locke indexes Stillingfleet's misunderstandings of the notions of ideas, certainty, and knowledge found in the *Essay* and Toland's *CNM*, Toland is still to this day somewhat received as Stillingfleet presents him. Originally portrayed by Stillingfleet as having brought the *Essay's* foundational principles to their true unorthodox end, and thus having out-Locked Locke, Toland is now portrayed as having heavily borrowed from the *Essay* and adapted its thought to his own heretical ends. This altered picture stands because while most are skeptical of or deny the accuracy of Stillingfleet's reading of Locke and the *Essay* in light of Locke's defense, they, for some reason, assume that the bishop's reading of Toland's *CNM* is correct.

As mentioned in the first chapter, scholarly assessments of Toland tend to abound with a few major, intertwined problems related to this prevailing view that Stillingfleet read *CNM* correctly and that Toland did greatly diverge from Locke despite the fact that both built on similar foundations.

Supporting or resulting from this view are three common assertions often made regarding the juxtaposition of Locke and Toland: 1) Toland appropriates the foundational principles of Locke's *Essay* to a significant degree, 2) Locke accepts above reason propositions, while Toland does not, and 3) Locke accepts divine revelation and Toland rejects, or essentially rejects, divine revelation. These three assertions, which are related to the prevailing view of *CNM*, are teeming with problems. First, assertion one is simply vague. Assertion two is the most widely known. There is clear textual evidence that Locke accepts "above reason" things and Toland rejects them. In fact, it seems as though this clear textual evidence is the best piece of evidence supporting the prevailing view that Toland, the disciple, attacked his master. But, due to the lack of specificity of assertion one, an imposing assumption actually undergirds assertion two. The assumption is that Locke and Toland are operating with the same notion of reason in Locke's acceptance of things that are above reason and Toland's rejection of things that are above reason. Surprisingly, no one has attempted an in-depth explanation of Toland's understanding of reason. To operate as if it is the same as Locke's is not only presumptuous but very problematic since Locke's understanding of reason is a significantly contested topic in Locke scholarship. Furthermore, due to the lack of comparison of Locke's and Toland's foundational, epistemological principles and their respective views of reason, assertion three is made. In fact, *some* incorrectly identify above reason propositions and revelation making assertions two and three identical. But of those who understand above reason propositions to be a subset of revelation or think the two to be overlapping somehow, they appear to think assertions two and three are mutually supportive for one reason or another.[1] Together the three assertions are coherent and they give a slightly more detailed explanation of the prevailing view's claim that Toland did greatly diverge from Locke. But while Locke scholarship is fraught with significant detailed analyses that work toward answering important questions that bear on the relationship between Locke and Toland, this is clearly not the case in Toland scholarship. It is riddled with reliance on second-hand information on or readings of

---

1. As indicated in chapter 2, some misunderstand propositions above (Lockean) reason to include propositions from natural sources about natural things. The correct understanding of the relationship of propositions that are above (vulgar) reason and revelation is that above reason propositions are revealed propositions that we would not have conceived of on our own, but if we had, we would have no reason to assent to them. All of Locke's examples are supernatural in nature. Above reason propositions do not exhaust revelation since revelation might provide us with natural or supernatural propositions that we could have arrived at on our own or that might deny propositions that we arrived at on our own without revelation. Revelation also deals with past, once observable matters of fact in history among other things.

Toland, which is likely due to the prolixity of the Locke-Stillingfleet debate and *CNM*'s hard-to-follow style. In short, there are numerous problems in Locke and especially Toland scholarship, some named above, which have caused Locke and Toland to be cast as very similar in some respects but greatly different in others.

Chapters 2, 3, and 4, whose ultimate goal is to compare the epistemologies of Locke and Toland, help correct and inform these three assertions and more. Chapter 2 set out to show that Locke's and Toland's notions of ideas and certainty comport and that the ensuing debate between Locke and Stillingfleet and its reception left little resolved regarding a comparison of Locke's and Toland's epistemologies. Chapter 2 went part way in clarifying assertion one and correcting assertion three, among other clarifications and corrections. Regarding assertion one, it was shown, as already stated, that Toland's notions of ideas and certainty actually comport with Locke's notions. It was thus shown that Stillingfleet's claim that *CNM* makes the sole duty of reason to be obtaining certainty and his related claim that certainty can only be had by clear and distinct ideas in *CNM* are false. Regarding assertion three, the suggestion was made in chapter 2 that the charge that Toland rejected revelation or at least undercut its authority actually came from Locke's discovery that Stillingfleet, at one point in the debate, makes an argument whose logical implications, unbeknownst to him, undercut the ability of revelation to be novel and correct natural probability. Locke notes that Stillingfleet actually is working with premises held by the position of those whom he opposes. And so it appears that many, like Roger Woolhouse, think the position which Stillingfleet was trying to oppose was that of John Toland, who stands at the beginning of the debate.[2] So, that is most likely where the idea came from that revelation, according to Toland's *CNM*, must be subordinate to a divinely unassisted, natural reason and thus is not able to be novel or correct natural probability. Chapter 3 is the completion of the exploration into Locke's epistemology and sets the stage for making corrections and improvements to the three assertions. While chapter 2 focuses on Locke's ideas, certainty, and knowledge, chapter 3 continues the investigation, focusing primarily on reason and its related faculties and reason's relationships with faith and revelation. It suggests what reason and its related faculties are and explains the relationships between reason and faith and reason and revelation.

Chapter 4 will finish the comparison of Locke's and Toland's epistemologies that will enable improvements or corrections to the three

---

2. Woolhouse, *Locke: A Biography*, 408–9; cf. Locke, *Mr. Locke's Reply . . . Answer to His Second Letter*, 419–20.

assertions discussed above. Chapter 4, the present chapter, will focus on the same questions regarding Toland that were asked of Locke in chapter 3: 1) According to Toland, what is reason?; 2) What is its relationship to faith?; and 3) What is its relationship to revelation? But, in chapter 4, a concurrent point-for-point comparison with Locke will be undertaken.

Thus, this chapter argues that the salient differences between Locke and Toland with respect to their understandings and treatments of reason, its related faculties, faith, and revelation are not based on or evidenced by their respective categorizations of propositions, but rather on Toland's attempt at working out the implications of Locke's epistemological principles in conjunction with Toland's interpretations of certain biblical passages and certain theological preferences and presuppositions. Had Locke ordered propositions according to his preferred consideration of reason, his categorization of propositions would be the same ascribed to Toland. The resultant, substantial differences between Locke and Toland in their understandings and treatments of epistemology are connected with Toland's definite or likely rejections of theological and philosophical positions that Locke does not dismiss: post-New Testament original revelation and miracles, non-materialism of the soul, and prior-to-the-close-of-the-New-Testament divine revelation requiring a supernaturally bestowed faculty and private miracles for believers.[3]

This chapter will follow the same outline as chapter 3. Part I will serve as the state of the question. Part II will touch on preliminary issues. It will give an expositional explanation of assent and the faculties of knowledge and judgment often associated with reason. Part III will describe Toland's conception of reason. Part IV will describe the relationship between reason and faith. An explanation of what above reason propositions are will be offered in part V. Part VI will describe the relationship of reason and revelation. Finally, the chapter will end with a section focusing on conclusions.

PART I: STATE OF THE QUESTION

The scholarship on Toland's epistemology is notably variegated and is intertwined with various supposed narratives that will be discussed in what follows. In the last chapter it was shown that nearly all miss Locke's distinction

---

3. As stated earlier and as will be shown, Toland would reject any claim of a private miracle that occurred in the presence of an unbeliever that was not to have been done by God and for the purpose of helping the unbeliever with her unbelief (*CNM* 151). John Locke does not specifically discuss the claims of believers in non-biblical religions regarding miracles done in favor of their religion.

between proper reason and vulgar reason. It is thus not surprising that most miss what Toland precisely intends by the faculty of reason, since all acknowledge Toland's epistemological principles are significantly dependent on or presuppose Locke's *Essay*.[4] Those who misunderstand Locke on reason and then move from Locke to Toland, presupposing an adoption of Lockean vulgar reason, will misunderstand Toland as well, at least on a few points. As said above, they will wrongly identify Locke and Toland as meaning the same thing in labeling propositions as being above reason. Whatever the case, in the end they see Toland as subordinating revelation to natural, unassisted revelation or rejecting revelation outright. Immediately below are cases in point for both conclusions.

Most often and especially, but not exclusively, in pre-1980's scholarship, Toland is portrayed as deistic or a deist—one who rejects an epistemological need of revelation for true religion. This scholarship can be divided into two groups, based on whether they argue that Toland thinks that Scripture is *useful* for Christians or not. These scholarly works tend to be brief in their treatments of Toland or his epistemology making their placement in one of the two groups only likely and placement based on further distinctions within the contours of these two groups conjectural. The first group's claims amount to this: regardless of his claimed intentions, Toland's primary intent with *CNM* is to argue that either acceptable divine revelation is superfluous or that divine revelation does not exist. These scholars can sometimes be read either way due to a lack of clarity. Moreover, they interpret Toland as arguing that we should make no *functional* distinction between the natural religion of reason, or morality, and Christianity. Such scholars are: Daniel C. Fouke, Gerald R. Cragg, Philip McGuinness, and Leslie Stephen.[5] The

---

4. See the following footnotes regarding what each scholar has to say about Toland's dependence on Locke's *Essay*.

5. Fouke, *Philosophy and Theology*. Fouke writes, "Toland advanced a number of powerful arguments for reducing Christianity to a purely natural religion based on reason alone" (237). It would have been helpful had Fouke given a definition of what he thinks Toland means by the faculty of reason. It is not even defined in his subsection "Reason and Enthusiasm" (81-86) or in his discussion of *CNM* (222-40). It appears that Fouke thinks that Toland does not believe that any propositions are actually revealed by God (221, 227, 236). Regarding his dependence on Locke, Fouke writes: "While *Christianity not Mysterious* set out an official epistemology that was clearly modeled on Locke's, Toland's mode of philosophizing revealed epistemological concepts that were far different from Locke's, with a strong emphasis on what we might now call the ideological functions of discourse" (23). At no point in the work does he give a treatment of Locke's *Essay*. Cragg, *Church and the Age of Reason*, 78, 160. Cragg notes that Toland presupposes the *necessity* of revelation in *CNM*, but then claims that Toland thinks revelation is *supplementary*. It is not clear what he means. It is possible that he means that for Toland revelation is not necessary for salvation, but is helpful

second group's claims amount to this: regardless of his claimed intentions, Toland's primary intent with *CNM* is to argue the primacy of reason in religion without denying the existence of revelation, unless a particular alleged revelation makes claims that do not match up with what one would think is reasonable under the consideration of purely natural sources of information. In other words, revelation can be accepted as such as long as it lends

---

in other areas. It is also possible that he means that Toland verbally committed to the necessity of revelation but in effect argues the opposite in *CNM* (78). What he says in a later passage supports this latter interpretation. From the context of the said later passage he groups Toland with the deists. The deists were those who thought revelation "was at best superfluous, at worse superstitious." Moreover, he also notes that Toland's *CNM* effectively banishes mystery, but without giving a definition as to what is meant by "mystery." "Reason" according to Toland, likewise, goes undefined (160). Regarding Toland's dependence on Locke, Cragg simply notes, "Toland presupposed Locke's views and expanded them, but he was more than Locke's echo . . ." (78). No clarity is lent by another work of Cragg: Cragg, *Reason and Authority*, 67, 78, 83. Welch, *Protestant Thought*, 1:36–38. He places Toland in a group whose shared conviction is: "genuine Christianity is identical with the religion of nature; natural religion is a perfect thing, and 'additions' are both unnecessary and false" (37). He notes, however, that Toland thought that "The essence of Christianity is the same as natural religion; there is nothing mysterious or above reason in the Gospel." This naked statement would leave open the possibility that Toland accepted things as being divinely revealed (36). Welch goes on to write: "Already in this second stage, the real primacy of natural religion is apparent. It was only a short step to the declaration that revealed religion was wholly unnecessary, or even opposed to the true religion of reason" (38). It is unclear what the difference between revelation being "unnecessary" (37) versus "wholly unnecessary" (38) might be. (Also, the grouping together of those that claim that revelation is "wholly unnecessary" with those that claim revelation might be opposed to religion is suspect). In the end, there is too little given by Welch to conclude what Toland thinks reason to be and whether or not he believes that there is such a thing as divinely revealed propositions. If we concentrate solely on his comments regarding the group in which he places Toland (37), however, it would seem that he thinks Toland rejects Scripture as being divine, or at least its novelty, because it has the unnatural gospel. McGuinness, "*Christianity Not Mysterious*," 233–37. McGuinness interestingly makes no direct assertions about Toland, only quoting what others have said about him. It appears as though he believes Toland to be a deist, someone who rejects miracles and thinks "Morality should thus be based on natural law rather than revelation" (237). This statement is why this chapter places him with those who reject revelation or think it superfluous. He does agree with John Biddle's claims of *CNM*'s dependence on the *Essay* (233–35). Stephen, *History of English Thought*, 1:94–118. Stephen claims that Toland, through *CNM*, attacked the authenticity of the Bible (94). He is admittedly confused because he says in certain respects Toland seems to indicate scholastic theology as a "possible science," but then writes: "The most obvious interpretation of Toland's words would admit of pure Deism" (109). This latter statement is why Stephen gets placed into this grouping of scholars. In respect to his relationship with Locke, he notes that the whole of Toland's philosophy was substantially derived from Locke (94).

clarity or confirmation but not novelty. Such scholars are: James Turner, John C. Higgins-Biddle, John Herman Randall, Jr., and Diego Lucci.[6]

6. Turner, *Without God, Without Creed*, 51–53. He defines deism thus: "Deism professed to be a religion founded on reason alone, composed solely of truths about God evident in the order of nature, subjecting all beliefs to the tests of reason and experience. In fact, it usually amounted to a severely stripped down version of Christianity, with all that smacked of mystery and superstition pared away" (51–52). This could be clearer. Do deists believe divine revelation is possible presently or in the past? If so, might revelation provide a better argument? Specifically regarding Toland, he notes that Toland believed revelation must submit to reason's judgment. In this light, it *appears* that Turner doubts that Toland actually considered revelation a legitimate category (52). However, he refers to "[t]horoughgoing Deists" as those who categorically rejected revelation, miracles, and "anything inaccessible to reason" (53). It thus appears he views Toland as secretly a thoroughgoing deist or possibly one that admitted revelation of some sort. Regarding Toland's epistemological dependence on Locke, Turner simply notes that Toland "argued from Lockean principles that only reason offered certitude and that revelation itself must submit to reason's judgment" (52). Based on this statement, I have placed him with those that understand Toland as accepting revelation as such as long as it does not lend novelty. Biddle, "Locke's Critique of Innate," 417–22. Biddle is unclear in his treatment of Toland. He notes that Toland is highly dependent on Locke but differs on one important point: whereas for Locke a revealed proposition cannot be believed if it is contrary to knowledge, for Toland it cannot be believed if it is contrary to "'natural' or 'common notions'" (419–20). Biddle thinks Toland and Locke differ on this point somehow (but, in truth, as this chapter will show, they are ultimately making the same assertions). It is also unclear what Biddle means by mysteries, above reason things, etc. He is clear that Toland might be read as "challenging the acceptance of Scripture as revelation" (420). Also, Higgins-Biddle, introduction to *The Reasonableness of Christianity*, xxviii–xxxv. The same vagueness regarding Toland and the differences between Toland and Locke are seen here as well. Due to his framing of Toland as considering revelation as such, even though it would be subordinate to natural reason, Higgins-Biddle is placed in this group. Randall, Jr., *Making of the Modern Mind*, 285–89. Randall understands two main factions to be disputing at the end of the 1600's: orthodox or supernatural rationalists—who insisted upon the "importance" of revelation—and the radicals or deists—who "rejected" revelation. That "[b]oth agreed that the core of religion was a set of doctrines that could be established by the unaided natural reason" (285) demonstrates the insufficiency of two categories at that time period when considering the orthodox Reformed and Lutheran, let alone Locke, none of who think very highly of our unaided reason in the area of religion. Nevertheless, it appears that Randall places Toland in the supernatural rationalist category. He notes that Toland combines Locke's according to reason and above reason categories and that Toland maintains "testimony may be given by revelation." But then he claims that Toland rejects revelation that contradicts anything experience teaches (289). He in the end is not fully clear. He does call Toland "Locke's disciple" (289). Lucci, *Scripture and Deism*, 72–73, 81–82. Lucci interprets Toland as teaching that a doctrine from Scripture must be demonstratively certain or probable upon purely natural sources of information to accept it as true and revealed (72–73). Regarding Toland's relationship to Lockean thought, Lucci says that Toland radicalized Lockean thought: while using Lockean principles, Toland collapsed faith into knowledge (81–82). (The collapsing of faith and knowledge is a common misunderstanding that was corrected in chapter 2.)

Many Toland scholars since the publication of Robert E. Sullivan's 1982 biography on John Toland—*John Toland and the Deist Controversy*—have concentrated on two levels of thought in *CNM*. While Toland is sometimes portrayed as undergoing radical theological and philosophical development through his thirty years of writing, which accounts for the increasingly un-Christian slant in his publications,[7] it has been widely accepted by recent scholars, at least in part due to Sullivan's arguments, that Toland was a pantheistic materialist through his entire career; and thus *CNM* offers Toland's public or exoteric theology, while his later works progressively reveal his esoteric or actual theology. There are two main reasons for this latter narrative, which has found a significant and favorable hearing in scholarship. First, Toland, although denying he ever wrote in this way, refers to those that do in *CNM* (1696) and *Tetradymus* (1720)—evidence that he is cognizant of the writing form. Second, significant Toland scholarship agrees that the anonymous *Two Essays Sent in a Letter from Oxford to a Nobleman in London*, which is more antagonistic to Christianity than *CNM* and was published before it, was written by John Toland.[8] Therefore, scholars reason that *CNM* cannot be Toland's real views and he must have been a pantheistic materialist his entire writing career, as is only revealed later.[9] Although a coherent narrative results, Rhoda Rappaport has argued effectively that Sullivan's line of reasoning that many have adopted is faulty on a few different counts. First, in her opinion, *Two Essays* is not pantheistic.[10] Second, Sullivan's reasoning on the authorship idea, according to Rappaport, is circular:

7. Cf. Sullivan, *John Toland*, 114–15. Here he assesses Chiara Giutini's proposal as found in Giutini, *Panteismo e ideologia repubblicana*.

8. E.g., Sullivan, *John Toland*, 43–47, 114–19. L. P., *Two Essays*; cf. Rappaport, "Questions of Evidence." Rappaport cites Giancarlo Carabelli as making a possible connection between Toland and the *Two Essays*. Carabelli, *Tolandiana*, 20–21. Rappaport smartly notes: "Carabelli's cautious attribution would require no comment, were it not for the fact that what began as conjecture has evolved into an established fact—all this without any notable addition to Carabelli's evidence" (339).

9. Toland explicitly rejects the notion that nature or the universe are God: Toland, *Letters to Serena*, 219–20. He also sharply criticizes Spinoza in the work. For a work that argues for Toland being a Spinozist: Israel, *Radical Enlightenment*, 609–14. His short section on Toland does not expound texts and deals very little with *CNM*. This massive and impressive tome on the Enlightenment sometimes, understandably, relies on secondary sources alone in support of assertions regarding Toland and his thought.

10. Rappaport, "Questions of Evidence," 347. I agree with Rappaport. There are no reasons one would or should arrive at the conclusion. The opening pages of the *Two Essays* are only taken by some to be materialistic or pantheistic or naturalistic-atheistic because of the author's *reserve* in accounting something as a miracle. Beiser, *Sovereignty of Reason*, 247. Beiser is another example of a scholar who thinks wrongly that the *Two Essays* is naturalistic. He gives no reasons other than a naked referencing of pages ii–iii, 2, and 4 of the *Two Essays* for support.

"He begins with the assumption that Toland wrote the *Two Essays*; there must therefore be clues to Toland's authorship in the text: and the discovery of such clues then confirms the initial assumption."[11] Her conclusion is that the evidence that John Toland wrote the *Two Essays* is "feeble."[12] An important implication that Rappaport does not mention is that her conclusion rocks Sullivan's argument for concluding that *CNM* taken at face value was not Toland's true beliefs at that time. Scholars have taken Sullivan's thesis unquestioned, however, and most since Rappaport have not heeded her conclusion or at least have not seen the major implication of it.

There are a few different groups of scholars that approach Toland's *CNM* from this esoteric/exoteric angle. The first group's claims, regarding *CNM*, can be summarized as follows: Toland's intentions are to legitimate revelation in *CNM* because revelation teaches right morals and civil order, even though he does not personally believe any propositions are divinely revealed. He additionally intends all readers to understand he is confirming the existence of revelation while plainly arguing that, nevertheless, Christianity is an instance of natural religion.[13] That is part of his exoteric program as unorthodox as it may be. The first scholar who is placed in this category, and who is most responsible for scholars reading *CNM* from an esoteric/exoteric angle, is Robert E. Sullivan, discussed above.[14] The most significant

11. Rappaport, "Questions of Evidence," 344.

12. Ibid., 348.

13. Sullivan, *John Toland*; Beiser, *Sovereignty of Reason*. They believe that *CNM* teaches that revelation is not necessary for salvation nor is belief in Christ necessary for salvation (Sullivan, 133, 228; Beiser, 243, 255). They also believe *CNM* was written to "legitimate revelation in light of reason" (quotation, Beiser, 243; cf. 220) because the moral principles in revelation were important for civil order, even though Toland knew that if reason were pushed to its limits it would lead rightly to naturalism or materialism (Sullivan, 119, 138, 173–74, 207–8; Beiser, 244). Thus they both agree that Toland, at face value, is affirming of revelation as such in his exoteric theology promulgated in *CNM*, while he is actually a materialist who denies revelation (Sullivan, 125, 127, 216, 275; Beiser, 247–49). They both believe that Toland does use complex arguments, however, to attack or criticize revelation that is not directly related to morals (Sullivan, 119, 126, 133, 135; Beiser, 254–57). Regarding Toland's relationship with Locke, Sullivan believes he adopted Locke's position on clear and distinct ideas (76) and his epistemology was reliant on both the *Essay* and Unitarian tracts (124). He does discuss the ways in which he thinks Toland differed from Locke in his epistemology, however (124–27). Regarding Toland's relationship with Locke from Beiser's perspective, Beiser writes that Toland took Locke's critical use of (Locke's) concept of reason one step farther; while Locke defended experimental philosophy and attacked scholasticism with Lockean reason, Toland did the same; but the latter also attacked doctrines with non-moral implications as they were useless for salvation and civil well-being, both being based on morality (256–57).

14. Sullivan, *John Toland*, 76, 124. He notes that *CNM*'s epistemology was rather

oversight made by Sullivan regarding his reading of *CNM*, other than not treating what reason means or his attribution of the *Two Essays* to Toland, is his taking Toland's claims about the book of Revelation for the New Testament. Sullivan writes: "In light of his conception of the New Testament as a 'Prophetical History of the External State of the Church' containing 'no new Doctrines,' its importance as a means of information seems doubtful."[15] Toland's claims here are clearly and explicitly about the book of Revelation and not the New Testament. If this is not the fundamental reason Sullivan thinks Toland argues that Christianity is an instance of natural religion, it at least fuels his faulty reading. He is also convinced that Toland taught that we can only accept clear and distinct ideas in *CNM* and that regarding the Bible this "precludes any discoveries."[16] In other words, revelation is subordinate to unassisted, natural reason or vulgar reason; or, if it is not thought at least probable on the consideration of purely natural sources of information, an alleged divinely revealed proposition is to be rejected.

The second scholar that can be placed in this group with Sullivan is Frederick C. Beiser. He does not simply echo Sullivan's claims, however. For instance, he portrays Toland in a slightly different way. He thinks that Toland has esoterically merged his pantheism with his earlier Christianity. Thus, according to Beiser, while maintaining both in his esoteric or true doctrine, Toland only incorporates his Christian thoughts exoterically.[17] In response to those who might object to this notion due to some materialistic points that appear in *CNM*, Beiser concludes that these are occasional slips of the pen where his esoteric materialism inadvertently comes out.[18] There are other epistemological claims that Beiser makes regarding *CNM* that are problematic. As chapter 2 shows, Beiser and Sullivan do not grasp what Toland and Locke mean by the terms clear and distinct ideas or how they incorporate them into their respective epistemologies. Furthermore, Beiser maintains that Toland is advocating a verifiability criterion for propositions in addition to Toland's insistence that we should not (or cannot) assent to anything but clear and distinct ideas (clear and distinct ideas understood by Beiser vaguely as being non-mysterious ideas). That is, according to Beiser, unless experience can verify what an alleged revelation is stating, we

---

opaque to all at its publishing (124). He affirms, however, *CNM*'s critical appropriation of the *Essay* (76).

15. Ibid., 125.

16. Sullivan, *John Toland*, 216; cf. 133, 139. Again, it is not clear that he understands how Locke uses clear and distinct ideas either (cf. 223).

17. Beiser, *Sovereignty of Reason*, 129–30.

18. Ibid., 247.

are not to assent to it.[19] Thus, anything we cannot obtain evidence for "in principle" is above reason and should be rejected.[20] But this is only part of Toland's attack, according to Beiser, and it is aimed at above reason propositions. Toland puts forth, Beiser claims, another argument more consistently. This argument is that it is irrational to hold any beliefs of no use to us; and therefore, anything in revelation not dealing with morality—the means of salvation—is irrational to entertain.[21]

The second group of scholars that approach John Toland from the esoteric/exoteric angle believe that Toland has a three-tiered intention in his writing. They do not think that Toland's true intent is to defend supposedly divine revelation that supports moral and civil order like the first group comprised of Sullivan and Beiser. The three-tiered intention is as follows: first, Toland wants *CNM* at face value to read like a Christian work—for instance, defending revelation; second, Toland wants to lead unwary readers to make for themselves the irreligious conclusions against which Toland pretends to be writing; and third, Toland wants to convey to the intelligent, irreligious readers his true beliefs. Hence, these thinkers are tied together with the common theme that John Toland is subversive in a fashion that is not readily apparent (thus these interpreters go beyond Justin Champion's claims that Toland is being openly and intentionally "subversive" against civil and spiritual tyranny—as Toland sees them).[22] These scholars admittedly believe their respective treatments point to Toland being a more brilliant thinker than his two major biographers, Pierre Desmaizeux and Robert E. Sullivan, as well as many others, have allowed.[23] David Berman and Daniel Fouke are two of the most notable scholars in this group.[24] Moreover, it is

19. Ibid., 250–52.

20. Beiser understands *CNM* to admit, occasionally, above reason truths that are above reason only in that one lacks evidence to confirm or deny them. Regardless, they are comprehensible. The above reason propositions that *CNM* officially rejects, according to Beiser, are those that are "incomprehensible" and cannot be empirically verified in principle. It is quite possible Beiser deems something incomprehensible based on the fact it cannot in principle be empirically verified. Ibid., 254. Beiser does express surprise at the radical implications of this criterion. Instead of doubting his reading of Toland, he doubts that Toland wanted to use this verifiability criterion in all applicable situations. Ibid., 252.

21. Ibid., 254–55.

22. Champion, *Republican Learning*, 35, 250–52; cf. Champion, "Enlightened Erudition," 140–141. In this later article, Champion discusses why "Toland's intellectual and religious identity has been, and remains, elusive to historical categorization" (141). Among other things, he outlines Toland's procedures in producing exoteric discourses that undermine (140).

23. Cragg, *Reason and Authority*, 67; Sullivan, *John Toland*, 43.

24. Berman, "Deism, Immortality, and the Art"; Berman, "Disclaimers as Offence

not just these broad conclusions that they share but some commonalities in their published treatments of Toland. Both presuppose Toland is insincerely Christian, a common position since Sullivan, and make assertions amidst scant exegetical work.²⁵

The major challenges that *should* confront their readings are formidable. First, there is Rappaport's implicit undercutting of the esoteric/exoteric reading of *CNM*. Second, while many doubt that Locke was orthodox in his beliefs, despite what he may have thought, few doubt his sincerity of admitting of divinely revealed propositions and related arguments.²⁶ This chapter

---

Mechanisms"; Berman, "Toland, John"; Fouke, *Philosophy and Theology*; cf. Berman, *History of Atheism*.

25. Berman believes Toland engages in the practice of "theological lying." Toland, like others, could not promulgate their unorthodox views overtly because of the oppression from the orthodox (Berman, "Disclaimers as Offence Mechanisms," 256). In one essay, Berman, with scant exegetical evidence to build on, writes: "The dilemma I am posing, in short, is that *either* Blount and Toland were orthodox, rather boring Christians, *or* they were theological liars." He doubts any of his own critics would conclude the first option is feasible and therefore they must agree with the second (Berman, "Disclaimers as Offence Mechanisms," 257). Little clarity and evidence supporting this argument are given by this or the other essay involving Toland. In his other essay, he argues that deists, by definition, minimally reject Christian mysteries and the authority of Scripture; and whenever they use arguments from Scripture or Scripture authoritatively their more intelligent readers would understand that they mean the opposite; and therefore, since Toland is a deist, when he makes conclusions that are dependent on Scripture he means the opposite (Berman, "Deism, Immortality and the Art," 61). What is more, this account given by Berman about Toland's deism is in fact a simplification of Toland's legerdemain. That is, *CNM* is a disguised deism. But Toland knows if one were to follow his reasoning, deism will yield pantheism and pantheism will yield atheism. Regardless as to whether he is right or wrong, Berman does not demonstrate how *CNM* inevitably leads to atheism. That would be very helpful to understand. Furthermore, Berman claims, like others, that Toland actually means the opposite in *CNM* when he says that he is not writing satirically (Berman, "Disclaimers as Offence Mechanisms," 271–72). Fouke, who also believes Toland is a theological liar, notes the difficulties of interpreting such a one: "[H]is [Toland's] philosophy reveals little of what he actually believed. Philosophy and theology, as he practiced them, had very little to do with the positive expression of his beliefs. He practiced philosophy to undermine, rent, and upheave the social basis of power and privilege" (Fouke, *Philosophy and Theology*, 12; cf. 187). Despite similar claims to this effect, ironically both Berman and Fouke are resolute in their assertions of what Toland does believe.

26. Conrad, "Locke's Use of the Bible." He arrives at a tentative conclusion that would not be welcomed in the majority of Locke scholarship: that Locke "is an esoteric writer who may have been attempting to undermine the authority of the Bible while simultaneously appealing to it" (abstract). Cf. Foster, "Bible and Natural Freedom." His earlier claims are in the same vein as Conrad's. Contrast these assessments with Justin Champion's assessment: "As many historians have established beyond doubt, Locke was a pious man, committed to exploring and understanding his Christian faith and belief with absolute rigor and industry." Champion, "Law of Continuity," 122.

will argue that Toland is heavily reliant on Locke. All Toland scholars would agree with that statement to a point. So if it is really Locke's arguments that inevitably lead to irreligious conclusions, might not Locke really be playing the esoteric/exoteric game, too? Or, is it that Toland is so intelligent that he sees holes in Locke's arguments and writes as if the intelligentsia, of which Locke is obviously not a part (coyly stated), will see these errors too? Either way, until they give a thorough exegetical treatment as to what Toland is arguing and how, their readers are left with little more than assertions (many of which the readers are left to check for themselves). Also, it matters little that Toland's contemporaries believed he wrote in a subversive manner—evidence thought to be substantial and relied upon heavily by Berman and Fouke. What is really important is that these scholars actually show how he did so.

Moreover, while most acknowledge that Toland adopts and appropriates Locke's principles to a significant degree but critiques Locke for allowing a category of above reason propositions (as noted above), Ian Leask believes that Toland ought to be read as undermining or subverting Locke not only by clearly denying a category of above reason propositions but because he also subtly does two things in *CNM*: 1) shows that Locke's own *Essay* undercuts Locke's above reason category; and 2) rejects Locke's critique on innate ideas, the foundation of the *Essay*. Leask begins his essay on Toland and Locke by rightly acknowledging that Toland's treatment of ideas, sensation and reflection, intuition and reason, and his musings on the performative self-undoing of 'total' skepticism, and his comments on 'real' and 'nominal' essences are "thoroughly Lockean," albeit not as detailed.[27] The problems with Leask's essay, however, from that point on are many. He takes Toland's rejection of above reason propositions to be an indication that Toland "refuses in any way to subordinate reason."[28] He thinks that the unintelligible mysteries that Toland rejects in *CNM* are all allegedly revealed propositions with novelty.[29] In short, he errs on this particular point by failing to make a distinction between revelation that contains some things that we would most likely not imagine unless told, but once told are imaginable, versus revelation that is true but not imaginable when revealed. The latter is what Toland (and Locke) rejects (recall from chapter 2 that Toland rejects any assertion or assertions, from any source, that cannot be imagined). This oversight made by Leask is also made by most, if not all, Locke and Toland scholarship. This crucial distinction is chapter 3's distinction between above

27. Leask, "Personation and Immanent Undermining," 234.
28. Ibid., 242–43.
29. Ibid., 243–46.

vulgar reason propositions, which are acceptable, and above proper reason propositions, which are unacceptable.

Moreover, Leask also incorrectly claims that Toland's priority of maintaining the supremacy of reason is to such an extent "that he will even declare an identity of faith and knowledge (*CNM*, 3.4.65)."[30] In other words, he like Beiser spots what he thinks is a verifiability criterion in *CNM* where one must reason from her personal experience before assenting to a proposition.[31] This last point was shown to be incorrect in chapter 2 of this book.

This theme of great divergence between Locke and Toland is further reinforced in other ways by Leask. For instance, it is reinforced by Leask's correct understanding of Toland's view of substance—that Toland does not allow things to be considered "above reason" because their real essences cannot be known—but with a wrong application—he thinks this is leveled against Locke's category of above reason. In short, Leask thinks that Toland has shown how Locke's *Essay* undercuts itself and a further way that much of revelation is ultimately to be denied.[32] Contra to Leask on this point and as shown in chapter 3 of this book, Locke never conceived of the above reason category in regards to substance or anything natural, but only supernatural things. As will be shown in this chapter, among other things, the actual critique made by Toland referenced by Leask, which in truth is against someone other than Locke, undercuts nothing in Locke and simply repeats in short order what Locke claims. With this clarification in mind, for anyone to think that Toland's argument that substance is not above reason is against Locke would be to suppose that Toland misunderstands Locke. What is more, Leask thinks that Toland undermines Locke's critique of innate ideas by conflating intuition and innate ideas, thus subtly critiquing Locke's rejection of innate ideas.[33] As was shown in chapter 2, this is patently

---

30. Ibid., 245.

31. Ibid., 245; Beiser, *Sovereignty of Reason*, 251, 254. Again, Beiser writes of Toland's verifiability criterion negating things that are "in principle" not empirically verifiable (254). For instance, he writes, "What we cannot verify in any possible experience is meaningless and therefore unbelievable" (251). Leask is less specific, but his evidence for such a criterion is that Toland claims faith is knowledge (245). Chapter 2 demonstrates Leask, Beiser, and Sullivan misunderstand what Toland was intending to convey when identifying faith and knowledge.

32. Leask, "Personation and Immanent Undermining," 250–52.

33. Ibid., 254. Leask writes: "... the founding principle of that philosophy [*Essay*] is never employed, either directly or indirectly, and is neither adumbrated or discussed; it is a kind of void or hole that is, paradoxically, all the more present in its absence. We might even say that the entirety of CNM is dominated by this absence—an absence that takes on extra significance when we consider the extent to which the direct engagement with Locke shapes so much else in CNM."

false. That Leask denies that Toland simply presupposes Locke's critique of innate ideas is due in part to the misinterpretations Leask has made on the earlier aforementioned points.[34] Finally, Leask claims that *CNM* "deserves to be treated as a work of philosophical significance" because Toland smartly undermines Locke with Locke's own *Essay* or because of his subtle divergence. This is incorrect. *CNM*, in truth, deserves to be treated as a work of philosophical significance because Toland seems to be a scholar of note who grasps Locke's epistemology.

On another issue, scholars typically believe that Toland does not believe in the occurrence of supernatural miracles. This is typically thought to be the case because of his esoteric naturalism (pantheistic materialism) or because some think that *CNM* actually argues against them. The latter reading is typically held by those who think *CNM* is a thorough-going deistic work. Those who think that Toland rejects miracles because he is a deist or pantheist often find support for their interpretations in their concurrent misunderstandings of what "mysteries," which *CNM* rejects, are.[35]

Another important issue that deals with the epistemologies of Locke and Toland is John C. Higgins-Biddle's hypothesis that Locke wrote *ROC* after seeing a draft of *CNM* because *CNM*, being deistic and using Lockean epistemology, would make Locke and his *Essay* appear deistic. This hypothesis was then incorporated into Sullivan's biography on Toland and has been treated as fact ever since.[36] The implication of this chapter for Higgins-Biddle's hypothesis is this: What happens to this hypothesis when it becomes evident *CNM* is not a thorough-going deistic work but affirms past supernatural miracles and divine revelation, while denying only current claims? Locke himself seemed somewhat suspicious of present-day claims of revelation and miracles in the *Essay* (IV.xviii.6) and *ROC*.[37]

---

34. Ibid., 254–55.

35. Beiser is an interesting example. Beiser, *Sovereignty of Reason*, 226, 247–48. Beiser thinks Toland trips himself up when he tries to write with orthodox content from a naturalistic frame of reference. He believes Toland vacillates on whether or not "miracles" are supernatural. Beiser also writes: "If miracles really are supernatural events, then there will be mysteries in Christianity after all" (248). Taylor, *Secular Age*, 223–24, 231. Taylor believes that Toland's rejection of mystery entails the dismissal of miracles.

36. Biddle, "Locke's Critique of Innate Principles"; Higgins-Biddle, introduction to *The Reasonableness of Christianity*, xxxiff; Sullivan, *John Toland*, 6; Fouke, *Philosophy and Theology*, 34; Leask, "Personation and Immanent Undermining," 245–46.

37. Locke, *ROC*, 161.

PART II: PRELIMINARIES

Before exploring reason, faith, and revelation in Toland and a concurrent point-for-point comparison with Locke, this section will cover preliminary concepts in Toland that are foundational to the discussion. The topics that will be covered here are, as in chapter 3's "Preliminaries" part, the following: knowledge, judgment, and assent. This part will answer the following two questions for each foundational concept: 1) What is it?; and 2) How does it compare to the analogue notion in Locke? Chapter 2 already compared Locke and Toland on other foundational epistemological concepts, namely, ideas, knowledge (sorts or resultant senses and degrees and the corresponding methods), and certainty. The upshot was that *CNM's* teaching on those foundational concepts and their associated distinctions was shown to be different from the *Essay's* corresponding treatment only on account of the former being less detailed and occasionally employing different terminology. This part will show that the same description applies to *CNM's* and the *Essay's* treatments of the aforementioned targeted concepts.

While Toland makes comments on judgment (and the concomitant notion of probability) now and then in *CNM*, he does designate two very brief chapters to the discussion of the concept in section I, the first entitled, "Of the Means of Information," and the next, "Of the Ground of Perswasion." Starting with the subject matter of the first chapter, means of information, he discusses the sources that inform our minds of the knowledge that we comprehend. Again, sometimes when Toland uses "knowledge," as in these chapters, he does not necessarily mean intuition or demonstration, but rather the mind's comprehension of ideas: something akin to Locke's identity and diversity sense of the term knowledge, or simply perception. In fact, Toland's definition of the means of information reflects that notion of knowledge: "*those Ways whereby any thing comes barely to our Knowledge, without necessarily commanding our Assent*" (16). In other words, some proposition can be introduced into our mind such that we perceive it—and thus have knowledge of it similar to the identity and diversity sense of the term—but that does not mean we will believe it. The means of information are experience and authority, but further distinctions can be made within these two. For instance, there is external experience or experience with external objects (sensation) and internal experience that help "us to the Ideas of the Operations of our own Minds" (16), which Locke calls reflection. These two, external experience or sensation and internal experience or internal awareness, are together "the common Stock of all our Knowledg; nor can we possibly have Ideas any other way without new Organs or Faculties" (16–17). In other words, all of our simple and distinct ideas, the "common

Stock" of our complex ideas that we have the ability to perceive, come from sensation and reflection in our confrontation with external, complex objects and a reflection on those experiences as discussed above.[38]

And just as the first means of information, experience, can be broken into two sorts so is authority broken into two sorts: human and divine. By human authority, Toland does not necessarily mean an expert in a certain field but rather either that or an everyday witness or testifier to any alleged fact (17). By divine authority, he means "divine revelation," and makes no other associated distinctions or qualifications (18).

While this part, at this point, will still concentrate on the chapters, "Of the Means of Information" and "Of the Grounds of Perswasion," it will be forced to go beyond them. Toland has some important thoughts in these chapters still. For instance, within these chapters he discusses the basis of our assent, which will be explained shortly, and he, like Locke, calls anything short of knowledge probability (15). And while our own experience speaks for itself, Toland does lay down rules regarding the heeding of authority. He explores assent to propositions specifically from human authority in these chapters and introduces assent to propositions of divine authority there too, but then refers the reader to section II, chapter 2, for a more thorough treatment of the topic (18). There he also gives additional thought to assent regarding issues involving human authority.

Regarding human authority, Toland offers a few basic principles that govern our assent. Toland writes:

> *all possible Matters of Fact, duly attested by coevous Persons as known to them, and successively related by others to different Times, Nations, or Interests, who could neither be impos'd upon themselves, nor be justly suspected of combining together to deceive others, ought to be receiv'd by us for as certain and indubitable as*

---

38. Beiser, *Sovereignty of Reason*, 251. It is precisely at this point in Toland's discussion that Beiser erroneously finds support for his idea that Toland promulgates a verifiability criterion for assent. Beiser notices that Toland says that "simple and distinct Ideas" are the "sole Matter and Foundation of all our *Reasoning*" (*CNM* 11-12). And he realizes that all of our ideas are derived from Toland's "experience" (*CNM* 16-17). Beiser wrongly concludes that simple and distinct ideas, which just means simple ideas in Locke's economy, mean clear and distinct ideas. So Beiser thinks that clear and distinct ideas are the sole matter and foundation of our reasoning and that anything that we assent to must be derived from our experience, which is similar to Stillingfleet's reading of *CNM*. He thus reasons that Toland made both clear and distinct ideas and verifiability two characteristics necessary for assent. He is wrong on both counts. Simple and distinct ideas are not identical to the category of clear and distinct ideas and it is simple and distinct ideas that must be derived from experience. In chapter 2 of this book Beiser was shown to be incorrect but from a different angle.

> *if we had seen them with our own Eyes, or heard them with our own Ears* (17).

When all of these rules concur, a matter of fact is to be *taken* for a demonstration, but, if not, it is to be taken as uncertain or perhaps probable (17–18). Toland does not explicitly give further degrees of surety of assent as Locke does, but does, like the latter, admit that in matters of "common Practice" we must "sometimes admit *Probability* to supply the Defect of *Demonstration*" (21).

There is another principle, however, that we must follow in governing our assent in every situation involving testimonies: evidence. "This infallible Rule, or Ground of all right *Perswasion*, is *Evidence*; and it consists *in the exact Conformity of our Ideas or Thoughts with their Objects, or the Things we think upon*. For as we have only Ideas in us, and not the Things themselves, 'tis by those we must form a Judgment of these" (18–19). Furthermore, "Ideas therefore being Representative Beings, their Evidence naturally consists in the Property they have of truly representing their Objects" (19). What he means in these passages, as is made clearer in *CNM*'s following paragraphs, is that we must correctly comprehend that to which we are considering assenting. Correctly comprehending something, such as the existence of a thing or other such proposition, entails having a *correct* collection and combination of simple ideas that represent the thing involved. Thus, the complex idea does not contain an inherent contradiction; a complex idea that contains a contradiction cannot be perceived. We would not believe anyone who told us that a particular ball was at the same time a black ball and a white ball (29), or that he saw a cane without two ends. In the latter case "I neither should nor could believe him; because this Relation plainly contradicts the Idea of a Cane." A wooden cane stuck into the ground that sprouts sprigs and branches is a proposition that could be believed upon the veracity of the testifier, however (39). According to Toland, "It is impossible for us to err as long as we take *Evidence* for our Guide; and we never mistake, but when we wander from it by abusing our *Liberty*, in *denying of any thing which belongs to it*, or *attributing to it what we do not see in its Idea*. This is the primary and universal Origin of all our *Errors*" (21). In fact, Toland claims that while we have no power to dissent from a self-evident proposition, we do have the power of "*suspending our Judgments about whatever is uncertain, and of never assenting but to clear Perceptions*" (22). Thus, we cannot rightly assent to something that we cannot comprehend or envision. So, if something about a complex idea is said to be true of the thing represented and believed to exist, but that something about that thing is not able to be perceived or is obscure at best, then we cannot rightly believe that

that something belongs to the thing that we believe exists. If this principle of requiring perceptibility of all propositions to which we consider assenting is maintained, we will have much better success than otherwise in rightly precipitating our assent regarding propositions pertaining to human authority, according to Toland. When we err it is our own fault (23–24). In short, the ground of persuasion is the evidence of a proposition, which is its capacity to be correctly represented, including the ideas from which it is built, in our minds. Moreover, this requirement of evidence or Toland's ground of persuasion includes Locke's rule that we cannot assent to anything contrary to knowledge, especially in the mentally irreconcilable sense.

After treating assent in matters concerning human authority, Toland turns to divine authority. He notes that he calls revelation a means of information because one must make sure it is such before assenting to the revealed proposition(s). Here Toland applies the ground of persuasion to instances of alleged divine revelation: "For *besides the infallible Testimony of the Revelation from all requisite Circumstances, we must see in its Subject the indisputable Characters of DIVINE WISDOM and SOUND REASON*; which are the only Marks we have to distinguish the Oracles and Will of God, from the Impostures and Traditions of Men" (41–42). Again, that is, the thing proposed must not involve a contradiction or certain falsehood *and* must be comprehensible to be considered for assent. "*Whoever reveals any thing*, that is, whoever tells us something we did not know before, *his Words must be intelligible, and the Matter possible*" (42). It is possible and intelligible that God formed man out of the earth and therefore believable (43), but it is not possible that God can create a something called a round square because a contradiction is nothing (39–40). We are, however, to also require a miracle for proof that God is the one who reveals the proposition or propositions. So the ground of persuasion is only part of accepting a revelation as such. In the Old Testament, if the prophet's prophecy did not come to pass he did not speak for God. In the New Testament, Mary did not determine that the angel spoke for God until she visited her aged cousin Elizabeth whom the angel told Mary was pregnant. Nevertheless, the miracle is not a guarantee alone. If a prophet does miracles while trying to have you believe in multiple Gods, part of his message is certainly false (and irreconcilable) and so one cannot assent to his propositions as directed in Deuteronomy 13:1–3 (43–44).[39] In short, evidence, as qualified above, and miracles mark divine revelation.

39. Beiser, *The Sovereignty of Reason*, 251; Sullivan, *John Toland*, 216; Leask, "Personation and Immanent Undermining," 244–45. This is yet another defeater of the notion held by Beiser and Leask that Toland required a verifiability criterion for assent and Sullivan's notion that Toland's epistemology "precluded any discoveries" in

Thus, when it comes to judgment and assent, *CNM* comports with the *Essay*. Both relegate uncertain issues to the realm of probability. While Locke discusses in detail the grounding of probabilities and the way in which they help develop varying degrees of conviction, Toland does not; but he does delineate the minimum requirements we need to assent to a proposition and the need of assenting in matters of common practice. It appears as though Toland presumes the reader has a basic grasp on how probability is grounded and how it guides our assent to varying degrees of surety. Regarding propositions coming from human testimony and allegedly divine sources, for Toland, all propositions must be perceivable and not inherently contradictory or certainly false. This is Locke's rule that we cannot believe anything that is contrary to knowledge both in the sense of being contrary to certain truths or inherently contradictory and the sense of being mentally irreconcilable or summarily un-envisionable. And like Locke, Toland requires a miracle as an external mark that a divinely revealed proposition is such. Although this chapter is several sections away from fully outlining Toland's treatment of revelation and reason, so far in Toland, as was found in Locke, an external mark of revelation has to do with miracles and internal marks are that the proposition is reconcilable with certain truths and logic and is itself representatively reconcilable or envisionable.

There are still more similarities between Locke and Toland on the issues of knowledge and judgment. It appears that Toland, like Locke, considers knowledge and judgment as distinct faculties and closely associates or identifies "faculties" and "powers." In an early section of *CNM*, Toland writes:

> Every one experiences in himself a Power or Faculty of forming various Ideas or Perceptions of Things: Of affirming or denying, according as he sees them to agree or disagree: And so of loving and desiring what seems good unto him; and of hating and avoiding what he thinks evil. The right Use of all these Faculties is what we call Common Sense (9).

In this quotation it is clear that he is referring to knowledge as a faculty among other faculties. And it is obvious that faculty and power are interchangeable for Toland. But, one question is, where does his description of the faculty of knowledge end? Although not completely clear, the "And so" after the second colon is likely to be taken as a transition moving onto the operations of other faculties building on what knowledge does. The other

---

religion. As demonstrated in chapter 2 of this book and here in this chapter there is no such criterion. One must simply be able to find the thing claimed intelligible and not certainly false.

operations he speaks of—loving and desiring and hating and avoiding—are two in which the ability to judge would play a part. Regardless, he does call knowledge a faculty or power as does Locke.

Elsewhere it is clearer that Toland understands judgment to be a faculty as well. In discussing propositions that are not self-evident he writes:

> But *God* the wise Creator of all . . . who has enabl'd us to perceive Things, and form Judgments of them, has also endu'd us with the Power of *suspending our Judgments about whatever is uncertain, and of never assenting but to clear Perceptions*. He is so far from putting us upon any Necessity of erring, that as he has thus privileg'd us on the one hand with a Faculty of guarding ourselves against Prepossession, or Precipitation, by *placing our Liberty only in what is indifferent, or dubious and obscure* (22).

As seen in this quote from *CNM*, as in the one preceding it, there is a close association or identification of the terms power and faculty. In this instance, the power that makes possible the suspension of judgment is also called a faculty. Again, this is precisely what Locke does: he uses the terms "faculties" and "powers" interchangeably. Locke is wary of talking of faculties as agents because of the conceptual mischief it causes, even though he himself does so from time to time (II.xxi.20). Apparently Toland follows Locke and, therefore, any abilities we can speak of can be referred to as faculties or powers. Therefore, the ability to "form Judgments" of the things we perceive is also a faculty as it is in Locke and this power of judgment can be suspended as is also the case in Locke. Toland even uses the same occasional personification that Locke does when he speaks of judgment: "I am pretty sure *he pretends in vain to convince the Judgment, who explains not the Nature of the Thing*" (36).

In summary, although *CNM*'s treatments of knowledge, judgment, and assent are less detailed than the *Essay* and both works occasionally use different terminology, they comport conceptually with one another. Toland does not conceptually contradict the *Essay* in any way. In fact, the lack of detail in explanation of concepts in *CNM* and the abundant similarities of both works point to a heavy dependence of *CNM* on the *Essay* regarding ideas, knowledge, and judgment. Toland's aforementioned veiled reference to Locke in discussing adequate and inadequate ideas is further evidence that dependence is the case.

PART III: REASON

As might be expected by one familiar with *CNM*, much of the information on Toland's understanding of reason comes from section 1 entitled, "Of Reason." That section consists of the following chapters: "What Reason Is Not," "Wherein Reason Consists," "Of the Means of Information," and "Of the Ground of Perswasion." There are still aspects of reason, however, that can be learned from the other two sections of *CNM*.

Interestingly enough, Toland begins his treatment of reason as Locke does. Both begin their respective treatments of reason acknowledging that there are multiple considerations of the term circulating in the philosophical literature and conversations (8–9). In Toland's introduction of the notion, he notes that the soul should not be identified with reason, but he finds it harmless to understand reason as "the Soul acting in a certain and peculiar Manner" (8–9).

More importantly, Toland's own description of reason is very similar to Locke's. For one, Toland does not consider the mind's passive reception of ideas from the basic senses and from the awareness or conscious observation of the mental operations (external and internal experience) as "strictly *Reason*" (10). He also, like Locke, conceives of reason as a faculty or power. This is evident from the beginning of his discourse on reason in the first chapter of section 1. There Toland calls reason "that whereby they define and explain all other things" (8). In other words, reason is an ability or power. In section 1's second chapter, "Wherein Reason Consists," a few similarities between Locke's and Toland's notions of reason come to the fore as well. There, Toland, like Locke, associates reason and demonstration. He writes that the method of knowledge known as demonstration can be called reason (14). Therefore, he defines reason there as, "*That Faculty of the Soul which discovers the Certainty of any thing dubious or obscure, by comparing it with something evidently known*" (14). In this same chapter, the reader also learns that the simple and distinct ideas are not technically reason even though they are used by it, just as in Locke. And just like Locke, Toland does not relegate the power or faculty of reason to demonstration alone. In *CNM*'s next chapter, "Of the Means of Information," he begins with the following: "BUT besides these Properties of *Reason* which we have explain'd, we are yet most carefully to distinguish in it *the Means of Information*, from *the Ground of Perswasion*: for the Neglect of this easy Distinction has thrown Men into infinite Mistakes, as I shall prove before I have done" (16). It appears as though his claim that the means of information and grounds of persuasion are in reason means that reason has something to do with assent. This relationship is pushed beyond any doubt when later Toland describes reason as "*that Faculty every one has of judging of his Ideas according to their Agreement or Disagreement, and so of loving what seems good unto him, and hating what he thinks evil: Reason*, I say, in this Sense is whole and entire in every one whose Organs are not accidentally indispos'd" (56–57). In the context of this quotation, Toland is pondering reason's consideration of divine truths or revelation, which means that he is considering areas of probability where judgment is required. Thus, reason must somehow take part in judging areas where certainty cannot be had, similar to the *Essay's* position. And, without a doubt, reason must undertake the weighing and considering of probabilities.[40]

What is even more interesting is that *CNM* and the *Essay* have similar answers as to whether all the faculties are reason! Locke treats reason at least as a faculty or group of faculties and he speaks of reason as being all the mental faculties when the mind is acting reasonably—that is, the mind acts reasonably when it heeds reason's advice based on its disquisitions and reason is employed to the degree of examinational thoroughness appropriate for the circumstance (and thus importance of the issue at hand). In what follows, this portion of this chapter of the book will show that Toland maintains the same position.

Toland similarly thinks of reason at least as a faculty or faculties and calls the right "Use" of all of the faculties "*Reason* in general." It has already been made evident that Toland conceives of reason as a faculty or group of faculties. That much can be gleaned from our discussion of reason above. Toland refers to the right use of all of our faculties in the following passage:

> Every one experiences in himself a Power or Faculty of forming various Ideas or Perceptions of Things: Of affirming or denying, according as he sees them to agree or disagree: And so of loving and desiring what seems good unto him; and of hating and avoiding what he thinks evil. The right Use of all these Faculties is what we call Common Sense, or Reason in general (9).

This definition appears to be rather all-encompassing of the mind even though the list of powers named is brief. That is, the quote includes a number of faculties by description, like perception, knowledge, and judgment, and describes the ultimate ends toward which the mind works, loving and desiring and hating and avoiding.

---

40. Toland never explicitly says that reason weighs probabilities, but one must infer it. If not everything can be known by reason, reason must have recourse to probabilities. This is again another example where Toland is simply assuming one understands some basic premises of the *Essay*.

Later on in *CNM*, Toland, however, makes it quite clear that the right use of the faculties is not constant and at those times we cannot be considered reasonable. He writes, "But if by *Reason* be understood a constant right Use of these Faculties, *viz. If a Man never judges but according to clear Perceptions, desires nothing but what is truly good for him, nor avoids but what is certainly evil*: Then, I confess it is extreamly *corrupt*" (57). We are prone to wrong conceptions and erroneous judgments, and we covet what "flatters our Senses, without distinguishing noxious from innocent Pleasures," and thoughtlessly give into inclinations and appetites (57). These proceedings are actually contrary to reason (58). He even notes those who judge contrary to their knowledge as Locke does (26–27). But we are under no necessity of making intellectual, moral, and spiritual errors because "There is no Defect in our Understandings but those of our own Creation" (58). In short, we are not always reasonable and deserving of that attribute.

That Toland like Locke makes a distinction between the sum total of mental faculties considered as reason and a particular faculty called reason is evident from other pages within *CNM*. The above description of reason as it stands so far, however, still leaves open the possibility of reason being simply the sum-total of all the mental faculties and deserving only of the name reason when operating correctly. There are a few reasons that this is not the case. Most importantly, Toland calls the faculty of reason and our associated liberty, which corresponds to our ability to suspend our judgment, perfect (60, 62). Thus, the perfect faculty or power does not make errors, something else does. So he must be considering reason in a second and more limited sense. As further support for this, Toland writes of people employing their reasoning faculties: "Were our reasoning Faculties imperfect, or we not capable to employ them rightly, there could be no Possibility of our understanding of one another in Millions of things, where the stock of our Ideas should prove unavoidably equal, or our Capacities different" (59). Thus, for Toland, like Locke, reason is a power among other powers and consists of some of them. And as a mere power, it only does anything in so far as it is employed by the mind or agent. So, in conclusion, Toland, like Locke, conceives of reason as a particular power or faculty, but all of the natural faculties are considered reason when the mind follows the disquisitions of that power or, in other words, acts reasonably.

What is more, that Toland, like Locke, believes not every issue deserves the same attention is also evident in *CNM*. In other words, acting reasonably entails not only the mind following the conclusions wrought from the employment of reason, but also giving the examinational thoroughness required by the circumstance and importance of the issue at hand. Early in *CNM* it appears as though Toland disapproves of probability: "When I have arriv'd at *Knowledg*, I enjoy all the Satisfaction that attends it; where I have only *Probability*, there I suspend my Judgment, or, if it be worth the Pains, I search after Certainty" (15). So Toland notes that some issues are worthy of the employment of our powers and energies in search of certainty, while it appears every other issue where probability is to be had ought to be suspended. Toland reasonably tempers this, however, and shows the aforementioned quote to be an overstatement. For instance, he notes that there are some important issues about which we cannot have certainty and some issues, like day-to-day living, where requirements of certainty would prove impractical (21).

So in light of all of this evidence, it is apparent that Toland has closely read and agreed with Locke's treatment of reason. They both understand reason to be a power. But they both also see that the mind can be called reason when it acts reasonably. And they both have the same notion of acting reasonably: heeding the disquisitions of reason and employing the power of reason to the examinational thoroughness required by the circumstance and importance of the issue at hand.

There are still other aspects of Toland's discussion of reason that are much like Locke's, some to which I have already alluded. First, Toland discusses our ability to suspend judgment (21–22). Second, he also treats liberty and reason, among others, as distinct powers. They are obviously related but there are no physical or metaphysical discussions as to their connections. There are mere assertions. This points to a third commonality between *CNM* and the *Essay*. Both are examples of experimental philosophy. This way of thinking is primarily descriptive of the way we find ourselves working. Great attention is given to descriptions of mental operations at our best, and thus in that way prescriptive. There is no attempt by either Locke or Toland to untangle the metaphysical discussions of free will, but simply assert that liberty is one power we have. In fact, Toland does not refer to his philosophy as a system of philosophy, or equally a "*Hypothesis*" (4–5, 15, 122–123). Toland's philosophy in *CNM*, like Locke's, is highly descriptive and generally avoids attempts to explain speculative things.

In summary, this section has shown a few very important points of commonality Toland holds with Locke pertaining to reason. In both, reason is the faculty or power employed to achieve demonstrative knowledge and probability when used by the mind. And all of the natural faculties can be considered reason, for all intents and purposes, when the mind acts reasonably—reasonably in the sense that the mind is dictated by its employment of reason and in the sense that the degree of reason's employment corresponds to the appropriate thoroughness that the circumstance warrants. Toland is also engaged in Locke's brand of experimental philosophy. Moreover,

Toland's focused treatment of reason in *CNM* is considerably shorter than that of the *Essay*.

PART IV: REASON AND FAITH

Toland's treatment of faith clearly connects it to reason and makes the former subordinate to the latter. *CNM*'s descriptions of faith and assent in the following two passages are reminiscent of Locke's teaching on proper faith or assent in general:

> The word [Faith as used by many in a variety of ways] imports *Belief* or *Perswasion*, as when we give Credit to any thing which is told us by God or Man; whence *Faith* is properly divided into *Human* and *Divine*. Again, *Divine Faith* is either when God speaks to us immediately himself, or when we acquiesce in the Words or Writings of those to whom we believe he has spoken (127).

> And seeing the Case stands really thus, all *Faith* or Perswasion must necessarily consist of two Parts, *Knowledg* and *Assent*. 'Tis the last indeed that constitutes the formal Act of *Faith*, but not without the Evidence of the first (128).

Thus, Toland, like Locke, essentially identifies all the words he uses for assent: persuasion, faith, and belief. And Toland is clear that one cannot assent to that which one does not conceive.[41] Also, there is no shifting when it comes to divine faith. Faith in divine matters is still faith. Again, this broad understanding of faith and assent corresponds to Locke's consideration of faith that chapter 3 of this book called proper faith. Furthermore, considering the discussion of reason above and the fact that faith is just assent in general, Toland's faith is therefore rightly governed by the mind's employment of reason to the uncertain issues being proposed to the mind. For instance, he writes, "All *Faith* now in the World is of this last sort, and by consequence entirely built upon *Ratiocination*" (127). Reason is to be used to sift through the matter and guide the mind in its judgments. If the mind does not heed

---

41. In a supporting passage, Toland also writes of only being able truly to assent to that which is conceived and an identification of concepts known as implicit faith and verbal assent: "A Man may give his verbal Assent to he knows not what, out of *Fear, Superstition, Indifference, Interest,* and the like feeble and unfair Motives: but as long as he conceives not what he believes, he cannot sincerely acquiesce in it, and remains depriv'd of all solid Satisfaction. He is constantly perplex'd with Scruples not to be remov'd by his *implicite Faith*; and so is ready to be shaken, and *carry'd away with every wind of Doctrine*" (36).

reason's recommendation or if the mind over- or under-employs its reason based on the gravity of the circumstance and issue at hand, then the mind's assent or faith will be irrational or unreasonable in one or more senses.[42]

So far this entire description of faith and its relationship to reason is indicative of Locke's understanding of the relationship between proper faith and proper reason. That is, Toland is not conceiving of reason operating in two possible offices—one that incorporates revelation, reason's proper office, and one that does not, reason's vulgar office—and he is not conceiving of two corresponding understandings of the term faith. In short, he is mirroring only Locke's proper senses of reason and faith. Thus it seems that John Toland is not desirous of conceding to common, erroneous ways of speaking to any degree. His final sentence of CNM speaks to this attitude: "I'm therefore for giving no Quarter to ERROR under any pretence; and will be sure, where-ever I have Ability or Opportunity, to expose it in its true Colours, without rendring my Labour ineffectual, by weakly mincing or softning of any thing" (174).

As in the preceding chapter, the next two sections will continue to build on the interaction of faith and reason by focusing on reason and revelation.

PART V: "ABOVE REASON" PROPOSITIONS

Toland is best known for his critique of those, Locke included, who accept "above reason" propositions. This is consistently seen as Toland's greatest point of departure from Locke, whose foundational epistemological principles Toland is said to employ. But as shown in the previous chapter, Locke ponders a concessionary contradistinction, the notions of vulgar reason and vulgar faith, which allows him to write of propositions being above (vulgar) reason. If propositions were to be categorized according to Locke's proper scope of reason employed throughout the *Essay* (up until IV.xviii), one would presumably categorize propositions according to (proper) reason and contrary to (proper) reason. He does not accept propositions above

---

42. It is possible that Toland, while expressly admitting that faith is assent, prefers to use faith with respect to belief in human and divine revelation and not with respect to the other means of information: our experience. This would be difficult to prove since CNM is focused primarily on divine authority matters. In other words, while faith is often used in the context of divine and human authority matters, there is comparatively little space given to the discussion of probability and assent derived from personal experience. Whatever the case may be—whether or not Toland would restrict faith to issues of divine and human authority and use only assent in the most general sense—the epistemological framework is unaffected and the epistemological agreement between CNM and the *Essay* goes undiminished.

(proper) reason as a legitimate category. That is the reason that Locke always uses summarily intelligible or comprehensible examples when he mentions the concessionary categorization of propositions, above (vulgar) reason. Since Toland does not concede to making room for vulgar conceptions of reason and faith it should be no surprise that he is likewise not too interested in making accommodations for an above reason category. In what follows we will explore what Toland does say about above reason propositions and the implications of his teaching.

Toland is adamant that nothing in the Gospel is contrary to reason or above reason. The thesis of CNM is, "that *there is nothing in the Gospel contrary to Reason, nor above it; and that no Christian doctrine can be properly call'd a Mystery*" (6). In fact, while the first of three sections of CNM is about reason, the next two sections are entitled "That the Doctrines of the Gospel are not contrary to Reason" and "That there is nothing *Mysterious*, or above Reason in the Gospel," respectively (xxxii). So, there is plenty said explicitly about propositions in CNM that allows a thorough comparison on the topic with the *Essay* and much that can be easily inferred from the comparison. In fact, CNM's discourse on the categorization of propositions is the only treatment of a major topic longer than the corresponding treatment in the *Essay*.

So, after his treatment of what reason is, he goes on to explain that nothing in the gospel is contrary to reason. He gives the following definition of contrary to reason propositions that is similar to Locke's: "that *what is evidently repugnant to clear and distinct Ideas, or to our common Notions, is contrary to Reason*" (25). Locke's definition of contrary to reason propositions is: "*Contrary to Reason* are such Propositions, as are inconsistent with, or irreconcilable to our clear and distinct *Ideas*" (IV.xvii.23). So, at least in both Toland and Locke, the propositions that are categorized as contrary to reason are propositions that assert claims that are contrary to knowledge in the mentally representative or mentally reconcilable sense. Or, in other words, they cannot be the subject of further reasoning. A notable difference between the two definitions is that Toland includes the reference to "*common Notions*" in his definition. While that is at least an obvious verbal difference it does not appear to result in a conceptual difference. It is clear that by "notions" he means ideas because he makes the two terms interchangeable in a few locations (14–15, 81). And by "common notions" he means our clear and distinct ideas that humans are commonly capable of forming.[43] This is evident by Toland's sarcastically speaking of doctrines contrary to common notions as "supra-intellectual Truths" (30; cf. 79, 118,

---

43. Those with faculty related injuries or impairments, especially those from birth, will not have the same set of simple ideas as is commonly held. For instance, a man born blind does not have the simple ideas of the variety of colors.

128–29) and his seriously claiming that "we cannot in this World know any thing but by our common Notions" (31).[44] So both Locke and Toland agree that anything that is summarily unenvisionble is to be rejected as being contrary to reason.

Further evidence for this reading of Toland is given in the same section. In his discussion of the aforementioned definition of contrary to reason he chides Christians for claiming "that tho the Doctrins of the latter cannot in themselves be contradictory to the Principles of the former [reason]; yet, that according to our Conceptions of them, *they may seem directly to clash*." He subsequently and disapprovingly notes what to him is bad reasoning: "tho we cannot reconcile them by reason of our corrupt and limited Understandings; yet that from the Authority of *Divine Revelation*, we are bound to believe and acquiesce in them" (25). He appears to be more concerned with whether or not something is summarily picture-able as opposed to whether or not it is definitively false or contradictory.[45] He does later acknowledge in the same section, however, that anything that we desire, believe, or do that is contrary to the right use of our mental faculties is contrary to reason (57–58). Nonetheless, his focus is primarily on the epistemological need of being able to envision doctrines or propositions before one can believe them.

This resultant principle that a proposition must be conceivable to be reasonable has some relationship with the ground of persuasion that is woven throughout *CNM* and explained in the "Preliminaries" section of this chapter. Just because one cannot quickly conceive of a certain doctrine or proposition does not mean, however, that it is contrary to reason. He believes that God "has endu'd us with the Power of *suspending our Judgments about whatever is uncertain, and of never assenting but to clear Perceptions*"

---

44. The prudence of Toland's appropriation of the term "common notions," one evidently used by those with whom Toland disagrees (cf. Locke, *Essay* I.ii.1), and his very different employment of the term is questionable. Such is liable to confuse the unwary reader. And while such a move might be considered "ridicule" of his interlocutors, from a Lockean epistemological standpoint, he is not without warrant in using common notions in this way.

45. Toland and Locke appear to group together propositions that are contrary to knowledge in the certainly false sense (contrary to known truths or inherently contradictory) with propositions that are contrary to knowledge in the summarily unenvisionable or mentally irreconcilable sense that are not definitively contrary to knowledge in the former sense. Many would be adamantly against such a pairing. As previously noted, John Norris taught that contrary to reason things should not be considered above reason in the incomprehensibility or mentally irreconcilable sense because the falsity of his category of contrary to reason propositions or doctrines can be pictured. He fought against the association of what to him should be two very different categories. Norris, *Account of Reason and Faith*, 100–136.

(22). Otherwise assent would be implicit and thus insincere (36). But if a proposition is definitively unintelligible or impossible then the proposition would be contrary to reason and if one assented to such a proposition one would be offending the rule of the ground of persuasion. He writes: "*Whoever reveals any thing*, that is, whoever tells us something we did not know before, *his Words must be intelligible, and the Matter possible*. This RULE holds good, let *God* or *Man* be the Revealer" (42). What he means by this is that we only pretend to assent to anything that we cannot so-far conceive or know that is impossible.

It is important to emphasize the point that "possible" in *CNM*, as used above, does not refer to the property of comporting to our typical every day experiences and thus credible upon natural considerations and therefore likely. Rather something that is "possible" is something that does not offend the law of non-contradiction. Toland asserts this clearly in the following passage:

> And that every *Contradiction*, which is a Synonym for *Impossibility*, is *pure nothing*, we have already sufficiently demonstrated. To say, for example, that *a thing is extended and not extended, is round and square at once*, is to say *nothing*; for these Ideas destroy one another, and cannot subsist together in the same Subject. But when we clearly perceive a perfect Agreement and Connection between the Terms of any Proposition, we then conclude it possible because intelligible (40).

So while contradiction and impossibility are synonyms for Toland, it appears that summarily conceivable (or perceivable or intelligible) and possible are *effectively* so. Again, if this were missed one might conclude that Toland would reject some or all of revelation because it asserts things we would not find credible based on purely natural considerations. This is not what Toland is saying. If a person said that he had seen a staff that had no ends, we could not believe him because infinite length is contrary to the idea of a staff. However, if the same person said that he had seen a staff that was in the ground in time sprout sprigs and branches, that is possible (39). Regarding an all-powerful God, it is possible and intelligible that He can immediately freeze a fluid, or that He created the world. Such propositions are not contrary to reason (40–41). But God cannot make a round square (40). In short, "When we say then, *that nothing is impossible with God*, or that he can do all things, we mean whatever is possible in it self, however far above the Power of Creatures to effect" (40).[46] Hence, we are not responsible

---

46. There is a difference between that which is by nature impossible—a round square—and that which is naturally impossible—the rapid formation of man out of

for believing things that are impossible or inherently contradictory. In fact it appears that anything inconceivable, whether definitively contradictory or not, at least *counts* as a contradiction or impossibility. Further evidence for this conflation will be drawn out of Toland's works in what follows (cf. 49, 108, 170–71). What is more, based on the lack of examples that Locke provides throughout the *Essay*, he could be uncharitably read as abiding by this same conflation. So, for Toland, contrary to reason frequently refers to propositions that one definitively cannot conceive of or imagine in his or her mind, and that is to say that they at least count as impossible. Most importantly, impossible does not mean improbable.

Toland also has a lengthy discourse denying that there are any above reason propositions in the gospel in the last section of *CNM*, which is entitled "That There Is Nothing Mysterious, or Above Reason in the Gospel" (66). He makes a very helpful distinction at the outset, defining for the reader what people typically mean when they say something is a mystery or that it is above reason:

> First, It denotes a thing intelligible of it self, but so cover'd by figurative Words, Types and Ceremonies, that *Reason* cannot penetrate the Vail, nor see what is under it till it be remov'd. Secondly, It is made to signify a thing of its own Nature inconceivable, and not to be judg'd of by our ordinary Faculties and Ideas, tho it be never so clearly reveal'd. In both these Senses *to be above Reason* is the same thing with MYSTERY; and, in effect, they are convertible Terms in *Divinity* (66–67).

So above reason can refer to a thing that could be comprehended and represented in the mind if the "Vail" obscuring it were removed. It also can refer to that which we cannot apprehend with our mental faculties although the propositions of which it consists are revealed.

Toland is convinced that neither sense of above reason propositions are found in the New Testament. Regarding the second sense, he says that many, who out of ignorance or passion, desire "to maintain what was first introduc'd by the Craft of Superstition of their Fore-fathers, will have some *Christian Doctrines* to be still *mysterious* in the second Sense of the Word, that is, *inconceivable in themselves, however clearly reveal'd*" (72). In fact, this sense of above reason amounts to Toland's most emphasized sense of contrary to reason: (summarily) unintelligible or incomprehensible. He goes on to use much ink in exposition of Scripture that supports his rejection of the claim that some New Testament doctrines are mysterious or above reason in the first sense of the terms or the veiled sense. He writes:

---

the earth.

> But, slighting so mean Considerations [the claims regarding the other sense of above reason], if I can demonstrate that in the New Testament *Mystery* is always us'd in the first sense of the Word, or that of the *Gentiles, viz.* for *things naturally very intelligible, but so cover'd by figurative Words or Rites, that Reason could not discover them without special Revelation*; and that the Vail is actually taken away; then it will manifestly follow that the Doctrines so reveal'd cannot now be properly call'd *Mysteries*" (73).

So, whenever the term mystery is used in the New Testament it refers to the very first sense of above reason that he refers to: "a thing intelligible of it self, but so cover'd by figurative Words, Types and Ceremonies, that *Reason* cannot penetrate the Vail, nor see what is under it till it be remov'd" (66). But, although the New Testament mentions these mysteries, there are no doctrines now in the New Testament that could be called mysteries.

The outline of his argument that there should be no sense of mystery or above reason applied to the New Testament is worth repeating in part. In chapter 2 of section III, "That Nothing Ought to Be Call'd a Mystery, because We Have Not an Adequate Idea of All Its Properties, Nor Any at All of Its Essence," he argues "That *nothing can be said to be a Mystery, because we have not an adequate Idea of it, or a distinct View of all its Properties at once; for then every thing would be a Mystery*" (74). That is, we have no adequate idea of any substance; and if that were a criterion to call something a mystery, practically everything would be a mystery. Also, something is not mysterious because we do not know all of its properties. Rather "*God has wisely provided we should understand no more of these than are useful and necessary for us*; which is all our present Condition needs" (75–76). In fact we are not to trouble ourselves about what is useless to be known or impossible to know (78). These principles hold true when it comes to doctrines, too. The doctrine need not be adequate or complete to be understood. It simply must be intelligible. For example, we don't know God's true essence but we are made aware of his attributes that are necessary and useful for us (86). In section III's third chapter, "The Signification of the Word Mystery in the New Testament, and the Writings of the Most Antient Christians," he attempts to show that every passage where the term "Mystery" is used ought to be read in one of three ways:

> First, *Mystery* is read for the *Gospel* or the *Christian* Religion in general, as it was a future Dispensation totally hid from the *Gentiles*, and but very imperfectly known to the *Jews*: Secondly, Some particular Doctrines occasionally reveal'd by the *Apostles*

are said to be *manifested Mysteries*, that is, unfolded Secrets. And, Thirdly, *Mystery* is put for any thing vail'd under Parables or Enigmatical Forms of Speech (95).

So, there is nothing unintelligible or inconceivable in itself (cf. 108). Toland argues throughout the chapter that all instances in the Bible that are of the above reason "vail'd" sense are all explained there. Although a more detailed treatment of Toland's categorization of biblical propositions is possible, it will not occupy this chapter any further.

A few things can be said about the comparison of Toland's and Locke's categorization of propositions so far. Propositions that are contrary to reason in *CNM* are the same or similar to those described by Locke in IV.xvii.23. Contrary to reason in both encompasses things that are summarily inconceivable or incomprehensible and things that are inherently contradictory or impossible. For both, only that which is conceivable can be the object of assent. But perhaps more importantly, possible does not refer to conforming to our everyday experience and thus naturally probable. Moreover, anything contrary to certain truths is contrary to reason. Regarding the category of above reason, Toland rejects it. Inadequate and incomplete ideas and everything now in the Bible are not above reason (or contrary to reason) in any sense of the term he treats. As discussed earlier, Locke, if he had listed the category of propositions with proper reason in mind, which appears to be in agreement with Toland's understanding of reason, would also have rejected the above reason category regarding propositions or doctrines that are clearly revealed yet inconceivable (I am not aware if Locke thinks that all veiled mysteries in Scripture were unveiled, however, as Toland does). In short, religious propositions that one might claim are above Locke's proper reason, and thus incomprehensible, would appear to fall into Locke's stated category of contrary to reason propositions. They cannot be reasoned about. Moreover, like Locke, Toland never expressly uses the term according to (proper) reason (the closest he comes is: 8–9, 56–57). But were both thinkers of the mind to approve or defend a categorization scheme of propositions it would be the following: according to reason and contrary to reason. If they were to both use their similar treatments of contrary to reason propositions discussed in their respective works, they would probably draw the same boundaries around the according to reason category. While we know that they have delimited themselves in a manner to two categories, it is not evident that they care to employ them.

Moreover, his defense of comprehensibility in doctrines and the attack on claims that certain doctrines we ought to accept are not comprehensible prevails in the other Toland works, namely those written by him in defense of *CNM*. This is important to show because nearly all think that Toland subordinates revelation to natural probability and some claim that *CNM* is not completely indicative of Toland's true thoughts. In *Apology*, Toland conveys that he is writing in defense of the Christian religion against the atheists and others who attack Christianity for being obscure or contradictory.[47] He explains that in his quote from *CNM*, "*all the Doctrines and Precepts of the New Testament (if it be indeed Divine) must consequently agree with Natural Reason, and our own Ordinary Ideas*," he means that our God-given reason must be able to comprehend what is being said.[48] In *Defence*, when defending his denial that any doctrines in the New Testament are mysterious, he notes that the common opinion concerning mysteries is that they are things revealed that we should know nothing of at all had they not been revealed, but we now know in part. Toland thinks that this type of seeing "*through a Glass darkly*" Christianity of which Paul writes is a "*Vulgar Faith*" not applicable to us who have the complete New Testament. Rather, "we perfectly *know, even as we are known*." He thus opposes the following claims of mystery:

> Some of them we look upon to be of such a Nature, that we are not able in the present state of our Faculties, to conceive beyond such a Degree, and which we expect a further Comprehension of in another state of more Perfection, such as are the Doctrines of the *Trinity, Incarnation, etc.* others there are which are but in part Reveal'd to us, and which we are capable of knowing further in this state, if God had been pleased to give us a clearer and fuller discovery of them, such as are the *Prophecies* contained in the *Revelations*, and other parts of Scripture.

In short, he opposes the notions that there are things revealed in the New Testament that we will better comprehend in the afterlife with new faculties (and in that sense not yet fully revealed or not able to be fully revealed) or are not yet fully revealed though comprehensible if they were. To this erroneous thinking he responds, "That there is nothing in Scripture but what is fully discovered to us, and what we fully comprehend." Basically, he is asserting that something is comprehensible or it is not and it is revealed and unveiled or it is not; and everything in the New Testament is revealed, unveiled, and comprehensible.[49] Finally, in *Vindicius*, he claims inconceivable doctrines or mysteries and contradictions are "only two emphatical Ways of

---

47. Toland, *Apology*, 27.
48. Ibid., 33–35.
49. Toland, *Defence*, 4–5.

saying *Nothing*."⁵⁰ Thus, he is consistent with the application of his rule of evidence or the ground of persuasion throughout his defenses of *CNM* and he shows it to have nothing to do with natural probability.

The pathway that Toland plows in arguing his case that there is nothing contrary to reason and that there is nothing above reason or mysterious in the New Testament in any sense of the word (the pathway that this part has followed to the above conclusions), is where all scholars have misread him, past and present. It is likely that all Toland scholars have approached *CNM* with the presupposition that Toland has adopted Locke's vulgar reason. So, perhaps they know that Locke conceives of above reason things as being comprehensible, at least in some cases (all of Locke's examples of above reason things are conceivable). Since they are unaware of Locke's proper reason, that which Toland has actually adopted, Toland's dismissal of above reason things, for them, must include what Locke included in above reason things—revealed propositions that we would not have conceived on our own, but if we did, we would have no basis to think them true. However, some seem incorrectly to identify any divine revelation as being above reason in Locke. Whatever the case is, it appears, from the readings of scholars, that Toland has effectively nullified any authority from revelation. In the first case, where revelation is not exhausted by the above reason category, revelation is subordinated to what amounts to a divinely unassisted, natural reason or Locke's vulgar reason. This comports with the erroneous reading that revealed "possible" propositions are propositions that are credible upon natural considerations and not simply conceivable propositions. Whether a scholar is put off course first by misunderstanding what above reason propositions are in *CNM* or the full understanding of what possible propositions are, the result is the same: revelation cannot offer us anything novel.

Of the few scholars that give what could be considered a detailed treatment of Toland's epistemology, they all fit into the description above. They all believe that revelation cannot offer us anything novel.⁵¹ They were all

---

50. Toland, *Vindicius*, 89–96 (quotation, 95). Again, John Norris would argue that the falsity of a contradictory proposition is conceivable and that is an important distinction from an above reason proposition or doctrine that cannot be conceived. Norris, *Account of Reason and Faith*, 100–136.

51. Sullivan is very clear, as will be shown, that he thinks that *CNM* rejects revelation that gives novelty. Leask, as has been shown in chapter 2, argues that *CNM* promotes a verifiability criterion for revelation and, as will be shown shortly, denies revelation that gives novelty. There is no evidence that he thinks these aspects are different. Beiser might be the same. He *explicitly* refers only to a verifiability criterion on top of a requirement that the ideas in the proposition and the resulting sum-total notion believed must be clear and distinct (chapter 2 argues Beiser does not grasp what Toland means by clear and distinct ideas, however). It is likely that Beiser intends his

treated in chapter 2 and shown to have misunderstandings about Toland's Lockean ideas and the relationship of faith and knowledge in *CNM*. It was also shown from where in the Locke-Stillingfleet debate the incorrect reading came that Toland subordinated revelation to natural, unassisted reason. This chapter could show how these misunderstandings on ideas, knowledge, and faith were influenced by this likely presupposed relationship of reason and revelation. That is, this section of the chapter could go through the arduous process of explaining each scholar's circular reasoning. Instead we will treat what these scholars say directly about above reason propositions and revelation.

The first scholar we will investigate is Sullivan. Sullivan notes that although Toland did not deny the possibility of revelation, his epistemological assumptions were "irreconcilable with allowing divine inspiration a role in the creation of humanity's religious opinions." Sullivan explains: "His conviction—that, should God use this means of information, the intelligence He conveyed would have to conform to the canons of human reason by presenting clear and distinct ideas, rather than mysteries—precluded any discoveries."[52] From this quote it appears that Sullivan understands that revelation must be intelligible. But he somehow (perhaps by misunderstanding what Toland means by "possible" and/or other aforementioned reasons) concludes that revelation informs us of that which comports to our unassisted, natural reason. So, in Sullivan's eyes, in *CNM* revelation can only tell us what we could conceive and assent to without the assistance of divine revelation—thus "precluded any discoveries." Sullivan supports this idea that the New Testament gives no new doctrines by mistakenly replacing "New Testament" in place of the book of Revelation in an important quote in *CNM*. In the quote Toland is making a reference to the book of Revelation and Sullivan apparently thinks he is making a reference to revelation. Sullivan writes: "In light of his [Toland's] conception of the New Testament as a 'Prophetical History of the External State of the Church' containing 'no

---

explanation of *CNM*'s use of a verifiability criterion to be an explanation of Toland's denial of revelation that gives novelty. There is a difference, however. The verifiability criterion will restrict, at least, the use of analogy in the supernatural world that the simpler novelty guideline does not. A theist or deist with the use of analogy would be able to accept the Bible's confirmation of immaterial beings (other than God) since the general notion is, according to Locke, acceptable from the consideration of purely natural sources. That is, it is possible some have reasoned that it is likely that there are ranks of intelligent beings, some of which are immaterial, that reach up to the infinite perfection of God (*Essay* IV.xvi.12). Such biblical claims of the existence of these immaterial beings would be rejected by the verifiability criterion.

52. Sullivan, *John Toland*, 216.

new Doctrines,' its importance as a means of information seems doubtful."⁵³ What Toland actually wrote, however, is:

> Having so particularly alledg'd all the Passages where there is mention made of *Mysteries* in the *New Testament*, if any should wonder why I have omitted those in the *Revelation*, to such I reply, that the *Revelation* cannot be properly look'd upon as a Part of the *Gospel*; for there are no new Doctrines deliver'd in it. Far from being a Rule of Faith or Manners, it is not as much as an Explanation of any Point in our Religion. The true Subject of that Book or *Vision* is a Prophetical History of the external State of the Church in its various and interchangeable Periods of Prosperity and Adversity. But that I may not fall under the least Suspicion of dealing unfairly, I shall subjoin the few Texts of the *Revelation* wherein the word *Mystery* is contain'd (105–6).

That Toland is referring to the book of Revelation and not the New Testament is beyond doubt from the quote. So Sullivan's likely bases for understanding that revelation cannot reveal anything not supported by purely natural considerations are undoubtedly incorrect.

The second scholar, Leask, misunderstands both what possible propositions are and Toland's discussion on above reason things. Regarding the first issue, Leask reads one of the above quotations—"*Whoever reveals any thing*, that is, whoever tells us something we did not know before, *his Words must be intelligble, and the Matter possible*" (42)—as pointing to the presence of novelty in an alleged revelation as actually invalidating that revelation. In discussing the fact that Locke allows revelation to overrule unassisted, natural probability, Leask mistakes Toland's possibility for Locke's natural probability: "For Toland, this Lockean criterion of 'probability' is simply not good enough: if revelation is not possible, it cannot be accepted in any way valid."⁵⁴ Among a few misinterpretations that fuel his misreading, one pertains to a quote from Toland that Leask rips out of context: "Now what is there in all this, but very strict Reasoning from Experience, from the Possibility of the thing, and from the Power, Justice, and Immutability of him that promis'd it" (132). Leask evidently thinks that reasoning from experience and the possibility of the thing implies that the thing assented to must be probable upon natural considerations.⁵⁵ But in context, Toland is discussing Abraham's arrival at the conclusion that God would revive Isaac after

---

53. Ibid., 125.
54. Leask, "Personation and Immanent Undermining," 244.
55. Ibid., 245.

being sacrificed. There is little reasoning in that biblical account that could be considered purely natural.

Leask reinforces his faulty reading of possible propositions with a faulty reading of Toland's above reason discussion, or vice-versa. Regarding Toland's dismissal of the category of above reason propositions, he claims that "Toland would go so far as to collapse the distinction that Locke is so keen to maintain."[56] Undergirding this notion is Leask's belief that above reason propositions are allegedly revealed propositions with novelty and incomprehensible doctrines, which is incorrect. As a result, for Leask, the collapse of the distinction does not mean that Toland thinks that all revelation is reasonable but rather he thinks that plenty of the so-called revelations are not divine.[57] Leask ends up operating under the notion that above reason things, unintelligible mysteries, and divine revelation with novelty are synonyms or effectively so in Toland.[58] What is more, Leask thinks that Toland's statements that essences are not above reason are leveled at Locke! He is unaware that Locke accepts above reason things as a concessionary category and Leask wrongly believes that this category would include essences which cannot be known, a position held by others as shown in chapter 3.[59] Recall that, with Locke, only a type of divinely revealed propositions can be considered "above reason." That is, above reason propositions in the *Essay* pertain to propositions regarding supernatural matters that we would not likely come up with ourselves, but if we did, we would have no basis to assent to them.

The third scholar is Frederick Beiser. He believes that Toland uses two arguments to attack revelation that gives novelty or tells us things that are (allegedly) above reason. The first argument he utilizes is that *CNM* advances a verifiability criterion with the result that one must reject anything that could not be verified in principle. Leask also sees a verifiability criterion in *CNM*. Chapter 2 argues against both thinkers. There it is shown that both scholars mistakenly understand Toland's use of knowledge (similar to the identity and diversity sense of the term or mere perception or conception) in reference to matters of faith as indicating a criterion that a thing must be verifiable if one is to assent to it. The second argument, which Beiser thinks is put forth more consistently by Toland, is that it is irrational to

56. Ibid., 243.
57. Ibid., 243–44.
58. Ibid., 244–45. Leask appears to identify unintelligible mysteries and revelation with novelty in *CNM*. This conflation is designated as above reason propositions by him. Add to this his apparent conflation of revealed propositions with novelty and unverifiable revealed propositions.
59. Ibid., 250–52.

hold any beliefs of no use to us, and this rules out anything in revelation not dealing with morality, what Beiser believes Toland thinks is the means of salvation.[60] Beiser finds support for the first part of his conclusion in the following quote from Toland: "The most compendious Method therefore to acquire sure and useful Knowledg, is *not to trouble our selves nor others with what is useless, were it known; or what is impossible to be known*" (78).[61] (Toland writes this following a discussion that God has given us capabilities only to understand what is useful and necessary for us.) Beiser writes: "If we apply this argument to the belief in religious mysteries, then Toland's point is that it is irrational to hold such beliefs because they are of no benefit to us."[62] If by religious mysteries Beiser means summarily incomprehensible things, then his statement is correct; but if he means religious mysteries that are novel and comprehensible but not observationally verifiable then his statement is not (it is possible that Beiser intends both to be labeled as mysteries).

Whatever the case is regarding what mysteries are in Beiser's conclusion, the bigger problem is what he thinks Toland deems useful and necessary. Beiser believes that "Toland's argument here clearly presupposes that there is a purpose behind religious beliefs, and in particular that this purpose consists in moral conduct. But Toland defends this very premise in some of his other religious writings."[63] In other words, Beiser is acknowledging that there is no actual evidence in *CNM* that explicitly states that Toland believes "Morality should be not only a necessary, but also a sufficient condition of salvation. But, if this is so, then the basis for a pragmatic defense of the belief in mysteries also disappears."[64] Contrary to Beiser, there is a wealth of evidence in *CNM* against this view that *CNM* promulgates a natural religion of morality. In arguing for our abilities to reason well despite the fall, Toland clearly states that not believing in Christ, in the case that one is privy to Him, is liable to condemnation: "Supposing a natural Impotency to reason well, we could no more be liable to Condemnation for not keeping the Commands of God, than those to whom *the Gospel* was never revealed for not believing on *Christ*" (59). Similarly, in arguing that we must be able to understand what is being said in the gospel, Toland writes: "It was reckon'd no Crime not to believe in *Christ* before he was reveal'd; *for how could they believe in him of whom they had not heard?* But with what better Reason

---

60. Beiser, *Sovereignty of Reason*, 255–56.
61. Ibid., 255.
62. Ibid., 255.
63. Ibid., 255.
64. Ibid., 256.

could any be condemn'd for not believing what he said, if they might not understand it?" (129). Still in the same vein, Toland remarks, "My next Observation is, That *the Subject of Faith must be intelligible to all, since the Belief thereof is commanded under no less a Penalty than Damnation*: He that believeth not, shall be damn'd" (134). Interestingly, these three quotes, although less detailed, are similar, if not the same, to Locke's position on the same matters in ROC.[65] In yet another part, Toland calls Christ and the gospel "gracious" and "wonderfully stupendous and suprizing" and a mystery to those that preceded the New Testament era (99, cf. 142–43). And in *Defence*, written by Toland in response to charges that he is a "*Deist*, or at best but a *narrow scanty Believer of Revelation*," he writes: "That 'tis very difficult for me to conceive how any Man, that owns the least tittle of *Natural Religion*, can publickly and solemnly profess to the World that he is firmly perswaded of the Truth of the *Christian Religion*, and the *Scriptures*, when at the same time he does not really and sincerely believe any thing of them."[66] In other words, if he were simply an adherent of natural religion he would believe it wrong to claim that he believed the Scriptures if it were the case that he did not think them revealed. In short, Toland is definitely not an adherent of natural religion but rather appears very Lockean.

It is clear that Toland is not professing or arguing for natural religion in *CNM*, contrary to what Beiser, Leask, and Sullivan claim. What this section has unearthed here runs counter to all those who think that *CNM* is professing a natural religion, which comprises a very large and notable segment of the scholarship. This section's findings also bear upon Berman's and Fouke's claims that Toland has a three-tiered intention with *CNM*: 1) to appear that he defends revelation, 2) to lead unwary readers to make the irreligious conclusions for themselves, and 3) to lead the intelligent to arrive at his true beliefs. Regarding the first intention, Toland not only *appears* to defend revelation, but he *does* defend it as Locke does. But with the great attention that Toland has evidently paid to Locke, what are these irreligious conclusions that one would come to make that would be different from Locke? Again, Fouke and Berman give their own bare assertions or assertions made by others about *CNM* as evidence. If Toland was a theological liar, as they claim, Locke would have to be a theological liar as well, unless they are willing to claim that Locke was too obtuse to see where his

---

65. Locke argues throughout *ROC* that the gospel is understandable to all and that one must believe in Christ when privy to His existence. He, like Toland, believes that one cannot be held liable, however, for not believing in Christ when one has never heard of Him. Locke, *ROC*, 254–56; cf. Marko, "Justification, Ecumenism, and Heretical Red Herrings."

66. Toland, *Defence*, 16–17.

own arguments led to irreligious conclusions. Even the slight deviations we are about to encounter in the next section regarding revelation and reason, which in no way help Berman's or Fouke's cause, are still in a sense largely Lockean.

PART VI: REASON AND REVELATION

Toland does not carve out a section in his work devoted solely to the taxonomy of divine special revelation as Locke does, but one can be pieced together and inferred. Although he does not use the term traditional revelation, he obviously treats Scripture as traditional revelation that was originally conveyed by God to humans and subsequently written down. In *CNM* he claims that he takes the divinity of the New Testament for granted (xxiv) and reiterates this presupposition in the *Apology*.[67] It is also clear that he is aware of the distinction between original revelation of the conveyable sort and unconveyable sort. He alludes to both concepts in one paragraph of *CNM*. There he notes that some try to defend incomprehensible doctrines by claiming that they are contrary to common notions, or incomprehensible, but "consistent with themselves." Toland comments on these allegedly incomprehensible doctrines further: "But supposing a little that the thing were so; it still follows, that none can understand these Doctrines except their Perceptions be communicated to him in an extraordinary manner, as by new Powers and Organs." In other words, even if some incomprehensible message were conveyed to one with new powers and organs, others could not be edified by the revelation as they could not comprehend it (30). Thus it is clear that he understands the distinction between the two types of revelation, both of which Locke would label original revelation.

Toland even incorporates the various conceptions of revelation with reason in the same way that Locke does, but with a few exceptions. This claim will be the topic of the bulk of the remainder of this chapter. Recall that for Locke, divine (special) revelation—original and traditional—must have the appropriate external and internal marks, which reason must identify, to be affirmed as revelation. The appropriate external marks for original revelation are a corresponding clear miracle or miracles and for traditional revelation are accompanying fair testimonies of a clear miracle or miracles. The first internal mark is that the interpretation of the revealed proposition is not contrary to knowledge both in the sense that it is not contrary to certain truths (false) or not inherently contradictory (also, false) and in the sense that it is not mentally irreconcilable. One would not expect it

---

67. Toland, *Apology*, 33–35.

to contradict knowledge in the first sense because if revelation could thus contradict knowledge—the goal and highest achievement of reason and the foundation of our further reasoning—it would be undercutting its source of validation that it is revelation. The second internal mark is that the interpretation of the revealed proposition is not definitively contradictory to assured revelation. Thus, Locke subordinates revelation to proper reason in a sense because the latter is used to affirm the external marks and determine and judge the internal marks or interpretation of the alleged revelation to legitimize it. It is evident from the *Essay* that Locke thinks the Bible fits these criteria and is the surest revelation available. In fact, all unattested, present day, original revelation, which Locke allows for in the *Essay*, must comport with vulgar reason on issues to which Scripture does not speak or Scripture. Moreover, Locke's *Essay* allows for revelation of the unconveyable sort.

Treating the various aspects, Toland does acknowledge miracles as the appropriate external marks. This chapter already noted this in the "Preliminaries" part. Some scholars, however, believe that Toland categorically rejects miracles or he would logically have to reject them in order to be consistent with his arguments in *CNM*. Charles Taylor is an example of scholars who portray Toland as rejecting anything "mysterious." Taylor understands things to be mysterious, apparently, in a sense different from that which Toland intended. Taylor thinks that Toland's dismissal of mystery from religion entails the dismissal of miracles.[68] But there is no evidence that Taylor has gone beyond a brief secondary account of *CNM*. He gives nothing from *CNM* that would lead one to that conclusion. Beiser's treatment of Toland, in contrast, is more in depth and demonstrates more than a passing notice of Toland. Beiser believes that Toland vacillates on the issue of whether or not miracles are supernatural events. Regarding Beiser's claim of Toland's vacillation, he thinks this is so because while Toland says "that miracles though happening according to natural law, occur with 'supernatural assistance,'" he "retracts his position entirely by admitting that miracles would not be miracles at all if they were explicable according to natural laws" (cf. 144–51). Beiser thinks that Toland, regardless of what he says, however, is obliged to dismiss so-called miracles as supernatural events: "If miracles really are supernatural events, then there will be mysteries in Christianity after all." What Beiser is arguing is that miracles are mysteries if supernatural and are according-to-natural-laws and non-mysterious if natural phenomena.[69]

Beiser's claim is, however, groundless; all of Toland's descriptions of miracles are contrary to them being simply natural phenomena. Toland's

---

68. Taylor, *Secular Age*, 223–24.
69. Beiser, *Sovereignty of Reason*, 247–48.

definition of a miracle is "*some Action exceeding all humane Power, and which the Laws of NATURE cannot perform by their ordinary Operations*" (144). Toland states that miracles are not just "some *Phenomenon* that surprizes only by its Rarity" (150). Also, if one could "tell how a *Miracle* was wrought . . . [that] is no *Miracle* at all" (150). God does not perform miracles, and thus does not alter the order of nature, unless there is a weighty reason and for some "special and Important End, which is either appointed by those for whom the Miracles is made, or intended and declar'd by him that works it" (146–47). In other words, God uses them as proof that He is communicating or He uses them to give credit to His agents. In fact, no miracle in the New Testament was performed, "but what serv'd to confirm the Authority of those who wrought it, to procure Attention to the Doctrines of the *Gospel*, or for the like wise and reasonable Purposes" (147). Miracles "are always wrought in favor of the Unbelieving" (149). What is more, we must reject miracles of witches, conjurers, and all heathens because there is in them no end worthy of God changing the course of nature and, also, "Diabolical Delusions would hereby receive equal Confirmation with Divine Revelation" (147–48).[70] Furthermore, and this gets at the root of Beiser's confusion regarding Toland's view of miracles, Toland states clearly that miracles must be "intelligible and possible," by which he means not contrary to reason in a particular sense (145). Miracles must follow the rule of the ground of persuasion. Therefore, claims of miracles such as a severed head speaking without a tongue or Jesus being born but not through an opening in the virgin are inherent contradictions or impossible because they are contrary to the nature of the thing. That is, speaking cannot be done without a tongue and being born means that a baby comes out of the mother through an opening (146).[71] So when Toland says that miracles are supernaturally assisted and that they are "produc'd according to the Laws of Nature" (150), this is what he means: speaking is done with speaking organs and a birth is when a baby exits through an opening in the mother's body (146). In Toland's economy, miracles are intelligible and therefore are not an inconsistent allowance of incomprehensibility or mystery in Christianity.

70. This is an interesting comment by Toland. He apparently does not believe that God would give demons any power to perform miracles or he thinks that demons do not exist. So, anything coming from a non-believer would have to be on the level of parlor tricks. The scholastic distinction between *mirabilia* and *miracula* is not employed. Cf. Muller, *Dictionary*, s.v. "mirabilia" and "miracula."

71. There is no indication that Toland would reject a claim of a miracle where a baby who was in the womb would suddenly and miraculously find itself outside of the womb without passing through the birth canal or through a cut in the mother's womb. One simply could not say the mother gave *birth* to the baby without redefining what birth means and the different notions it includes under its conceptual umbrella.

Furthermore, bound up with the external miracles is veracity of the testifier. Toland notes that our faith is built on ratiocination. Ratiocination must consider three things at least before it can assent to divine revelation as such: the book is written by whom the book says it is, the person's actions and state of the person comports with what a divine agent would be, and the work is intelligible (127). The first two deal with the veracity of the testifier who has supposedly received divine revelation and believes the message he or she brings to be divine revelation. And as said above, miracles would provide the indication. The third corresponds to the principle that God communicates to us such that the ground of persuasion is a sure and steadfast rule.

So, while miracles are the external mark for revelation, Toland also operates with at least two of the same internal marks that Locke does. It is abundantly clear in what has been said before that a revealed proposition, if it is to be even considered as such, must be mentally reconcilable or, in other words, summarily envisionable. Toland's primary emphasis throughout the work is that anything we believe must be comprehensible, whether it is from human or allegedly divine authority. And, it is beyond doubt that purported revelation that was contrary to certain knowledge must be rejected (cf. 57–59). Furthermore, Toland, although not explicitly saying so, would have to follow Locke in giving the best interpretation of a revealed proposition priority over a proposition that is deemed probable by unassisted, natural reason. If this were not the case, Toland would have no argument for his claims that belief in Christ is necessary for salvation, at least to those aware of Christ. That is, all are responsible for considering and weighing the claims for themselves and are responsible for acknowledging Christ as Savior regardless of what their unassisted, natural or vulgar reasons might think about such claims. Thus, marks for revealed propositions are that they are not contrary to knowledge in both aforementioned senses; they can be contrary to natural probability though.

Whether or not Toland believes a further internal mark of revelation is that the alleged revelation must not be definitively contrary to assured revelation must be considered. As said already, Toland takes the divinity of the New Testament for granted (xxiv). And he thinks God's revelation must be everywhere "uniform and self-consistent" and cannot "cast down or destroy it self" (125). So, while this internal mark is operational within *CNM* it is not explicit. Therefore the books that were added as part of the canon must have comported with the books already assumed as such or, at least, did not contradict them. Interestingly, as already stated, none of the testimonies of miracles associated with the books of the other religions in Toland's view are acceptable. The works' very messages disqualify them.

There are a few other questions that still must be answered. First, while it is obvious that Toland believes that there was original revelation in the time of the writing of Scripture, does he believe original revelation of the conveyable sort still exists today? Second, does unconveyable original revelation exist today or has it ever existed according to *CNM*? Third, does Toland believe that the Old Testament is divine revelation as well?

While Locke does not officially rule out modern-day original revelation of the conveyable sort, Toland's *CNM* does. When Toland originally alludes to the concepts of conveyable and unconveyable original revelation, he does not say whether he thinks unconveyable original revelation ever existed or if either currently exist (30–31). As just noted above, he obviously thinks that original revelation of the conveyable sort existed at one time, at least, since we have Scripture (135–37). In chapter IV of section III, "Objections Brought from Particular Texts of Scripture and from the Nature of Faith, Answer'd," he focuses on the nature of propositions delivered in Scripture. There he categorically denies present-day original revelation of the conveyable sort. He writes: "Again, *Divine Faith* is either when God speaks to us immediately himself, or when we acquiesce in the Words or Writings of those to whom we believe he has spoken. All *Faith* now in the World is of this last sort, and by consequence entirely built upon *Ratiocination*" (127). He apparently finds support for his view that faith is based on ratiocination or reasoning in Hebrews 11:1–3:

> The Author of the Epistle of the *Hebrews* do's not define FAITH a Prejudice, Opinion, or Conjecture, but Conviction or Demonstration: *Faith, says he, is the confident Expectation of things hop'd for, and the Demonstration of things not seen.* These last Words, *things not seen,* signify not (as some would have it) things incomprehensible or unintelligible, but past or future Matters of Fact. . . . Besides, there can be properly no *Faith* of things seen or present, for then 'tis Self-evidence, and not Ratiocination (129–30).

Thus, faith cannot be implicit and regard incomprehensible things and it cannot pertain to things one is witnessing or has witnessed as those notions are obtained by the senses, and, therefore, they are, as discussed in the "Preliminaries" section, essentially certain. Furthermore, faith now must be based on reasoning without God immediately revealing to us what he wants us to believe. He uses another portion of Hebrews 11 to give an example of the nature of this latter aspect of modern-day faith. In attempting to sacrifice his son, Abraham was trusting God, amidst what to many would appear a contradiction between God's present command of sacrifice and his former promises, by reasoning that God would raise Isaac from the dead (131–32).

The bulk of chapter IV of section III defends the idea that religious faith is now always based on reasoning with previously given divine revelation, the real point of interest currently at hand, and that the doctrines and propositions of divine revelation are always intelligible. Using verses from 1 Corinthians and Hebrews he claims that if faith were not from reasoning we would have no degrees of understanding (133–34). He writes, "*if Faith were not a Perswasion resulting from previous Knowledge and Comprehension of the thing believ'd, there could be no Degrees nor Differences in it*" (133). And, in 1 Peter 3:15, "*Faith signifies an intelligible Perswasion*" (136).

The denial of present-day original revelation has two obvious implications and another that is possible. The first obvious implication is that there can be no more traditional revelation added to Scripture. In *Vindicius*, he even alludes to the "*dreadful Curse which the Author of the* Revelation *pronounces against such as shall add or take away from that Book*" as pertaining to the entire Bible and not just the book of Revelation.[72] The other clear implication is that he leaves no room for so-called enthusiasts who base their persuasion or conviction of different faith claims solely on the operation of the Holy Spirit.[73] For Toland, revelation is purely a means of information (cf. 45). The possible implication is that miracles have ceased. Toland connects them with confirmation of revelation. If they are *only* for the confirmation of original revelation then there are no more miracles. Toland, however, never explicitly says this. He does claim that miracles are "to procure Attention to the Doctrines of the *Gospel*, or for the like wise and reasonable Purposes" (147). But that statement does not tell the reader what he thinks might be a reasonable purpose. And when he refers later to the fact that they are wrought to confirm doctrines he mentions no other viable occasions (150).[74] Whatever the case is, the modern-day miracles he explicitly rejects are those that are claimed by heathens, whose views are contrary to our idea of God, and those of the Roman Catholics, whose miracles of tran-

---

72. Toland, *Vindicius*, 22.

73. Those, like the Reformed, who rely on the distinction between the internal principle of knowing (faith resting on the testimony of the Holy Spirit) and the external principle of knowing (Scripture) could be the objects of Toland's derision as well. Muller, *Dictionary*, s.v. "principia theologiae."

74. One might claim *CNM* could allow that a miracle might occur in front of a church one Sunday morning for giving attention and confirmation to the gospel that will be preached or read there that day. But that would likely make the sermon given that day a candidate for modern-day, original revelation. And, presumably, the text being read already has the historical testimonies of miracles and thus would not require any further confirmation.

substantiation are not for the benefit of the unbelieving (147–49). Anyone who approaches Toland thinking that he holds the view that God does not interact with the created order could, if not exceedingly careful, read him as rejecting modern-day miracles without much thought. Many presume him to be a thorough-going deist. Nonetheless, it would not be at all surprising, considering the above, that he does reject modern-day miracles.

While it is clear that Toland rejects present-day original revelation, it is not completely clear whether or not he rejects original revelation of the unconveyable sort in the time of the writing of the Bible and before. In the same chapter referenced directly above—chapter 4 of section III—he remarks: "Now since by *Revelation* Men are not endu'd with any new Faculties, it follows that God should lose his end in speaking to them, if what he said did not agree with their common Notions" (128). At face value the text appears to be saying that God does not endow us with new faculties for the purposes of revelation and it would therefore be useless for Him to communicate to anyone with revelation of the unconveyable sort. One could argue, however, that he means Scripture by the term "Revelation," since the focus of the chapter is that there is nothing in Scripture that is incomprehensible. Thus, perhaps Toland allows that revelation of the unconveyable sort could have happened in non-scriptural revelation. That last statement is a possible conclusion but it seems forced, especially in light of a few other reasons to the contrary, all of which are intertwined. First, revelation for Toland is, again, simply a means of information and does not include anything like the operation of the Holy Spirit where He is the cause of our conviction and thus overrides our reason or bestows new powers. He writes:

> I am not ignorant how some boast they are strongly perswaded *by the illuminating and efficacious Operation of the Holy Spirit*, and that they neither have nor approve other Reasons of their *FAITH* . . . So far of REVELATION; only in making it a *Mean of Information*, I follow *Paul* himself, who tells the *Corinthians*, that he *cannot profit them except he speaks to them by* Revelation, *or by* Knowledg, *or by* Prophesying, *or by* Doctrine (45).

Thus there appears to be no allowance, according to *CNM*, of a supernaturally bestowed faculty or power associated with revelation, even for the purposes of understanding original revelation that to others would be gibberish. Revelation is only a means of information. This citation pertains to the present as well as the time of Paul, which is in the midst of the era of the writing of the New Testament. Second, a new faculty would require a miracle and it is hard to square a miracle, in such an instance, with the requirement that it be for the benefit of the unbelieving since, third, unconveyable original revelation is not profitable to others (30, 45). Fourth, Toland writes, "*God has wisely provided we should understand no more of these than are useful and necessary for us*; which is all our present Condition needs" (76). So, while Locke is not deterred by his own principle of utility in his allowance of unconveyable original revelation, perhaps Toland is. Finally, Toland is a type of materialist and thinks that there is no immaterial soul. In defending his claims that we do not have to know the essence of a thing to know the thing, he writes: "The Idea of the *Soul* then is every whit as clear and distinct as that of the *Body*; and had there been (as there is not) any Difference, the *Soul* must have carri'd the Advantage, because its Properties are more immediately known to us, and are the Light whereby we discover all things besides" (85–86). So, perhaps, additionally, there is some sort of repugnancy in God's mind about altering the make-up of his human material masterpieces by adding a supernatural organ or faculty to them. Thus, it is possible that Toland would reject any revelation of the unconveyable sort because it would require a miracle, perhaps an alteration to our souls is contrary to a particular divine policy, and the information revealed would be unedifying to others. But perhaps his denial that there is anything above reason in any sense in the Christian religion would be better evidence for excluding the unconveyable sort of revelation. In the end, while not certain, it seems very likely that Toland would categorically deny original revelation of the unconveyable sort.

Moreover, it appears that Toland believes the Old Testament to be traditional revelation as Locke does. While Toland only explicitly states that he takes the New Testament's divinity for granted, the context explains why. Toland writes, "*In the following Discourse, which is the first of three, and wherein I prove my Subject in general, the Divinity of the New Testament is taken for granted; so that it regards only Christians immediately, and others but remotely*" (xxiv). So perhaps this is just an odd way of saying that the focus of the book is predominantly on the doctrines from the New Testament. Recall, the thesis of *CNM*: "*there is nothing in the Gospel contrary to Reason, nor above it; and that no Christian Doctrine can be properly call'd a Mystery*" (6). Furthermore, he treats the Old Testament as he does the New, quoting from both and using examples from both throughout *CNM*. He also acknowledges miracles connected to the Old Testament books. For all we know, he might follow the reasoning that since the New Testament presupposes the truth of the Old Testament then even the Old Testament books without miracles associated with them are to be considered Scripture. In short, it seems conclusive that Toland would accept the Old Testament as divine revelation. What is more, every time that he uses the term revelation to stand for a legitimate divine revelation, it points to Scripture.[75] Thus, the entire Bible is not only a paradigm for revelation, at least for the most part, but it is the written product of, perhaps, all the divine revelation given to humans.

Taking stock of the conclusions so far, there appear to be a few differences between *CNM* and the *Essay*. *CNM* denies modern-day original revelation of the conveyable sort and the *Essay* does not. Likewise, Toland apparently rejects original revelation of the unconveyable sort and Locke does not. And, while *CNM* probably denies miracles today, Toland also has the rule that miracles were always done for the benefit of the unbeliever. Locke allows miracles for today and does not explicitly state Toland's additional rule. Furthermore, *CNM* promulgates materialism while the *Essay* does not. And, whenever Toland refers to a legitimate divine revelation he is referring to Scripture or some part of it. For Locke, in the *Essay*, Scripture does not necessarily exhaust traditional revelation. He clearly discusses the possibility of traditional revelation in addition to the Bible.

Interestingly, one or two of these differences disappear when combining the theological opinions of John Locke given in *ROC* with his official experimental philosophy pertinent to revelation given in the *Essay*. *CNM* and *ROC* are more theological and include far more interpretations of biblical passages in their arguments than does the *Essay*, which is more of a philosophical work. While Locke's official stance in the *Essay* is that an immaterial human soul is a possibility (IV.iii.6), his personal belief conveyed in *ROC* is that the likely stance from Scripture is that there is no consciousness without a material body.[76] If there is a connection between materialism and the rejection of unconveyable original revelation, perhaps Locke would agree with Toland's assessment from a biblical vantage point, except for Paul's reception of unconveyable revelation in the third heaven, which Locke upholds (1 Cor 2:9) (*Essay* IV.xviii.3).

Another possible difference between *CNM* and the *Essay* is worth mentioning and it pertains to the logical priority of certain major elements regarding revelation. This logical priority is not, however, necessarily the order in which these elements are presented. *CNM* states up front that the

---

75. In one passage, Toland uses the term revelation in a general manner to indicate divine *and* human varieties. He writes, "Others will say that this Notion of *Faith* make *Revelation* useless. But, pray, how so? for the Question is not, whether we could discover all the Objects of our *Faith* by Ratiocination: I have prov'd on the contrary, that no Matter of Fact can be known without *Revelation*" (140; cf. 42). He is saying that all matters of fact come to our minds through various sources of revelation. In another place he refers to "*Humane* and *Divine Revelation*" (18).

76. Locke, *ROC*, 4–15.

divinity of Scripture is taken for granted. It also presupposes the existence of God and our epistemological endowment from Him of everything we need for our own good. This last notion rules out the need of assenting to anything incomprehensible. That is *CNM's* starting point. It is thus from Scripture that the external and internal marks are extracted. There is probably no other extant (bodies of) revelation of the traditional sort, in Toland's mind, by virtue of the fact that all alleged revelation will fail in one way or another when it comes to the marks. The *Essay*, namely book IV, begins with presuppositions of the existence of God and our epistemological endowment of all powers needed for our own good. From there it moves to the marks of revelation. Then it moves to presenting the Bible as conforming to the marks.[77] After that it entertains and makes allowances for alleged revelation beyond Scripture. The *Essay* is thus more objective in its approach to Scripture.

In the end, Toland's treatment of revelation and reason, however, is very much akin to Locke's. Revelation is considered as such by virtue of its external marks, miracles, and its internal marks, its being not contrary to knowledge in two senses and not definitively contrary to assured revelation. Both see the Bible as the paradigm of traditional revelation. But, while Locke makes allowances for present-day original revelation and extra-biblical traditional revelation, Toland rules both out, or at least rules the former out and shows utter disinterest in the latter. Clearly, the alleged revelation of other faiths could not even be considered as revelation; and Scripture, in Toland's mind, rules out the potential of any further revelation to Christians. And while Locke conceives of and allows for immediate revelation of the unconveyable sort in the *Essay*, it would be surprising if Toland finds it a legitimate category of revelation based on God's exhibited parameters for working miracles, the inability to convey the associated propositions, and possibly Toland's stated materialism.

CONCLUSION

This chapter has argued that the differences between Locke and Toland with respect to their understandings and treatments of reason, its related faculties, faith, and revelation are not based upon or evidenced by their respective categorizations of propositions, but on Toland's attempt at working out

---

77. Locke does clearly presume Scripture to be traditional revelation without proving it, however, in such passages like *Essay* III.ix.23. There he says that the Old and New Testaments are infallible without proving it. Book IV is, nonetheless, the focus at present.

the implications of Locke's epistemological principles in conjunction with Toland's interpretations of certain biblical passages and certain theological preferences and presuppositions. Had Locke ordered propositions according to his preferred consideration of reason, his categorization of propositions would be the same ascribed to Toland. The resultant, substantial differences between Locke and Toland in their understandings and treatments of epistemology are connected with Toland's definite or likely rejections of theological and philosophical positions that Locke does not dismiss: post-New Testament original revelation and miracles, non-materialism of the soul, and prior-to-the-close-of-the-New-Testament divine revelation requiring a supernaturally bestowed faculty and private miracles for believers.[78]

There are a few possible connections amidst these five differences. It is likely that the rejections of past divine revelation requiring a supernaturally bestowed faculty (i.e., original revelation of the unconveyable sort), non-materialism of the soul, and private miracles for believers are connected. Perhaps Toland has scriptural reasons for these but they are not stated. Locke, however, is a materialist based on biblical considerations in *ROC*, which Toland may have read. Furthermore, Toland's likely rejection of modern-day miracles is based upon his rejection of modern-day original revelation. And Toland's rejection of that is apparently based upon his reading of certain passages from Scripture, which he presupposes to be writings of God's revelation.

Some final words can be mentioned regarding the three common assertions often made regarding the juxtaposition of Locke and Toland: 1) Toland appropriates the foundational principles of Locke's *Essay* to a significant degree, 2) Locke accepts above reason propositions, while Toland does not, and 3) Locke accepts divine revelation and Toland rejects, or essentially rejects, divine revelation. As to comment one, it is clear that Toland has appropriated the foundational principles of the *Essay* with very little deviation. Regarding comment two, Locke rejects summarily unintelligible propositions just as Toland does. So, comment two is greatly misleading as discussed. Comment three is false. Both Locke and Toland clearly accept the existence of divine revelation. They do, however, differ on some minor details.

---

78. Again, Toland would reject any claim of a private miracle that occurred in the presence of an unbeliever that was not to have been done by God and for the purpose of helping the unbeliever with her unbelief (*CNM* 151). John Locke does not specifically discuss the claims of believers in non-biblical religions regarding miracles done in favor of their religion.

5

Conclusions and Implications

INTRODUCTION

THIS CHAPTER WILL FOCUS on high-lighting some important conclusions and implications of this book as well as offering suggestions for further, needed studies. First, it will briefly revisit and comment upon the argument that this book has laid out and the new narrative that it has brought to the fore. This chapter will then discuss the implications for the history of philosophy, namely in the specific area of the rise of natural religion in England. A new, corresponding categorization scheme for organizing thinkers during this rise and for orienting students of this period will be suggested. This will be followed by a few comments on Locke's and Toland's treatments of categorizations of propositions and doctrines in relation to reason and then a brief discussion on the implications of Locke's and Toland's teaching that revealed propositions are not made more credible by support from natural philosophy or what is commonly referred to today as science. This chapter then will comment on scholarship that has argued that *CNM* is not indicative of Toland's true thoughts. This chapter will end with a section describing a very important study that this book begins. A comparative study of Locke's and Toland's prolegomena, namely regarding the attributes of Scripture and hermeneutics, could nicely build upon the epistemological foundations laid in this book.

PART I: RE-VISIONING REASON, REVELATION, AND REJECTION IN JOHN LOCKE'S *AN ESSAY CONCERNING HUMAN UNDERSTANDING* AND JOHN TOLAND'S *CHRISTIANITY NOT MYSTERIOUS*

As was said throughout this book, scholarship mostly denies that Stillingfleet correctly read Locke but they affirm or, at least, assume that he correctly read Toland. The strange truth of the matter is that Stillingfleet connects two thinkers for particular shared notions and terminology, which they did indeed share, but ends up misinterpreting what both were saying. And partly due to Locke's loud and articulate protestations in his own defense, it has been accepted by scholarship that there was insufficient warrant for Stillingfleet, or anybody for that matter, to frame the *Essay* and *CNM* as being very similar. Besides, says scholarship, how close could they be when Locke clearly accepts doctrines above reason and Toland's utmost concern was to attack them? But few took the time to even glance at what Locke said of Stillingfleet's reading of *CNM*, let alone the entire debate and the implicated works and related defenses.

Another major stumbling block directly for Locke scholars and indirectly for Toland scholars is Locke's concessionary definitions of faith and reason that he introduces in IV.xviii. Throughout most of IV, Locke is developing his understanding of what this book calls proper reason and proper faith, the very same that Toland appropriates, which negates the category of above reason propositions. So, when Locke starts to use his concessionary or vulgar set of faith and reason definitions, Locke scholars have historically been confused by the switch and those comparing Locke and Toland in a more superficial manner think that this in some way is proof of their significant differences.

But in the end, as indicated in the last chapter, Toland deviates very little from Locke. In fact, when he does it is due to his working out the implications of Locke's epistemological principles in conjunction with his own interpretations of certain biblical passages and certain theological preferences and presuppositions, some of which, one might argue, are still in some sense Lockean. And while *CNM* might not thus be considered a very original work, it is significant, at least, by how well Toland demonstrates his grasp on the epistemological principles of the *Essay*.

PART II: HISTORICAL IMPLICATIONS FOR THE NARRATIVE OF THE RISE OF NATURAL RELIGION IN ENGLAND, CORRESPONDING THINKERS, AND THE BIDDLE HYPOTHESIS

Historians of philosophy have labored hard to categorize the seventeenth- and eighteenth-century English philosophical theologians into various groups in order to economically convey to their readers the movement of thought that gave rise to natural religion in England. These categories often cannot be pressed too far and have limited utility. At times the criteria used to define groups are too loose or vague and the groups overlap leaving a thinker or thinkers in two groups or the criteria are too rigid, leaving some notable thinkers outside of all of the groups. The former situation is far more common than the latter. In what follows, this part will briefly discuss the figures typically incorporated in the narrative of the rise of natural religion in England, a couple of examples of the attempted groupings of these thinkers by more recent literature, and these specific groupings' respective shortcomings. This part will then note the implications of the findings of this book on the rise of natural religion, namely a suggestion of new criteria by which to group some of these thinkers, a related need for the further study of particular figures, and a rebuttal to John Higgins-Biddle's hypothesis regarding one of Locke's reasons for writing *ROC* related to *CNM*.

A few names commonly appear in the narrative of the rise of natural religion in England. They are all considered to be outside of the pale of Protestant scholasticism. Lord Herbert of Cherbury (1583–1648) is often the first or one of the first named. In his *De Veritate* (1624) he puts forth the common axioms or precepts of universal natural religion and for this reason is sometimes fashioned as the father of deism. Chronologically he is followed by John Locke and sometimes by Archbishop John Tillotson. Locke's and Tillotson's epistemologies and defenses of religion have numerous affinities and are thus discussed together. The subsequent group treated is the next generation of thinkers, some of which were writing at the same time as Locke. It includes such thinkers as John Toland, Anthony Collins, and Matthew Tindal, to name a few. Most, if not all, placed in this next generation are considered Lockean in one sense or another. And each thinker's major defining work, except for Toland's *CNM*, appears after Locke's death.[1] All of

---

1. Most would agree that the works for which Toland and Tindal are best known today are *CNM* and *Christianity as Old as the Creation*, respectively. Toland's career began with *CNM* and Tindal's ended with *Christianity as Old as the Creation*. Anthony Collins has several works for which he is noted that span throughout his writing career. Thus, there does not seem to be significant agreement in scholarship regarding what

these thinkers are often portrayed as de-emphasizing the role of the supernatural in our lives and religion compared to the previous generation. But the shorter a particular treatment of the rise of natural religion in England is, the fewer there are who will be named from this post-Locke generation. Toland is almost always mentioned because of the much-touted deviation from Locke made popular by Stillingfleet. Tindal is also almost always mentioned because his *Christianity as Old as the Creation*, published in 1730, is the clearest articulation of Christianity as merely natural religion.[2] It marks the height of the natural religion narrative before its decline in prominence, helped along by such minds as David Hume.

James Livingston attempts the difficult task of dividing the thinkers above into separate groups in one of his recent works. After mentioning Herbert of Cherbury and *De Veritate*, he groups John Locke and John Tillotson as "rational supernaturalists" and John Toland and Matthew Tindal as "deists." He writes the following:

> By the end of the seventeenth century most of the ablest thinkers were divided into two camps. The orthodox or rational supernaturalists insisted on the unique role of revelation and on the distinction between what could and what could not be known by the exercise of reason alone. The more radical thinkers, who came to be known as the Deists, rejected the necessity of revelation and insisted on the sufficiency of unaided natural reason in religion.[3]

One of the first problems is that the two groups are based on different criteria or the answers to different questions. That is, the rational supernaturalists are said to affirm "the unique role of revelation," a vague claim, and a distinction between what reason can and cannot conclude for itself, while the deists, in the passage above, are said to reject the necessity of revelation and apparently thought natural reason was capable of determining the way of salvation for itself. If they were intended to be the same criteria, it seems the best interpretation of these two groups would be that the rational

---

Collins's most influential work is.

2. Tindal has appropriated the epistemological thought of Locke regarding ideas and knowledge. Cf. Tindal, *Christianity as Old*, 159–60. It is beyond doubt as well that he deviates from him. Anthony Collins was a student and close personal friend of Locke. His works have many similarities to Locke. Collins, *Essay*; Collins, *Philosophical Inquiry*.

3. Livingston, *Modern Christian Thought*, 1:16. Livingston's rational supernaturalist and deist categories are likely based to some degree on John Herman Randall, Jr.'s categories: supernatural rationalists and deists. It is unclear to me into which group Randall intends to place John Toland. Randall, Jr., *Making of the Modern Mind*, 285–89.

supernaturalists believed that revelation was necessary for salvation and the deists did not. The problem stemming from that is that the paradigm of the rational supernaturalists, John Locke, did believe that humans had the potential to be saved by responding to the natural light they had. While it was not likely, it was possible.[4]

Another commendable categorization scheme comes from Claude Welch in *Protestant Thought in the Nineteenth Century*, vol. 1. After naming Lord Herbert of Cherbury as being a significant first articulator of the precepts of natural religion, he goes on to categorize key figures into three chronologically overlapping but progressing stages of natural religion. The first stage, where John Locke is the paradigm, includes those who assert, "Essential Christianity, though its content transcends what alone reason is able to discover, is harmonious with natural religion."[5] "The second stage was characterized by the assertion that Christianity (insofar as it is acceptable) does not transcend natural religion but is an instance of it. At no point may Christianity go beyond it."[6] Toland and Tindal are placed in this stage. The third and final stage is marked by those who think revelation is "wholly unnecessary, or even opposed to the true religion of reason."[7]

The problems with Welch's scheme are few but important. First, stage one encompasses, in reality, those like Locke who do not, in principle, accept anything inconceivable into religion but also those who do. That is a rather significant difference to allow in the same stage. Secondly, moving from the first to the second stage, an important common point, Christianity, is necessarily defined differently in those different stages; and it is not even present in the description of the third stage. Thirdly, the appropriateness of putting those who see revelation as wholly unnecessary and those who think it opposed to true religion is doubtful. On a related point, it would seem that those who think revelation is wholly unnecessary (but not opposed to true religion) might fit better into the second stage.

While both of these models of thinking through the rise of natural religion could possibly be improved, this chapter suggests another and simpler categorization scheme that is inherent within this book. There are a series of sifting questions regarding revelation that one asks of and answers for a certain thinker. By virtue of these questions a thinker's approach to revelation *in principle* is used to group him or her with similarly principled individuals. The first question is: Does this thinker claim that assent to revelation as

---

4. Locke, *ROC*, 254–93.
5. Welch, *Protestant Thought*, 1:35.
6. Ibid., 36.
7. Ibid., 38.

being such can be legitimate? If no, the thinker denies revelation. If yes, the next question is asked: Does this thinker claim assent to revealed doctrines or propositions not comporting with natural probability can be legitimate?[8] If no, then the thinker teaches that divine revelation must comport with natural probability to be legitimate; in other words, legitimate revelation and its associated doctrines are according to or subordinate to the dictates

---

8 A proposition that does not comport with natural probability is one that runs counter to natural probability based upon purely natural considerations or a proposition asserted that could not rightly be affirmed upon purely natural considerations.

The following are some helpful reminders regarding natural probability. Natural probability includes the testimony of humans that does not originate in divine sources. The King of Siam hearing about particulars regarding Holland from a Dutch Ambassador may believe him about many things but stop short of assenting to the claim that an elephant could walk on a lake made hard by the bitter cold. The proposition, while not touching on the experience of the king, can be verified or could rationally be believed upon the veracity of the ambassador. All that is to say, natural probability is not necessarily the simple results of mental calculations based on the collections of the experiences and observations of an isolated individual (cf. Locke, *Essay* IV.xv.5). Also, one might through analogy and observation assent to propositions regarding the supernatural realm through divinely unassisted reasoning. For instance, it is possible some have reasoned that it is likely that there are ranks of intelligent beings, some of who are immaterial, that reach up to the infinite perfection of God (*Essay* IV.xvi.12). While this is a proposition focused on supernatural things it could come about from reasoning from natural sources. Locke's above (vulgar) reason category transcends divinely unassisted or natural probability. Locke's above (vulgar) reason propositions must be divinely revealed and they always pertain to supernatural things that we could not otherwise rationally assent to even in the unlikely scenario that we happened to imagine them (*Essay* IV.xvii.23; IV.xviii.7–8).

These things are important to understand in considering the second group—those that admit of traditional revelation but deny that it can go beyond natural or vulgar probability or run counter to it. For instance, if a divine revelation seems to suggest that the universe contains powerful, immaterial beings subordinate to God, a thinker in the second group could affirm that, while he or she might not affirm that one-third of them rebelled against God; the person might not be able, even with others, to come up with good reasons from purely natural considerations why this might be so. In addition, if one is convinced that the Bible teaches that God made humans in one day but is convinced that science says otherwise, science is to be followed. Thus the second group operates with the presupposition that God does not communicate propositions that we are unable to derive ourselves and assent to in principle or to observe ourselves and verify without divine assistance. In other words, they believe that God does not communicate to us that which is above (vulgar) reason or counter to or beyond natural probability. Traditional revelation for the second group can still be helpful in reminding us of or teaching us our moral duties or showing us the conclusions that reasoning should arrive at (and does), filling in the gaps in our reasoning, etc. It is possible that there are some who subordinate revelation to natural probability in only salvific matters—so as to give no geographical people group more of an advantage in being saved—and thus would claim assent to the proposition that one-third of the angels fell as being legitimate. But these would fall into the third group that this section will treat shortly.

of natural or vulgar reason.⁹ But if the answer is yes, another question is asked: Does this thinker claim assent to one or more revelations (namely revealed doctrines or groups of related propositions) that are ultimately inconceivable or irreconcilable can be legitimate? If the answer is no, the thinker denies revealed inconceivable doctrines but not conceivable ones that transcend natural probability; in other words, legitimate revelation and its associated doctrines are according to or subordinate to Locke's proper reason and its rules and thus can be above vulgar reason. If the answer is yes, another question *could* be asked: Does this thinker think that revealed doctrines or groups of propositions that offer so-called "human-logical contradictions" are acceptable? If no, the thinker accepts revelation as such that results in summarily incomprehensible doctrines but not those that are "human-logically contradictory" (In fact, most in the era would deny that it is theologically appropriate to separate human logic from divine logic.) If yes, then the thinker posits that we might be required to believe human-logical contradictions (that are not so according to God's logic). This final distinction, however, is found more at home within the discussions and debates among the orthodox thinkers and will not take up notable space here.¹⁰ On a similar note, one who accepts things above vulgar reason might consider things above proper reason to be considered logical contradictions or effectively so. Thus, based upon the questions being asked in the order they are, concrete groups are formed: 1) those that categorically reject revelation and divine doctrines as such; 2) those that categorically reject revelation and divine doctrines as such that do not comport with natural probability; 3) those that categorically reject revelation and divine doctrines

---

9. I say that they subordinate revelation to natural or vulgar reason because according to these thinkers revelation cannot run counter to natural probability or be above vulgar or natural reason to be considered as such. Nonetheless, these thinkers claim traditional revelation exists so they are technically operating with proper reason. The difference, however, is in the nature of revelation. According to them, it will never assert something or present an argument, if it is truly divine, that natural or vulgar reason would dismiss if the claim were merely based on human testimony or other natural sources without any admixture of divine assistance. This counters Locke's stance that revelation can trump natural probability and even convey propositions beyond our natural or vulgar reasoning abilities.

10. Francis Turretin answers the following question with a yes for the Reformed tradition: May the judgment of contradiction be allowed to human reason in matters of faith? He charges the Lutherans (namely the ubiquitarians) with ruling out the judgment of contradiction in so-called matters of the faith. Turretin, *Institutes of Elecntic Theology*, 1:32. Anthony Collins, one of the foremost thinkers frequently labeled a deist, chides those who dismiss the use of human logic in theology. For him, while God is far more perfect and intelligent, our human logic is a subset of the divine logic. Collins, *Essay*.

CONCLUSIONS AND IMPLICATIONS   181

as such that go beyond natural conceivability or reconcilability; 4) those that can accept inconceivable, albeit logically non-contradictory, revelation or doctrines; 5) those that can accept revelation or doctrines with so-called human-logical contradictions (but would not accept that the divine logic could be transgressed).[11]

The advantages of this scheme are a few. For one, this concentrates on the nature of reason, faith, and traditional revelation. While other types of revelation are discussed during this period in history, most of these English thinkers are predominantly concerned with the Bible, the accepted traditional revelation of Christianity. While modern-day original revelation was also an important topic, allowances for it or categorical rejections of it could be based upon Scriptural considerations. Presumably, most would agree that these thinkers' stances on the question of modern-day revelation are less important than their stances on traditional revelation from past original revelation. These questions give a better sense of the thinkers' positions on the latter (One would be hard pressed to find a notable thinker in the era who explicitly denies ancient revelation while accepting only contemporary revelation. Besides, the questions could easily be reconfigured to specify Scripture as the revelation of concern.) Also, concentrating on the nature of revelation from the standpoints of thinkers is more orderly than grouping thinkers based upon what they think is necessary for salvation, or some other complicated issue. Furthermore, this scheme is based upon Lockean categories. This is important because the epistemologies of thinkers typically found in the narrative are variations of the epistemology laid out in the *Essay*. Locke looms large into the eighteenth-century and his *Essay* undoubtedly helped guide conversations about revelation. Asking the above questions for thinkers such as Anthony Collins or John Tillotson, who himself was likely formative to the *Essay,* are areas for further study, while a cursory read of Tindal, at least toward the end of his life, would seem to place him in the second group, those who subordinate revelation to natural probability.[12] What is more, from this book it is apparent that Locke and Toland fit into the third group together.

11. The first question asked in the series of questions groups thinkers into one of two groups, the first being group one, the second containing groups two, three, four, and five. The second question divides this second group into two groups, the first being group two, and the second being comprised of groups three, four, and five. The third question then further divides the combined grouping of groups three, four, and five into group three and a grouping consisting of groups four and five. The fourth question then divides group four and five.

12. Tindal, *Christianity as Old*. He is quite explicit that his desire is to "advance the Honour of *External* Revelation; by shewing the perfect Agreement between *That* and *Internal* Revelation" (8). He also remarks that external revelation and natural religion

Moreover, the fact that Toland is placed in the same group as Locke and not the group that subordinates revelation to natural or vulgar reason or the group that denies revelation would tend to overturn John Higgins-Biddle's hypothesis regarding the writing of *ROC*, now taken as a matter of fact by some. He thinks it is possible that Locke had a copy of *CNM* prior to its publication. If so, he wonders if Locke's noting of its epistemological connections to his *Essay* and its deistic conclusions might have caused him to write *ROC*, in part, to show his *Essay* does not end up in deism, but on the contrary is against it.[13] What is more, Higgins-Biddle's account appears to be a tacit affirmation of Stillingfleet's reading of *CNM*. Nonetheless, the conjectured motivations for Locke's writing of *ROC* lose their force when it is seen that the gulf between the *Essay* and *CNM* is not as wide as once thought.

Finally, there is some warrant for the frequent grouping of Toland together with Tindal as opposed to Locke, but scholarship has not properly identified these connections. Again, first and foremost the grouping occurs in scholarship because Toland is thought to have subordinated revelation to natural reason as does Tindal. While this is incorrect, there are still important affinities between the two thinkers. In the end, Toland seems to strip Christianity of God's original revelation of the unconveyable sort, modern-day miracles, and modern-day revelation. Tindal also seems to attack unconveyable original revelation, modern-day original revelation, and miracles, albeit from different angles.[14] Thus, Toland and Tindal both limit God's interaction. So, when only considering their conclusions as stated, Tindal and Toland appear to be more alike than Locke and Toland. A further study juxtaposing Toland and Tindal more thoroughly than done here, however, is needed and would likely prove a helpful and fruitful project.

---

may not differ in one aspect (51). He also gets rid of Locke's rule that revelation can trump natural probability (158). While Tindal is operating with a version of Locke's proper reason (he *is* claiming traditional revelation is such), his expunging of the rule effectively subordinates revelation to natural probability or, in this book's terms, vulgar reason. It is possible, however, that Tindal means that the way of salvation as explained in revelation cannot differ from natural religion (cf. 59). So, Tindal might claim beliefs in above natural or vulgar reason propositions not regarding the message of salvation, such as one-third of the angels rebelled, could be reasonably accepted. While this latter explanation is doubtful, more investigation and closer readings of Tindal would be needed.

13. Higgins-Biddle, introduction to *The Reasonableness of Christianity*, xxvii–xxxvii; Biddle, "Locke's Critique of Innate."

14. Tindal, *Christianity as Old*, 162, 170, 199.

PART III: CATEGORIZATION OF PROPOSITIONS AND DOCTRINES

It is worthwhile mentioning a few observations regarding categorizations of propositions or doctrines in the *Essay* and *CNM*. This book has shown that Locke's stated acceptance of above reason propositions or doctrines and Toland's rejection of doctrines with the same label amounts to no epistemological differences between the two thinkers. Had they organized propositions and doctrines according to their preferred conception of reason, proper reason, they would have the same categorization of propositions. Interestingly, neither thinker explicitly produces such a categorization. The explicit categorization Locke does give, as mentioned in chapter 3, is concessionary, having been based upon his concessionary vulgar reason notion. Toland defines contrary to reason things and above reason things to discuss those categories but never presents a full taxonomy including an according to reason category. In short, while this book asserts that they have apparently limited themselves to have according to reason and contrary to reason proposition categories ready to hand, they never expressly employ them. While it could be the case that both thinkers never offer a full and preferred categorization of propositions because they believe that the reader should infer it, it also might be that both decided not to offer an express and preferred categorization of propositions due to the confusion that could arise.

In their era, such categorizations of propositions in relation to "reason" abounded. Reading *CNM* alone gives you the sense of the confusion that could arise and the effort one might expend in trying to explain what is or should be meant by the different categories. Perhaps additional evidence that Toland and Locke were far more interested in undoing the harm done by what they considered haphazard employment of labels (Locke with far more subtlety) and that they were not very interested in positively advocating a particular way of categorizing are comparisons of their works with those of Robert Boyle (1627–91). While acknowledging that employment of such labels are liable to misunderstanding, Boyle, undeterred, carefully explains, for instance, how we can understand and organize all of the different things that often come to be spoken of as being "above reason."[15] In short, Locke's, Toland's, and Boyle's pertinent works all share a careful criticism of the then-current categorizations of propositions, but it is only Boyle's that are also clearly constructive in that respect.

---

15. Marko, "Above Reason Propositions."

PART IV: LOCKE'S AND TOLAND'S HERMENEUTICS AMIDST THE INFLUENCES OF THE NATURAL SCIENCES AND BIBLICAL CRITICISM

Locke and Toland operate with a certain epistemological and hermeneutical principle that guards against the Bible's authority being usurped by extra-biblical sources. Locke is adamant in his debate with Stillingfleet that a particular doctrine derived from Scripture is not to be thought more or less credible depending on the probability for or against it supplied by vulgar or natural reason.[16] What can be inferred from this is that while vulgar reason may provide us with a possible interpretation, one should not be compelled in any sense to use or favor such an interpretation. So, an interpretation of a passage that is supported by a prevailing theory of natural science, for instance, is not, because of that support, to be given more weight than an interpretation that does not seem as probable under only natural considerations. When it comes to multiple, possible interpretations, the only advice Locke has is that one proposition of Scripture cannot contradict another. If that cannot be done with two propositions, for instance, after "fair endeavours," one must suspend one's judgment.[17]

Now this rule clearly affects passages that might be or are commenting on metaphysics, miracles, or divine agency. But that is not all. This rule even applies to passages where one might claim that archaeological findings "support" Scripture's historical claims. Again, Locke and Toland would counter that Scripture is not made more credible by finding support in archaeological findings but rather the Bible confirms the probable interpretations of the unearthed data that conform to it. For Locke and Toland there is comparatively little knowledge for us in this world. We are immersed in probability.

How well they employed this principle is another question. Both men have works in other areas beyond theology where Scripture is employed. How much biblical support did they *find*, for instance, for their political views? Does it appear they are guilty of eisegesis? If so, might this offer some insight to the next generations of political writers who eschew the Bible?

---

16. Locke, *Mr. Locke's Reply . . . Answer to his Second Letter*, 136–39, 418–29, 443–44.

17. Locke, *ROC*, 304.

PART V: THE QUESTION OF STYLISTIC CAMOUFLAGE AND HIDDEN PANTHEISM VERSUS DEISM FORTHRIGHTLY STATED

In the 1980s a rift in Toland scholarship was created. Toland's *CNM* had been fashioned as a "deistic" work and the progenitor of Tindal's so-called "Deist's Bible," *Christianity as Old as the Creation*. In the 1982 publication of *John Toland and the Deist Controversy*, Robert E. Sullivan advanced his notion that Toland is truly a pantheistic materialist at the time of writing *CNM*.[18] Sullivan thinks that Toland argues for revelation because the Bible supports civil order and morals, but concurrently argues that Christianity is simply an instance of natural religion.[19] In truth, according to Sullivan, Toland, however, does not believe in the possibility of divine revelation.[20] This was received into scholarship by some with slight alteration and by others with significant alterations. That latter scholarship hypothesizes that *CNM* has a three-tiered intention as follows: first, Toland wants *CNM* at face value to read like a Christian work—for instance, defending revelation; second, Toland wants to lead unwary readers to make for themselves the irreligious conclusions against which Toland pretends to be writing; and third, Toland wants to convey to the intelligent, irreligious readers his true beliefs.[21] So while the older line of Toland scholarship and much of the recent Toland scholarship label Toland as a deist, some since Sullivan understand *CNM* to be masking Toland's pantheism.

There are problems with all of these views. First, as already discussed, epistemologically Toland is closer to Locke than he is to Tindal. Regarding Sullivan's claims and the assertions of many others, *CNM* does not subordinate revelation to natural reason and Christianity requires faith in Christ for those who have heard the gospel. So it cannot simply be promulgating natural religion or deism. Also, Sullivan's argument that Toland was a pantheist all of his life is based on circular reasoning as discussed in chapter 4.[22] And, those with the complicated three-tiered notion of *CNM* have just as many problems. What are these irreligious conclusions that Toland intended his reader to make and that his irreligious counterparts understood? Again, these authors simply make assertions amidst scant exegetical work

18. Sullivan, *John Toland*, 43–47, 114–19.
19. Ibid., 119, 138, 173–74, 207–8.
20. Ibid., 125, 127, 216, 275.
21. Berman, "Deism, Immortality, and the Art"; Berman, "Disclaimers as Offence Mechanisms"; Berman, "Toland, John"; Fouke, *Philosophy and Theology*; cf. Berman, *History of Atheism*.
22. Cf. Rappaport, "Questions of Evidence."

and depend on the claims of Toland's adversaries that he has underhanded intentions. Toland is shown in this book to echo Locke in so many respects to the degree that they are left with one of two conclusions if they want to persist with their hypothesis: 1) Locke is oblivious to his mistakes that Toland mischievously replicates and there are plenty of people on a higher mental level than Locke that recognize them; or 2) Locke is doing the same thing that they claim Toland to be doing. Assuming they would choose the latter option, they still must be pressed to deliver precisely how Toland and Locke intend to undercut Christianity with hidden snares. This will also require that they enter the lists with some very formidable Locke scholars, few of whom doubt that Locke earnestly thought himself a believing Christian under the authority of Scripture.[23]

If there is any charge of knowing misconduct, it is unlikely in either thinker's epistemology. Some have charged Locke with the abuse of Scripture intentionally or unintentionally, but that question could be investigated regarding Locke and Toland in the suggested study below.

PART VI: A COMPARISON OF LOCKE AND TOLAND REGARDING THE NATURE OF SCRIPTURE AND HERMENEUTICS

A final area of study involving Locke and Toland that could build on this book is a comparative look at Locke's and Toland's bibliologies in this time period. This would involve exploring both thinkers regarding their views of the nature of Scripture, namely the attributes of Scripture. The thinkers' respective views on hermeneutics in principle and in practice could also be explicitly incorporated. Such a study would go beyond the subsections involving reason and revelation in this book. While *CNM* is a combination of

---

23. There is another way that one might attempt to argue that Toland's, and even Locke's, 1695–96 works are undergirded by pantheism: that anything mentally irreconcilable should be dismissed. Many theists claim that we should not expect to be able to reconcile all ideas as there are supernatural things for which we have no direct experience. A Trinitarian might say, for instance, that God is one with respect to substance and three with respect to persons (and thus not a logical contradiction), even though in our experience one human substance results only in one human person; our experience of a material world and faculties do not provide us with ideas by which to reconcile the doctrine of the holy Trinity. So, one might argue that Locke and Toland do not accept irreconcilable things because there is actually nothing that is supernatural: all is nature. But that would directly contradict them in their works either regarding pantheism or their trust that God has equipped us for what is helpful (and that apparently excludes some supernatural things). What is more, they both admit supernatural miracles as an external mark of divine revelation.

a theological work and an exploration of experimental philosophy, the *Essay* is predominantly an exploration of experimental philosophy. Thus, to get a better grasp on Locke's hermeneutics and his positions on several aspects of Scripture, *ROC* and its vindications, which are primarily theological, would be necessary to study.

This proposed study of Locke's and Toland's views of the nature of Scripture and hermeneutics is, in fact, one logical next step to this book. While in recent decades scholarship has become increasingly focused on Locke's theology, little has been done specifically with Locke's bibliology. It is possible that Locke's views on the nature of Scripture have received so little attention because treatments of biblical authority are impossible to separate from Locke's epistemology regarding faith, revelation, and reason, all challenging interrelated topics. In other words, what has made an exploration of Locke's bibliology formidable is that Locke's epistemology has been interpreted very differently by the many scholars involved in the on-going conversation. Thus, there is no consensus view of Locke's epistemology from which to build. Moreover, there has been some scholarly treatment of Toland regarding Scripture, and those are typically on his hermeneutics. But these have approached Toland as one who thinks the Bible does not or cannot give humans anything that transcends natural probability.[24]

I hope this present work opens new vistas for the prolegomena and hermeneutics of John Locke and John Toland and spurs on further studies into the theology and epistemology of John Tillotson, Anthony Collins, and Matthew Tindal, just to name a few.

---

24. Works for beginning the exploration of the scholarship on Locke's understandings of Scripture and hermeneutics are: Champion, "'Directions for the Profitable Reading"; Champion, "'Law of Continuity"; Foster, "The Bible and Natural Freedom"; Kuehne, "Reinventing Paul"; Sell, *John Locke*, 92–104; Conrad, "Locke's Use of the Bible"; Weinsheimer, *Eighteenth-Century Hermeneutics*; Lucci, *Scripture and Deism*. These last two works treat Locke and Toland.

Bibliography

PRIMARY WORKS

Bacon, Francis. *Instauratio Magna: Of the Advancement and Proficiencie of Learning of the Partitions of Sciences in IX Bookes.* Translated by Gilbert Wats. Oxford: Leonard Lichfield, 1640.

Bayle, Pierre. *A General Dictionary, Historical and Critical.* Vol. 4. Translated and edited by John Peter Bernard et al. London: James Bettenham, 1736.

"Bibliotheque Raisonnée des Ouvrages des Savans de l'Europe pour les Mois d' Avril, Mai & Juin 1730." Amsterdam: Wetsteins & Smith, 1730.

Boyle, Robert. *The Christian Virtuoso: Shewing, That by Being Addicted to Experimental Philosophy, a Man Is Rather Assisted, than Indisposed, to Be a Good Christian. The First Part.* London: printed by Edw. Jones for John Taylor, 1690.

———. *Reflections upon a Theological Distinction. According to Which, 'tis Said, That Some Articles of Faith Are Above Reason But Not Against Reason. In a Letter to a Friend.* London: printed by Edw. Jones for John Taylor, 1690.

———. *The Works of the Honourable Robert Boyle.* Edited by Thomas Birch. 6 vols. Vol 1. London: printed for John and Francis Rivington et al., 1772. Vols. 2–6. London: printed for W. Johnston et al., 1772.

Bramhall, John. *A Defence of True Liberty from Antecedent and Extrinsicall Necessity, Being an Answer to a Late Book of Mr. Thomas Hobbs of Malmsbury, Intituled, A Treatise of Liberty and Necessity.* London: John Crook, 1655.

Clarke, Samuel. *Remarks upon a Book Entituled, A Philosophical Enquiry Concerning Human Liberty.* London: n.p., 1717.

———. *Samuel Clarke, The Works.* 4 vols. London: J. and P. Knapton, 1738. Reprint. New York: Garland, 1978.

Collins, Anthony. *An Answer to Mr. Clark's Third Defence of His Letter to Mr. Dodwell.* 2nd ed., cor. London: J. Darby, 1711.

———. *A Discourse of Free-Thinking, Occasion'd by the Rise and Growth of a Sect Call'd Free-Thinkers.* London: n.p., 1713.

———. *A Dissertation on Liberty and Necessity: Wherein the Process of Ideas, from Their First Entrance into the Soul, until Their Production of Action, Is Delineated. With Some Remarks upon the Late Reverend Dr. Clarke's Reasoning on This Point. And an Epistle Dedicatory to Truth.* London: J. Shuckburgh, 1729.

———. *An Essay Concerning the Use of Reason in Propositions, the Evidence whereof Depends upon Human Testimony*. 2nd ed., cor. London: 1709.

———. *A Philosophical Inquiry Concerning Human Liberty*. 2nd ed., cor. London: n.p., 1717.

———. *Reflections on Mr. Clark's Second Defence of His Letter to Mr. Dodwel*. 2nd ed., cor. London: J. Darby, 1711.

———. *A Vindication of the Divine Attributes. In Some Remarks on His Grace the Archbishop of Dublin's Sermon Intituled, Divine Predestination and Foreknowledge Consistent with the Freedom of Man's Will*. London: n.p., 1710.

Gretton, Phillips. *Remarks upon Two Pamphlets Written by the Late A. C. Esq; Concerning Human Liberty and Necessity*. London: Stephen Austen, 1730.

Hare, Francis. *Church Authority Vindicated in a Sermon Preach'd at Putney, May 5, 1719: At a Visitation of the Peculiars of the Most Reverend the Lord Bishop of Canterbury, before the Right Worshipful Dr. Beetesworth, Dean of the Arches, and Commissary of Those Peculiars, to Which Is Added, a Postscript, Occasioned by the Right Reverend the Ld. Bishop of Bangor's Answer*. 4th ed., cor. London: J. Roberts, 1720.

Harvey, Gideon. *Archeologia Philosophica Nova*. London: J. H. for Samuel Thomson, 1663.

Hobbes, Thomas, and John Bramhall. *Hobbes and Bramhall on Liberty and Necessity*. Edited by Vere Chappell. Cambridge: Cambridge University Press, 1999.

Hobs, Thomas. *Of Libertie and Necessitie*. London: W. B. for F. Eaglesfield, 1654.

Jackson, John. *A Vindication of Humane Liberty: In Answer to a Dissertation on Liberty and Necessity; Written by A. C. Esq*. London: J. Noon, 1730.

King, William. *Divine Predestination and Fore-knowledge, Consistent with the Freedom of Man's Will, a Sermon Preached at Christ-Church Dublin, May 15, 1709*. Dublin: J. Gowan, 1727.

———. *Essay on the Origen of Evil*. 2nd ed., cor. 2 vols. Translated by Edmund Law. London: J. Stephens, 1732.

Lessing, Gotthold Ephraim. *Philosophical and Theological Writings*. Translated and edited by H. B. Nisbet. Cambridge: Cambridge University Press, 2005.

Locke, John. *An Answer to Remarks upon An Essay Concerning Humane Understanding*. Appended to Locke's *A Letter to Edward Ld Bishop of Worcester, Concerning Some Passages Relating to Mr. Locke's Essay of Humane Understanding: In a Late Discourse of His Lordships, In Vindication of the Trinity*. London: printed for A. and J. Churchill, 1697.

———. *An Essay Concerning Human Understanding*. Edited by Peter H. Nidditch. Oxford: Clarendon, 1979.

———. *An Essay Concerning Humane Understanding*. 3rd ed. London: printed for Awnsham and John Churchil and Samuel Manship, 1695.

———. *A Letter to Edward Ld Bishop of Worcester, Concerning Some Passages Relating to Mr. Locke's Essay of Humane Understanding: In a Late Discourse of His Lordships, In Vindication of the Trinity*. London: printed for A. and J. Churchill, 1697.

———. "L1804: Locke to Phillipus van Limborch, 26 October 1694." In *The Correspondence of John Locke*, vol. 5, edited by E. S. De Beer, 169–75. Oxford: Clarendon, 1979.

———. "L2202: Locke to William Molyneux, 22 February 1697." In *The Correspondence of John Locke*, vol. 6, edited by E. S. De Beer, 4–9. Oxford: Clarendon, 1981.

———. "L2243: Locke to William Molyneux, 10 April 1697." In *The Correspondence of John Locke*, vol. 6, edited by E. S. De Beer, 86–93. Oxford: Clarendon, 1981.

———. "L2254: Locke to William Molyneux, 3 May 1697." In *The Correspondence of John Locke*, vol. 6, edited by E. S. De Beer, 105–8. Oxford: Clarendon, 1981.

———. "L2277: Locke to William Molyneux, 15 June 1697." In *The Correspondence of John Locke*, vol. 6, edited by E. S. De Beer, 142–45. Oxford: Clarendon, 1981.

———. *Mr. Locke's Reply to the Right Reverend the Lord Bishop of Worcester's Answer to His Letter, Concerning Some Passages Relating to Mr. Locke's Essay of Humane Understanding: In a Late Discourse of His Lordships, In Vindication of the Trinity*. London: printed by H. Clark for A. and J. Churchill and E. Castle, 1697.

———. *Mr. Locke's Reply to the Right Reverend the Lord Bishop of Worcester's Answer to His Second Letter*. London: printed by H. C. for A. and J. Churchill and E. Castle, 1699.

———. *A Paraphrase and Notes on the Epistles of St. Paul to the Galatians, Romans, I & II Corinthians, Ephesians. To Which Is Prefix'd, An Essay for the Understanding of St. Paul's Epistles, by Consulting St. Paul Himself*. London: printed by J. H. Awnsham and John Churchill, 1707.

———. *The Posthumous Works of Mr. John Locke: viz. I. Of the Conduct of the Understanding. II. An Examination of P. Malebranche's Opinion of Seeing All Things in God. III. A Discourse of Miracles. IV. Part of a Fourth Letter for Toleration. V. Memoirs Relating to the Life of Anthony First Earl of Shaftsbury. To Which Is Added, IV. His New Method of a Common-Place-Book, Written Originally in French, and Now Translated into English*. London: printed by W. B. for A. and J. Churchill, 1706.

———. *The Reasonableness of Christianity as Delivered in the Scriptures*. Edited by John C. Higgins-Biddle. Oxford: Clarendon, 1999.

———. *The Reasonableness of Christianity, as Delivered in the Scriptures*. 2nd ed. London: Awnsham and John Churchil, 1696.

———. *A Second Vindication of the Reasonableness of Christianity, etc*. London: A. and J. Churchil, 1697.

———. *A Vindication of the Reasonableness of Christianity, from Mr. Edwards's Exceptions*. Appended to *The Reasonableness of Christianity, as delivered in the Scriptures*. 2nd ed. London: Awnsham and John Churchil, 1696.

———. *The Works of John Locke Esq*. 3 vols. London: printed for John Churchil and Sam. Manship, 1714.

L. P. Master of Arts. *Two Essays in a Letter from Oxford to a Nobleman in London*. London: R. Baldwin, 1695.

Molyneux, William. "L2189: William Molyneux to Locke, 3 February 1697." In *The Correspondence of John Locke*, vol. 5, edited by E. S. De Beer, 766–67. Oxford: Clarendon, 1979.

———. "L2269: William Molyneux to Locke, 27 May 1697." In *The Correspondence of John Locke*, vol. 6, edited by E. S. De Beer, 132–35. Oxford: Clarendon, 1981.

Norris, John. *An Account of Faith and Reason: In Relation to the Mysteries of Christianity*. London: printed for S. Manship, 1697.

Nye, Stephen. *The Agreement of the Unitarians with the Catholick Church: Being also A Full Answer, to the Infamations of Mr. Edwards; and the Needless Exceptions, of My Lords the Bishops of Chichester, Worcester, and Sarum, and of Monsieur De Luzancy*. London: n.p., 1697.

Pope, Alexander. *An Essay on Man. Enlarged and Improved by the Author. Together with His MS. Additions and Variations, as in the Last Edition of His Works. With the Notes of Mr. Warburton*. London: printed for J. and P. Knapton, 1755.

Sennert, Daniel. *Thirteen Books of Natural Philosophy*. London: Peter Cole, 1660.

Spencer, Thomas. *The Art of Logick Delivered in the Precepts of Ramus*. London: John Dawson, 1628.

Stillingfleet, Edward. *The Bishop of Worcester's Answer to Mr. Locke's Letter, Concerning Some Passages Relating to His Essay of Humane Understanding, Mention'd in the Late Discourse in Vindication of the Trinity*. London: printed by J. H. for Henry Mortlock, 1697.

———. *The Bishop of Worcester's Answer to Mr. Locke's Second Letter; wherein His Notion of Ideas Is Prov'd to Be Inconsistent with It Self, and with the Articles of the Christian Faith*. London: printed by J. H. for Henry Mortlock, 1698.

———. *A Discourse in Vindication of the Trinity with an Answer to the Late Socinian Objections against It from Scripture, Antiquity and Reason*. 1st ed. London: printed by J. H. for Henry Mortlock, 1697.

———. *A Discourse in Vindication of the Trinity with an Answer to the Late Socinian Objections against It from Scripture, Antiquity and Reason*. 2nd ed. London: printed by J. H. for Henry Mortlock, 1697.

Tillotson, John. "Sermon XI: Of the Miracles Wrought in Confirmation of Christianity." In *Fifteen Sermons on Various Subjects*, edited by Ralph Barker, 301–42. London: Ri. Chiswell, 1703.

———. "Sermon XII: Of the Miracles Wrought in Confirmation of Christianity." In *Fifteen Sermons on Various Subjects*, edited by Ralph Barker, 343–70. London: Ri. Chiswell, 1703.

———. "Sermon XIII: Of the Miracles Wrought in Confirmation of Christianity." In *Fifteen Sermons on Various Subjects*, edited by Ralph Barker, 371–96. London: Ri. Chiswell, 1703.

Tindal, Matthew. *Christianity as Old as the Creation: or, The Gospel, a Republication of the Religion of Nature*. London: n.p., 1730.

Toland, John. *An Apology for Mr. Toland, in a Letter from Himself to a Member of the House of Commons in Ireland; Written the Day before His Book Was Resolv'd to Be Burnt by the Committee of Religion. To Which Is Prefix'd a Narrative Containing the Occasion of the Said Letter*. London: n.p., 1697.

———. *Christianity Not Mysterious: or, A Treatise Shewing, That There Is Nothing in the Gospel Contrary to Reason, Nor above It: and That No Christian Doctrine Can Be Properly Call'd a Mystery*. 1st ed. London: n.p., 1696.

———. *Christianity Not Mysterious: or, A Treatise Shewing, That There Is Nothing in the Gospel Contrary to Reason, Nor above It: and That No Christian Doctrine Can Be Properly Call'd a Mystery*. 2nd ed. London: printed for Sam Buckley, 1696.

———. *A Collection of Several Pieces of Mr. John Toland*. 2 Vols. London: printed for J. Peele, 1726.

———. *A Defence of Mr. Toland in a Letter to Himself*. London: printed for E. Whitlock, 1697.

———. *Letters to Serena: Containing, I. The Origin and Force of Prejudices. II. The History of the Soul's Immortality among the Heathens. III. The Origin of Idolatry, and Reasons of Heathenism. As also, IV. A Letter to a Gentleman in Holland, Showing Spinosa's System of Philosophy to Be without Any Principle or Foundation*.

V. Motion Essential to Matter; in Answer to Some Remarks by a Noble Friend on the Confutation of Spinosa. To All Which Is Prefix'd, VI. A Preface: Being a Letter to a Gentleman in London, Sent Together with the Foregoing Dissertations, and Declaring the Several Occasions of Writing Them. London: printed for Bernard Lintot, 1704.

———. *Vindicius Liberius: or M. Toland's Defence of Himself, against the Late Lower House of Convocation, and Others*. London: printed for Bernard Lintott, 1702.

Turretin, Francis. *Institutes of Elenctic Theology*. 3 vols. Translated by George Musgrave Giger and edited by James T. Dennison, Jr. Phillipsburg: P. & R., 1992.

SECONDARY WORKS

Antognazza, Maria Rosa. *Leibniz on the Trinity and the Incarnation: Reason and Revelation in the Seventeenth Century*. Translated by Gerald Parks. New Haven: Yale University Press, 2007.

Ashcraft, Richard. "Faith and Knowledge in Locke's Philosophy." In *John Locke: Problems and Perspectives*, edited by John W. Yolton, 194–223. Cambridge: Cambridge University Press, 1969.

Ayers, Michael. *Locke*. 2 vols. New York: Routledge, 1991.

Beiser, Frederick C. *The Sovereignty of Reason: The Defense of Rationality in the Early English Enlightenment*. Princeton: Princeton University Press, 1996.

Berman, David. "Anthony Collins: Aspects of His Thought and Writing." *Hermathena* 119 (1975) 49–70.

———. "Anthony Collins' Essays in the Independent Whig." *Journal of the History of Philosophy* 13, no. 4 (October 1975) 463–69.

———. "Collins, Anthony (1676–1729)." In *The Continuum Encyclopedia of British Philosophy, vol. 1 A–C.*, edited by Anthony Grayling et al., 681–84. New York: Thoemmes Continuum, 2006.

———. "Deism, Immortality, and the Art of Theological Lying." In *Deism, Masonry, and the Enlightenment*, edited by J. A. Leo Lemay, 71–78. Newark, NY: University of Delaware Press, 1987.

———. "Disclaimers as Offence Mechanisms in Charles Blount and John Toland." In *Atheism from the Reformation to the Enlightenment*, edited by Michael Hunter and David Wooton, 255–72. Oxford: Clarendon, 1992.

———. *A History of Atheism in Britain: From Hobbes to Russell*. New York: Croom Helm, 1988.

———. "Toland, John." In *The New Encyclopedia of Unbelief*, edited by Tom Flynn, 749–51. Amherst, MA: Prometheus, 2007

Biddle, John C. "Locke's Critique of Innate Principles and Toland's Deism." *Journal of the History of Ideas* 37, no. 3 (1976) 411–22.

Brown, Stuart. "Locke as Secret 'Spinozist': The Perspective of William Carroll." In *Disguised and Overt Spinozism Around 1700: Papers Presented at the International Colloquium Held at Rotterdam, 5–8 October 1994*, edited by Wiep Van Bunge and Wim Klever, 213–34. New York: Brill, 1996.

Buckley, Michael J. *At the Origins of Modern Atheism*. New Haven: Yale University Press, 1987.

Champion, Justin. "'Directions for the Profitable Reading of the Holy Scriptures': Biblical Criticism, Clerical Learning and Lay Readers, c. 1650–1720." In *Scripture and Scholarship in Early Modern England*, edited by Ariel Hessayon and Nicholas Keene, 208–30. Burlington, VT: Ashgate, 2006.

———. "Enlightened Erudition and the Politics of Reading in John Toland's Circle." *The Historical Journal* 49, no. 1 (2006) 111–41.

———. "'A Law of Continuity in the Progress of Theology': Assessing the Legacy of John Locke's *Reasonableness of Christianity*, 1695–2004." *Eighteenth-Century Thought* 3 (2007) 111–42.

———. *Republican Learning: John Toland and the Crisis of Christian Culture, 1696–1722*. Manchester: Manchester University Press, 2003.

Christophersen, H. O. *A Bibliographical Introduction to the Study of John Locke*. New York: Franklin, 1930.

Clarke, Desmond M. "Toland on Faith and Reason." In *John Toland's Christianity Not Mysterious: Text, Associated Works and Critical Essays*, edited by Philip McGuiness et al., 293–302. Dublin: Lilliput, 1997.

Conrad, Jonathan Donald. "Locke's Use of the Bible in *The Two Treatises*, *The Reasonableness of Christianity*, and a *Letter Concerning Toleration*." PhD diss., Northern Illinois University, 2004.

Copleston, Frederick. *A History of Philosophy*. 9 vols. Westminster, UK: Newman, 1964.

Cragg, Gerald R. *The Church and the Age of Reason, 1648–1789*. Rev. ed., 1967. Reprint, New York: Penguin, 1990.

———. *Reason and Authority in the Eighteenth Century*. Cambridge: Cambridge University Press, 1964.

Cranston, Maurice. *John Locke: A Biography*. New York: MacMillan, 1957.

Daniel, Stephen H. *John Toland His Methods, Manners, and Mind*. Kingston, Ontario: McGill-Queen's University Press, 1984.

Dunn, John. *The Political Thought of John Locke: An Historical Account of the Argument of the 'Two Treatises of Government.'* Cambridge: Cambridge University Press, 1969.

Dworetz, Steven M. *The Unvarnished Doctrine: Locke, Liberalism, and the American Revolution*. Durham, NC: Duke University Press, 1990.

Foster, David. "The Bible and Natural Freedom in John Locke's Political Thought." In *Piety and Humanity*, edited by Douglas Kries, 181–212. Lanham, MD: Rowman and Littlefield, 1997.

Fouke, Daniel C. *Philosophy and Theology in a Burlesque Mode: John Toland and "The Way of Paradox."* Amherst, MA: Humanity, 2007.

Gerrish, B. A. *The Old Protestantism and the New: Essays on the Reformation Heritage*. Chicago: University of Chicago Press, 1982.

Harris, James A. *Of Liberty and Necessity: The Free Will Debate in Eighteenth-Century British Philosophy*. Oxford: Clarendon, 2005.

Heinemann, F. H. "John Toland and the Enlightenment." *The Review of English Studies* 20, no. 78 (1944) 125–46.

Helm, Paul. "Locke on Faith and Knowledge." *The Philosophical Quarterly* 23, no. 90 (1973) 52–66.

Higgins-Biddle, John C. Introduction to *The Reasonableness of Christianity*, edited by John C. Higgins-Biddle, xv–cxv. Oxford: Clarendon, 1999.

Israel, Jonathan I. *Radical Enlightenment: Philosophy and the Making of Modernity 1650-1750*. Oxford: Oxford University Press, 2001.
Jolley, Nicholas. "Locke on Faith and Reason." In *The Cambridge Companion to Locke's "Essay Concerning Human Understanding,"* edited by Lex Newman, 436-55. Cambridge: Cambridge University Press, 2007.
Klever, Wim. "Slocke, Alias Locke in Spinozistic Profile." In *Disguised and Overt Spinozism Around 1700: Papers Presented at the International Colloquium Held at Rotterdam, 5-8 October 1994*, edited by Wiep Van Bunge and Wim Klever, 235-60. Leiden: Brill, 1996.
Kuehn, Manfred. "Reason and Understanding." In *The Routledge Companion to Eighteenth Century Philosophy*, edited by Aaron Garret, 167-87. New York: Routledge, 2014.
Kuehne, Dale S. "Reinventing Paul: John Locke, the Geneva Bible, and Paul's Epistle to the Romans." In *Piety and Humanity*, edited by Douglas Kries, 213-32. Lanham, MD: Rowman and Littlefield, 1997.
Leask, Ian. "Personation and Immanent Undermining: On Toland's Appearing Lockean." *British Journal for the History of Philosophy* 18, no. 2 (2010) 231-56.
Lewis, C. S. *Letters to Malcolm: Chiefly on Prayer*. San Diego: Harcourt, 1992.
Livingston, James C. *Modern Christian Thought*. 2nd ed. 2 vols. Minneapolis: Fortress, 2006.
LoLordo, Antonia. *Locke's Moral Man*. Oxford: Oxford University Press, 2012.
Losonsky, Michael. "Locke and Leibniz on Religious Faith." *British Journal for the History of Philosophy* 20, no. 4 (2012) 703-21.
Lucci, Diego. *Scripture and Deism: The Biblical Criticism of the Eighteenth-Century British Deists*. New York: Lang, 2008.
Marko, Jonathan S. "Above Reason Propositions and Contradiction in the Religious Thought of Robert Boyle." *Forum Philosophicum* 19, no. 2 (2014) 227-39.
———. "Justification, Ecumenism, and Heretical Red Herrings in John Locke's *The Reasonableness of Christianity*." *Philosophy and Theology* 26, no. 2 (2014) 245-66.
———. "The Promulgation of Right Morals: John Locke on the Church and the Christian as the Salvation of Society." *Journal of Markets and Morality* 19, no. 1 (2016) 41-59.
———. "Revisiting the Question: Is Anthony Collins the Author of the 1729 *Dissertation on Liberty and Necessity*." *Philosophy and Theology* 22, nos. 1 & 2 (2010) 77-104.
———. "Why Locke's 'Of Power' Is Not a Metaphysical Pronouncement: Locke's Response to Molyneux's Critique." *Philosophy and Theology* 29, no. 1 (2017) 41-68.
Marshall, John. "Locke, Socinianism, 'Socinianism', and Unitarianism." In *English Philosophy in the Age of Locke*, edited by M. A. Stewart, 111-82. Oxford: Clarendon, 2000.
McGuinness, Philip. "*Christianity Not Mysterious* and the Enlightenment." In *John Toland's Christianity not Mysterious: Text, Associated Works and Critical Essays*, edited by Philip McGuiness et al, 231-42. Dublin: Lilliput, 1997.
Mooney, T. Brian, and Anthony Imbrosciano. "The Curious Case of Mr. Locke's Miracles." *International Journal for Philosophy of Religion* 57, no. 3 (2005) 147-68.
Mossner, Ernest Campbell. "Collins, Anthony." In *The Encyclopedia of Philosophy, vol. 2 Cabala to Entropy*, edited by Paul Edwards, 144-46. New York: MacMillan & Free, 1967.

Mossner, Ernest Campbell. "Collins, Anthony." In *Encyclopedia of Philosophy: vol. 2 Cabanis-Destutt De Tracy*, 2nd ed., edited by Donald M. Borchert, 330–32. Detroit: Thomas Gale / Macmillan Reference USA, 2006.

Muller, Richard A. *Dictionary of Latin and Greek Theological Terms: Drawn Principally from Protestant Scholastic Theology.* Grand Rapids: Baker Academic, 1985.

———. "Philip Doddrige and the Formulation of Calvinistic Theology in an Era of Rationalism and Deconfessionalization." In *Religion, Politics and Dissent, 1660–1832: Essays in Honour of James E. Bradley*, edited by Robert D. Cornwall and William Gibson, 65–84. Farnham, UK: Ashgate, 2010.

Nuovo, Victor. "Locke's Theology, 1694–1704." In *English Philosophy in the Age of Locke*, edited by M. A. Stewart, 183–216. Oxford: Clarendon, 2000.

O'Higgins, James. *Anthony Collins: The Man and His Works.* The Hague: Nijhoff, 1970.

———. *Determinism and Freewill: Anthony Collins' A Philosophical Inquiry Concerning Human Liberty Edited and Annotated with a Discussion of the Opinions of Hobbes, Locke, Pierre Bayle, William King and Leibniz.* The Hague: Nijhoff, 1976.

Plantinga, Alvin. "Reformed Epistemology." In *A Companion to Philosophy of Religion*, edited by Philip L. Quinn and Charles Taliaferro, 383–93. Oxford: Blackwell, 1997.

Peterson, Michael, William Hasker, Bruce Reichenbach, and David Bassingerer. "Faith and Reason: How Are They Related?" In *Reason and Religious Belief*, 4th ed., edited by Michael Peterson et al., 52–70. New York: Oxford University Press, 2009.

Polinska, Wioletta. "Faith and Reason in John Locke." *Philosophy and Theology* 11, no. 2 (1999) 287–309.

Popkin, Richard H. "The Philosophy of Bishop Stillingfleet." *Journal of the History of Philosophy* 9, no. 3 (1971) 303–19.

Rabieh, Michael S. "The Reasonableness of Locke, or the Questionableness of Christianity." *Journal of Politics* 53, no. 4 (1991) 933–57.

Randall, John Herman, Jr. *The Making of the Modern Mind: A Survey of the Intellectual Background of the Present Age.* 1926. Reprinted with a forward by Jacques Barzun. New York: Columbia University Press, 1976.

Rappaport, Rhoda. "Questions of Evidence: An Anonymous Tract Attributed to John Toland." *Journal of the History of Ideas* 58, no. 2 (1997) 339–48.

Reedy, Gerard. "Socinians, John Toland, and the Anglican Rationalists." *The Harvard Theological Review* 70, nos. 3 & 4 (1977) 285–304.

Rogers, G. A. J. Introduction to *The Philosophy of Edward Stillingfleet*. Vol. 1. Edited by G. A. J. Rogers, vii–x. Bristol: Thoemmes, 2000.

Rowe, William L. "Causality and Free Will in the Controversy between Collins and Clarke." *Journal of the History of Philosophy* 25, no. 1 (1987) 51–67.

———. *Thomas Reid on Freedom and Morality.* Ithaca, NY: Cornell University Press, 1991.

Russell, Paul. "Hume's Treatise and the Clarke-Collins Controversy." *Hume Studies* 21, no. 1 (1995) 95–116.

Schuurman, Paul. "Vision in God and Thinking Matter: Locke's Epistemological Agnosticism Used against Malebranche and Stillingfleet." In *Studies on Locke: Sources, Contemporaries, and Legacy*, edited by Sarah Hutton and Paul Schuurman, 177–93. Dordrecht: Springer, 2008.

Sell, Alan P. F. *John Locke and the Eighteenth-Century Divines.* Cardiff: University of Wales Press, 1997.

Smith, Donald Thomas. "John Locke's Concept of Reasonable Christianity." PhD diss., Southern Methodist Seminary, 1997.
Snobelen, Stephen D. "Socinianism, Heresy and John Locke's Reasonableness of Christianity." *Enlightenment and Dissent* 20 (2001) 88–125.
Snyder, David C. "Faith and Reason in Locke's Essay." *Journal of the History of Ideas* 47, no. 2 (1986) 197–213.
Stephen, Leslie. *History of English Thought in the Eighteenth Century.* 3rd ed. 2 vols. New York: Smith, 1949.
Stewart, M. A. "Stillingfleet and the Way of Ideas." In *English Philosophy in the Age of Locke*, edited by M. A. Stewart, 245–80. Oxford: Clarendon, 2000.
Strauss, Leo. *Natural Right and History.* Chicago: University of Chicago Press, 1953.
———. *Persecution and the Art of Writing.* Chicago: University of Chicago Press, 1952.
Sullivan, Robert E. *John Toland and the Deist Controversy: A Study in Adaptations.* Cambridge: Harvard University Press, 1982.
Taylor, Charles. *A Secular Age.* Cambridge: Harvard University Press, 2007.
Tetlow, Joanne. "John Locke's Covenant Theology." *Locke Studies* 9 (2009) 167–99.
Thiemann, Ronald F. *Revelation and Theology: The Gospel as Narrated Promise.* Notre Dame, IN: University of Notre Dame Press, 1985.
Turner, James. *Without God, Without Creed: The Origins of Unbelief in America.* Baltimore: John Hopkins University Press, 1985.
Uzgalis, William. "Anthony Collins." In *Stanford Encyclopedia of Philosophy.* First published August 25, 2003 with substantive revisions February 23, 2009. Accessed on March 13, 2009. http://plato.stanford.edu/entries/collins
Wallace, Dewey. "Socinianism, Justification by Faith, and the Sources of John Locke's *The Reasonableness of Christianity.*" *Journal of the History of Ideas* 45, no. 1 (1984) 49–66.
Weinsheimer, Joel. C. *Eighteenth-Century Hermeneutics: Philosophy of Interpretation in England from Locke to Burke.* New Haven: Yale University Press, 1993.
Welch, Claude. *Protestant Thought in the Nineteenth Century.* 2 vols. New Haven: Yale University Press, 1972.
Winkler, Kenneth P. "Anthony Collins." In *Routledge Encyclopedia of Philosophy, vol. 2 Brahman-Derrida, Jacques*, edited by Edward Craig, 415–18. New York: Routledge, 1998.
Woolhouse, R. S. *Locke.* Minneapolis: University of Minnesota Press, 1983.
———. *Locke: A Bibliography.* Cambridge: Cambridge University Press, 2007.
Wolterstorff, Nicholas. *John Locke and the Ethics of Belief.* Cambridge: University Press, 1996.
———. "John Locke's Epistemological Piety: Reason is the Candle of the Lord." *Faith and Philosophy* 11, no. 4 (1994) 572–91.
Yolton, John W. *Locke: An Introduction.* Oxford: Blackwell, 1985.
———. "The Way of Ideas: A Retrospective." *The Journal of Philosophy* 87, no. 10 (1990) 510–16.

Name Index

Ashcraft, Richard, 6, 10, 68, 88, 111
Ayers, Michael, 6, 28, 70, 73, 80–81, 85

Beiser, Frederick C., 4–5, 7, 8, 10, 19–21, 35, 130, 131, 132–33, 136–37, 139, 141–42, 157–58, 160–62, 164–65
Berman, David, 8, 133–35, 162–63, 185–86
Biddle, John C., *See* Higgins-Biddle, John C.
Boyle, Robert, 95, 98, 183

Champion, Justin, 7, 8, 17–18, 20–21, 133, 134, 187
Christophersen, H. O., 14, 15
Clarke, Samuel, 72, 83
Collins, Anthony, 6, 10, 56, 72, 83, 176–77, 180, 181, 187
Conrad, Jonathan Donald, 135, 187
Copleston, Frederick, 6, 66
Cragg, Gerald R., 5, 6, 66, 127–28, 133

Foster, David, 134, 187
Fouke, Daniel C., 5, 8, 127, 133–35, 137, 162–63, 185

Hare, Francis, 17, 55–56
Harris, James A., 73, 83, 99
Helm, Paul, 5, 6, 10, 19, 59, 69, 71, 78, 109–11, 116
Higgins-Biddle, John C., 5, 6, 8, 9, 10, 12, 19, 67, 113, 128, 129, 137, 176, 182

Israel, Jonathan I., 8, 130

Jolley, Nicholas, 6, 10, 70, 80–81, 85, 89

Kuehn, Manfred, 6, 66–67
Kuehne, Dale S., 187

Leask, Ian, 5, 6, 7, 10, 18, 20, 21–22, 34–37, 67, 102, 135–37, 141, 157, 159–60, 162
Lewis, C. S., 85
Livingston, James C., 5, 6, 66, 177
L. P. Master of Arts, 8, 130
LoLordo, Antonia, 6, 70
Losonsky, Michael, 6, 69, 72
Lucci, Diego, 5, 7, 21, 129, 187

Marko, Jonathan S., 9, 34, 72–73, 83–84, 95, 97, 98, 113, 162, 183
McGuinness, Philip, 5, 127–28
Molyneux, William, 10, 15, 17, 53
Muller, Richard A., 165, 168

Norris, John, 15, 96, 151, 157
Nye, Stephen, 17–18, 54–55

O'Higgins, James, 6, 66, 72, 73, 83, 100

Polinska, Wioletta, 6, 10, 68–69, 72, 111
Pope, Alexander, vi
Popkin, Richard H., 18

NAME INDEX

Randall, John Herman, Jr., 5, 6, 66, 129, 177
Rappaport, Rhoda, 8, 130–31, 134, 185
Reedy, Gerard, 18
Rogers, G. A. J., 3, 18
Rowe, William L., 73, 83

Schuurman, Paul, 18
Sell, Alan P. F., 6, 10, 18, 68–69, 111, 187
Snyder, David C., 6, 69–70, 71–72, 88–89
Stephen, Leslie, 2, 5, 127–28
Stewart, M. A., 18
Sullivan, Robert E., 4, 5–7, 8, 10, 19–21, 34, 54, 57–58, 59, 66, 130–34, 136, 137, 141–42, 157, 158–59, 162, 185–86

Taylor, Charles, 137, 164
Tillotson, John, 10, 56, 64, 119, 176–177, 181, 187
Tindal, Matthew, 10, 176–78, 181–82, 185, 187
Turner, James, 5, 129
Turretin, Francis, 106, 113, 180

Uzgalis, William, 6, 66

Weinsheimer, Joel. C., 187
Welch, Claude, 5–6, 66, 128, 178
Woolhouse, R. S., 6, 15, 17, 18, 20, 57–59, 69–70, 88–89, 102, 125
Wolterstorff, Nicholas, 6, 10, 70–71, 72, 85–87, 119

Yolton, John W., 22, 54

www.ingramcontent.com/pod-product-compliance
Lightning Source LLC
Chambersburg PA
CBHW070327230426
43663CB00011B/2241